E. M. Forster
the personal voice

E. M. Forster

the personal voice

John Colmer

Professor of English
University of Adelaide

Routledge & Kegan Paul
London, Boston, Melbourne and Henley

First published in 1975
by Routledge & Kegan Paul Ltd
39 Store Street,
London WC1E 7DD,
9 Park Street,
Boston, Mass. 02108, USA,
296 Beaconsfield Parade,
Middle Park, Melbourne,
3206, Australia and
Broadway House, Newtown Road,
Henley-on-Thames, Oxon,
RG9 1EN
Reprinted and first published
as a paperback in 1983
Set in Monotype Bembo
and printed in Great Britain by
The Thetford Press Ltd,
Thetford, Norfolk

ISBN 0 7100 8209 6 (C)
ISBN 0 7100 9496 5 (P)

Contents

Contents

Preface

When E. M. Forster said that he belonged to 'the fag-end of Victorian liberalism', he not only provided his own guide to his cultural origins but hinted at their limitations. What were the main characteristics of the liberal tradition he inherited? What were its strengths? What were its weaknesses? And what did Forster himself do to maintain the first and mitigate the second? These questions are prompted by his work as a novelist and essayist because he habitually saw himself in relation to this tradition and because all his writings explore the paradoxes and tensions inherent in it. He was never simply a story-teller, a witty entertainer, but was always an ironic moralist imbued with a profound vision of man and society based on the contrast between the fine-spun issues of private morality and the coarse-woven or patched up solutions of society, a representative figure in a transitional age, conscious of his relation to the main movements of mind and society.

Although much has been done to interpret Forster's writings in relation to their appropriate historical context, especially by John Beer, Malcolm Bradbury, Wilfred Stone, and Lionel Trilling, the time has now come for a fresh assessment. New evidence has come to light about his life and writings since his death in 1970, particularly through the publication of *Maurice* (1971) and the homosexual tales in *The Life to Come and Other Stories* (1972). And much remains among the Forster papers in King's College Library, Cambridge, that must alter our view of the novelist, including manuscripts of part of a novel, *Arctic Summer*, manuscript variants of the published novels, personal memoranda, biographical reminiscence, and unpublished lectures, talks, and essays. The present study draws on this rich material, but until the Abinger Edition of his works is complete and P. N. Furbank's biography appears, some things must remain in doubt.

Recent cultural studies of the late-Victorian and Edwardian period, details of which are given in the bibliography, have thrown new light on Forster's intellectual and literary background. In addition, the newly published memoirs and biographies of his friends and contemporaries present valuable sidelights on the novelist's personality, the reception of his work, and his general relation to the age. Of especial interest are Leonard Woolf's volumes of autobiography, Michael Holroyd's biography of Lytton Strachey, and Quentin Bell's life of Virginia Woolf. 'To write of the culture which produced Forster and Virginia Woolf', W. W. Robson has remarked, 'would be to write a whole chapter in the intellectual and social history of England. They belong to the last phase of liberal humanism.' The present book aims to place Forster's various works in their appropriate social and cultural context, using, as far as possible, Forster's own accounts of the climate of thought in which his powers as a writer developed.

Acknowledgments

I am deeply indebted to the Trustees of E. M. Forster's Estate, the Provost and Scholars of King's College, Cambridge, for permission to quote from the manuscripts of the novels, the published extracts from the incomplete novel, *Arctic Summer*, and much miscellaneous unpublished material in King's College Library. The copyright of the Forster Papers is owned by the Provost and Scholars of King's College, Cambridge, and may not be reproduced without permission. For their unfailing kindness and co-operation in making the Forster Archive available to me, I wish to thank the Vice-Provost, Dr D. A. Parry, the Librarian, Dr A. N. L. Munby, and the Forster Archivist, Mrs P. Bulloch.

I am grateful to Edward Arnold (Publishers) Ltd., for their generosity in allowing me to quote extensively from *Abinger Harvest, Aspects of the Novel, Goldsworthy Lowes Dickinson, The Hill of Devi, Howards End, The Life to Come and Other Stories, The Longest Journey, Marianne Thornton, Maurice, A Passage to India, A Room with a View, Two Cheers for Democracy, Where Angels Fear to Tread*, and Forster's Introduction to the Oxford University Press, World's Classics edition of *The Longest Journey* (1960); Doubleday & Co., Inc. has granted me permission to quote from *Alexandria: A History and a Guide*; Harcourt, Brace Jovanovich, Inc. has allowed me to quote from *Abinger Harvest, Aspects of the Novel, The Eternal Moment, Goldsworthy Lowes Dickinson, The Hill of Devi, Marianne Thornton, A Passage to India, Two Cheers for Democracy*; the Hogarth Press has agreed to let me quote from *Pharos and Pharillon*; Alfred A. Knopf, Inc. has kindly granted me permission to quote from *Howards End, The Longest Journey, A Room with a View, Where Angels Fear to Tread*; W. W. Norton & Co., Inc. has granted me permission to quote from *The Life to Come and Other Stories* and *Maurice*, and I am also grateful to Mr Christopher Isherwood and the National Institute of Arts and Letters for permission to quote from *Maurice*; I am grateful to the Society of Authors as literary representatives of the Estate of E. M. Forster for permission to quote from *The Collected Short Stories, Pharos and Pharillon,* and other works.

I am also grateful to Professor H. H. A. Gowda for permitting me to reproduce passages from my essay 'Howards End Revisited', in *A Garland for E. M. Forster* (1969); to Sir Dennis Proctor for permission to quote from *The Autobiography of G. Lowes Dickinson* (1973); and to Mr Oliver Stallybrass for allowing me to quote from his invaluable introductions and notes to the Abinger Edition of Forster's works, published by Edward Arnold.

I wish to acknowledge the grant of Study Leave from the University of Adelaide in 1973–4 that enabled me to complete this book.

Finally I wish to thank: Mr Benjamin Britten for answering queries about his friendship and collaboration with Forster; Mr P. N. Furbank for supplying biographical details; Miss Elizabeth Ellem for making available her researches on the early versions of *A Room with a View* and on *Arctic Summer*; Keith Cable for details of Forster's association with the Aldeburgh Festival; John Edge, Geoffrey Thurley, and Haydn Moore Williams for valuable comments on separate chapters; Robin Eaden for help during the final stages of the book; Joan Craik for her patient and accurate typing; and Dorothy Colmer for criticism and encouragement.

Abbreviations

References are normally incorporated into the text. For critical works the identification is by the author's name and further details are given in the Bibliography. The following abbreviations are used for Forster's own work, and for other frequent references.

	Title and date of publication
WAFT	*Where Angels Fear to Tread* (1905)
LJ	*The Longest Journey* (1907)
RWV	*A Room with a View* (1908)
HE	*Howards End* (1910)
CO	*The Celestial Omnibus* (1911)
GE	*The Government of Egypt* (1920)
AHG	*Alexandria: A History and a Guide* (1922)
PP	*Pharos and Pharillon* (1923)
PI	*A Passage to India* (1924)
AN	*Aspects of the Novel* (1927)
EM	*The Eternal Moment* (1928)
GLD	*Goldsworthy Lowes Dickinson* (1934)
AH	*Abinger Harvest* (1936)
CSS	*Collected Short Stories* (1947)
TCD	*Two Cheers for Democracy* (1951)
HD	*The Hill of Devi* (1953)
MT	*Marianne Thornton* (1956)
IE	'Indian Entries' (1962)
M	*Maurice* (1971)
LTC	*The Life to Come and Other Stories* (1972)

Abinger   Volumes in the new Collected Abinger Edition of Forster's Works, edited by Oliver Stallybrass and published by Edward Arnold, are identified by the word

	Abinger, followed by appropriate abbreviation for the specific work
CB	Forster's Commonplace Book, formerly Bishop John Jebb's, now in King's College Library, Cambridge
IR	*Independent Review*
KCL	Manuscript or typescript material in the Forster Archive, King's College Library, Cambridge
WAFT:BM	Manuscript of *Where Angels Fear to Tread*, now in the British Museum

I

Life and Times

The spirit of muddle that he delighted to explore in his novels and short stories presided over Forster's baptism. He was to have been christened Henry, but his father, distrait, handed his own name to the verger, and the child was called Edward. The father, Edward Morgan Llewellyn Forster, was an architect, a descendant on his mother's side of the Thorntons, who were rich bankers and prominent members of the Evangelical 'Clapham Sect'. Forster's mother, Alice Clara Whichelo (known as Lily), was a daughter of Henry Mayle Whichelo, a poor drawing master. When he died suddenly in 1866, he left his wife, Louisa, with no money and ten children. Providentially the family doctor introduced twelve-year-old Lily into the Thornton family, where she became the protégée of the wealthy Marianne Thornton, and subsequently married Marianne's favourite nephew. The novelist, Edward Morgan Forster, was born on 1 January 1879 at his parents' house, 6 Melcombe Place, Dorset Square, London. The pattern of premature bereavement repeated itself. In October 1880 Forster's father died. At twenty-five, Lily was left 'with a small baby, and without any support except what was extended to her by her husband's relatives' (MT, p. 258). Thus Forster never knew his father; and his early upbringing was dominated by three women: his great-aunt, Marianne Thornton, an affectionate but dictatorial woman; his lively, witty maternal grandmother, Louisa Graham Whichelo, whom he adored and later remembered affectionately in the character of Mrs Honeychurch in *A Room with a View*; and his mother, Lily, who provided a series of happy homes, accompanied the novelist in his early travels abroad, and continued to influence him until her death in 1945. This female-dominated world appears in various guises in the novels and probably helped to determine the pattern of his psychological development.

Of the three women, Marianne Thornton was the most important. In his biography of his great-aunt, Forster writes: 'I succeeded my father as the favourite nephew. . . . I received the deplorable nickname of The Important One, and when my mother showed signs of despondency she was reminded that she had me to live for' (MT, p. 259). On her death in 1887, Marianne Thornton left the eight-year-old boy £8,000. Without this legacy, he would never have been able to go to Cambridge, or to travel in Europe and India. Forster later wrote, 'she and no-one else made my career as a writer possible, and her love, in a most tangible sense, followed me beyond the grave' (MT, p. 289). It was a debt that he repaid – perhaps overpaid – in two major themes of his novels: the theme of continuity, and the theme of people no longer alive, but 'living in other lives' (Cowley, 1958, p. 29), as Mrs Wilcox lives on through Margaret Schlegel in *Howards End*, and as Mrs Moore lives on in the minds of her children and of Dr Aziz in *A Passage to India*. Moreover, Marianne Thornton's tendency to substitute money for love established a pattern that Forster was to explore later in his novels. But it would be a mistake to see any of these later preoccupations in purely personal terms: the idea of continuity and the power of memory dominate early twentieth-century literature; and the relationship between love and money is one of the central themes of Victorian and Edwardian fiction.

The early years of Forster's life exerted a crucial influence on his later development. Soon after the death of his father, his mother retired to a house in the country. She 'provided me', Forster writes, 'with a sheltered and happy childhood'. The house near Stevenage, in Hertfordshire, was called 'Rooksnest', and Forster's earliest piece of writing is a loving description of it; with its neighbouring farm and protective wych elm, it was the original for the house in *Howards End* where it becomes a symbol of harmony and happiness, of the 'elemental hunger for continuance' that, Leavis notes, is so central to all Forster's work. Religion played its part in his upbringing. His mother 'read morning prayers', but 'was never intense' about it. Like Mrs Wilcox in *Howards End*, her 'interests lay elsewhere: in helping her neighbours: in running her little house and garden: in district visiting: and in criticizing Queen Victoria's Jubilee.' When he was eight, Forster was sufficiently impressed by his mother's high-principled decision not to respond to the sentimental request to 'give the dear Queen one penny', that he was determined not to cheer when the Queen rode by. But the sight of a policeman made him take off his sailor hat and cheer with the rest.

This trivial incident reflects the nation's growing dissatisfaction with imperial pomp and foreshadows Forster's later anti-imperialism, developed at Cambridge, and powerfully reinforced by his residence in Egypt (1915–19) and India (1912–13 and 1921).

Forster's early life at Rooksnest was important in two further ways. It was there that he formed his first friendship. This initiation into the life of 'comradeship' – a word of special significance for Forster, as we shall see – was with Ansell, the garden-boy, who was given an afternoon-a-week to play with him. His tutor disapproved of their 'childish and undignified' pranks. From Forster's later accounts of these boisterous Wednesday afternoon games, which sometimes involved hiding in a dark straw penthouse together, it is clear that the friendship was not only a source of intense joy, but came to symbolize an ideal of naturalness and fraternity. The posthumously published short story, 'Ansell', the tale of a Cambridge scholar who gives up the life of learning under the affectionate influence of the former garden-boy, provides additional confirmation (LTC). The relationship may have served to create a model for many subsequent friendships in fiction and in life. Some of the most intense personal relations in the novels involve two men who are separated by difference of either class or nationality (Maurice and Alec in *Maurice*, Dr Aziz and Fielding in *A Passage to India*); moreover, in *Maurice*, the hero's first vision of friendship comes through George, the garden-boy, whose naked image haunts his dreams. Incidents of violence and physical horseplay occupy a disproportionate importance in the male relationships from the early novels to the later homosexual short stories, as in 'What does it Matter? A Morality', in *The Life to Come* volume, while in real life Forster frankly confessed a preference for 'a strong young man of the lower classes and to be loved by him and even hurt by him' (Personal Memorandum, 1935, quoted Abinger: LTC, p. xiv).

The abrupt departure from Rooksnest also influenced Forster's development. While his early boyhood there has been accepted as the source of his ideal of domestic harmony, the traumatic effect of his sudden exile from this rural paradise has not so often been recognized. In a paper on Memory to the Bloomsbury Memoir Club, in the early 1930s, Forster speaks feelingly of how, when he was fourteen, the owners turned his mother and himself out of Rooksnest. This is followed by the illuminating but enigmatic statement: 'If I had been allowed to stop on there I should have become a different person, married, and fought in the war' (KCL). In fact, Forster remained

3

unmarried and was strongly pacifist in sympathy, although he did serve with the Red Cross in Alexandria; but, in retrospect, he seems to have thought that the move from Rooksnest snapped the tender fibres of growing affection that might have flowered into marriage, the making of a home, and the willingness to defend home and country from the enemy. The uprooting from Rooksnest cut him off from a life lived in harmony with the earth and from a sense of belonging to the permanence and continuity of English life, a life that he later celebrated – perhaps idealized – in *Howards End*. In that early carefree existence, 'running about over the fields or muddling around in the farm or chasing the chickens or being chased by a cow or fingering the wych elm' (which later assumed a mystic significance in *Howards End*), he was, without knowing it, 'breathing in a notion of the continuity of England and the desirability of her continuance' ('Three Countries', KCL). The three novels, *The Longest Journey* (1907), *Howards End* (1910), and *Maurice* (written 1913-14, but not published until 1971), all explore this theme of continuity, which was also a major preoccupation of the age: 'one of the main achievements of the nineteenth century was the elaboration and application of the principle of *continuity*' (Cox, 1963, p. 154). But the twentieth century shattered that ideal. Forster's novels dramatize the conflicts of two ages as well as the divisions in the author's sympathies and beliefs.

Forster's education left its mark on his vision of life by opening his eyes to the shallowness of middle-class culture, the rigidity of its constricting conventions, its neglect of the emotional and spiritual life. In 1890, at the age of eleven, he was sent to a preparatory school at Eastbourne kept by the Rev. C. P. Hutchinson, a clergyman as remarkable for his lack of religious enthusiasm as for his intolerance of others, notably the neighbouring agnostic, the famous scientist T. H. Huxley. Although the school contributed little to Forster's positive development, the first chapter of *Maurice* probably records accurately enough the pathos and futility of his sex education there: well-meaning but a fraud. As a 'pious child', he was shocked to discover that another boy called Henson with whom he was left on Good Friday, 1891, knew nothing about either Easter or Ascension Day; and his ambivalent attitude towards this unpopular boy may be reflected in the creation of Varden, the victim of bullying in *The Longest Journey*. The same 'spiritual shallows' existed at his public school, Tonbridge, where he was sent as a day boy. There he suffered the worst of both worlds, since he was subjected to a standardizing process he despised, and, as a day boy, was regarded as an outsider. In *The Longest Journey*, when the pompous housemaster, Mr Pembroke, indignantly pictures the unorganized life of a day boy for the new master, Rickie Elliot, the reader, like Rickie, can think of nothing more natural than boys being 'at home for meals, at home for preparation, at home for sleep', and nothing more unnatural than the boarding school system, with its separation from home and artificial *esprit de corps* (ch. 17).

In this novel, Forster criticizes the system through the hero, Rickie, who first struggles against its pernicious effects and finally succumbs, under the influence of his devious wife, Agnes, and her complacent brother, Herbert Pembroke. In addition, a day boy is bullied, tortured and victimized, and Rickie is compelled to become an accomplice in getting rid of him. Since Forster has confessed that a great deal of his own experience has gone into *The Longest Journey*, we are justified in reading much of it as thinly veiled autobiography.

Forster's experience of his public school provided him with two vital elements in his vision of life: first, a hatred of the conventional values that were taught there; second, a recognition that the public school system was responsible for the characteristic weakness of the English middle classes – their inability to give to the emotional life its proper importance. In some 'Notes on the English Character', originally given as a talk in India, but later worked up for publication (AH), he speaks of the way English public school boys are taught to believe that the school is the world in miniature and are therefore quite unprepared to understand the complexities they face when they go out into the world. 'They go forth into it', he writes, 'with well-developed bodies, fairly developed minds, and undeveloped hearts. And it is this undeveloped heart that is largely responsible for the difficulties of Englishmen abroad. An undeveloped heart – not a cold one. The difference is important.'

The doctrine of 'the undeveloped human heart' is embodied in all Forster's fiction. *The Longest Journey* illustrates poignantly the processes that produce it, while its actual effects may be seen in all those male characters who represent the world of convention and spiritual unreality in the novels. Typical products are the unimaginative, self-righteous official Ronny Heaslop, in *A Passage to India*, and Henry Wilcox, an epitome of the business mind, in *Howards End*. We are not primarily concerned here with Forster's dislike of the public school system, a system that has perhaps changed considerably, but with one of the essential ingredients in his vision of life. Believing that to lead the good life a man must learn to establish personal relations and acknowledge the equal claims of body and spirit, heart and head, Forster recognized that most Englishmen of the middle classes are ill-prepared to do either. They cannot therefore connect. The phrase 'only connect', used as an epigraph to *Howards End*, sums up his ideal of harmony. His novels are dramas in which the goal is the achievement of personal salvation, not worldly success; they are also novels in which the vision of truth is enjoyed only by those who trust their emotions and guard their inner integrity from the corrupting influences of convention.

In Forster's novels, as in the novels of his predecessors and contemporaries, a whole set of religious terms – salvation, grace, conversion, transfiguration – become assimilated into an essentially secular vision (Ellmann, 1960, pp. 191–203). Men now seek their happiness on this earth not in heaven; they develop what Pater calls, in *Marius the Epicurean* (1885), 'a religious veneration for life as such'; when men can no longer find the true ground of their being in God they look for it in personal relations; consequently their ideals become self-realization, self-fulfilment, or just sheer getting on, as in Wells's comic novels about the careers of Mr Kipps, Mr Polly and Mr Lewisham. What distinguishes Forster from other Edwardian secular salvationists is his visionary, other-worldly quality and his harking back to an older religion with pagan rites and priestesses guarding the holy shrines (Mrs Moore and Mrs Wilcox), a religion related to the *fin de siècle* and Edwardian worship of Pan, but developing differently.

Cambridge liberated Forster from a world he despised and provided him with a symbol of the good life. He discovered that 'the public school is not infinite and eternal, that there is something more compelling in life than teamwork, and more vital than cricket, that firmness, self-complacency and fatuity do not between them compose the whole armour of man' (GLD, p. 26). He entered King's College in 1897, took a Second in the Classics Tripos in 1900, then switched to History, with the same result, in 1901. He studied Classics under Nathaniel Wedd and History under the notorious Oscar Browning, who was as likely to listen to essays in his bath as with a red handkerchief over his sleeping face. Wedd – 'a cynical, aggressive, Mephistophelian character who affected red ties and blasphemy', was not an old Etonian as so many King's men were, but a product of the City of London School. As an undergraduate, he had taken an active part in the feud against the arrogance of the Best Set, whose leader was A. C.

Benson and whose criterion was 'good form'. As a don, he became an eccentric, anti-authoritarian figure. He undoubtedly helped to form Forster's political and social attitudes, especially his distrust of authority, his sympathy for the outsider, particularly of a lower class, and his hostility to notions of good form. Wedd also awoke a passionate interest in all things Greek, including Greek ideals of male friendship. With a wide knowledge of modern European literature, he introduced Forster to the daring moderns – as they then seemed in Cambridge: Ibsen, Zola, and George Moore. And, perhaps, most important of all, he gave Forster his first, typically Cambridge, encouragement to be a writer: 'I don't see why you should not write' (Jones, 1959, p. 11). Forster was delighted and began to write: at first, whimsical essays for undergraduate magazines, such as 'On Grinds', 'On Bicycling', 'A Long Day'; then later, once his imagination had been fired by foreign travel, more mature essays and short stories, first published in the *Independent Review*.

In the sceptical atmosphere of Cambridge Forster soon discarded religion. During his first year, when he lived out of college, he ran through St Edward's Passage in his pyjamas and dressing gown to sign on at the porter's lodge instead of attending morning chapel. In his second year, when he moved into college, his faith in Christianity 'quietly and quickly disappeared'. This was partly due to the influence of his closest friend, H. O. Meredith, but also to his almost total absence of any sense of sin and his dislike of the personality of Christ, who failed to provide him with a sufficiently attractive 'father-figure, brother-figure, son, friend' and lacked both intellect and humour and much else that Forster valued; as he later said, 'I would on the whole rather not meet the speaker [of the gospels] either at an Eliot cocktail party or for a quick quaker talk.' That one of the sources of Forster's agnosticism was the personality of Christ is a striking illustration of the centrality of personal relations in his visions of life. His agnosticism was also the product of 'the general spirit of questioning' that was 'associated with the great name of G. E. Moore'. Forster did not receive Moore's influence direct – 'I was not up to that and have never read Principia Ethica.' But, as he admits in his retrospective account to the Humanist Society sixty years later, Moore's ideas were part of the air he breathed and they came to him 'through those who knew the Master'. That the most valuable things in life are inner states of being and that the most valuable of these states are those that arise from personal relations and from the contemplation of beauty, were ideas that Forster found immediately congenial and later embodied in his fiction.

More important than any indirect influence from Moore was Forster's election, in his third year ('the year that an undergraduate comes into his own and the University belongs to him'), to the Society of Apostles. This was a private university society founded in the early nineteenth century that met on Saturday nights, when a paper was read and members spoke in turn, drawing lots for order. Such were the externals, but the 'soul' of the thing was 'incommunicable', said Goldsworthy Lowes Dickinson. This may be so, but the account given by Henry Sidgwick, who was elected in 1856–7, surely comes close to evoking its essential spirit. Moreover, it establishes that it was something more than 'the dream of a coterie of lapsed Protestants' (Stone, 1966, p. 58).

> Absolute candour was the only duty that the tradition of the
> society enforced. No consistency was demanded with opinions
> previously held – truth as we saw it then and there was what we
> had to embrace and maintain, and there was no proposition so
> well established that an Apostle had not the right to deny or
> question, if he did so sincerely and not from mere love of paradox.
> The gravest subjects were continually debated, but gravity of
> treatment . . . was not imposed, though sincerity was. In fact it
> was rather a point of the apostolic mind to understand how
> much suggestion and instruction may be derived from what is in
> form a jest – even in dealing with gravest matters.

The Apostolic spirit, as defined in the last sentence, finds perfect expression in Forster's art of suggestion and in his moral vision, with its characteristic blend of gravity and humour. In Cambridge a temperament and a tradition had magically fused.

For Forster Cambridge was not simply an ancient university, but the symbol of the good life. In his biography of Goldsworthy Lowes Dickinson, he takes up and elaborates phrases from his friend's manuscript autobiography to describe Dickinson's happiness there, but in reality to describe his own.

> As Cambridge filled up with friends it acquired a magic quality.
> Body and spirit, reason and emotion, work and play, architecture
> and scenery, laughter and seriousness, life and art – these pairs
> which are elsewhere contrasted were there fused into one. People

and books re-inforced one another, intelligence joined hands with affection, speculation became passion, and discussion was made profound by love (GLD, ch. 7).

Cambridge, it is clear, became the symbol of the undivided life, and all Forster's novels explore the possibility of men and women achieving such a harmony. In three of the novels, the task of achieving it, is complicated by difference of national temperament: in *Where Angels Fear to Tread* (1905) and *A Room with a View* (1908), the difference is between English and Italians; in *A Passage to India* the contrast is between English and Indians, between Moslems and Hindus. The main clash in *The Longest Journey* is between the characters that represent convention and those that represent private integrity; in *Howards End* it is between the representatives of commercialism and of spiritual values, while in *Maurice* it is between those who remain faithful to the wisdom of the body and those who do not. And there are other great divisions; in all Forster's fiction we are conscious of three societies: the elect who live by personal relations, the pseudo-elect, and conventional society that lives by the laws of 'the tribe'. But it is not always clear whether it is culture or nature that admits one to the society of the elect. Faith in culture links Forster to the great tradition of nineteenth-century liberalism; faith in nature to the Romantic tradition.

The tradition of nineteenth-century liberalism had its philosophic and its political sides and they were not identical – liberalism with a small or a large 'L', in fact: and some writers have mistakenly associated Forster with the now discredited ideas of old-fashioned political liberalism of which he was one of the most clear-sighted critics. In essence philosophical liberalism sprang from a belief in reason, individualism and the inevitability of progress. It embraced many forms of thought that were strictly speaking incompatible. One form had its roots in the eighteenth-century Enlightenment and was rational, agnostic, and utilitarian; another developed out of the English Romantic Movement and was imaginative and religious. John Stuart Mill typifies the first, with his reverent agnosticism, his belief in the principle of the greatest happiness for the greatest number, his championing of liberty and freedom of speech. An example of the second was the Clapham Sect, associated with the anti-slavery and missionary activities of William Wilberforce, Zachary Macaulay, and the Thorntons. Forster regarded the Clapham Sect with special esteem, in spite of its development of the religious sense at the expense of the imaginative and emotional,

9

because of his family ties with the Thorntons. The first of these traditions was sceptical, worldly, progressive: the second was cautious, unworldly, devoted to the relief of suffering. Forster drew something from both. In general, the Victorian upper and middle classes, inspired by the nineteenth-century myth of progress, evolved a comfortable faith in moral and economic *laissez-faire*: only remove external restraints and authoritarian rule, and a new era of freedom and happiness would follow. In his novels and political essays, Forster draws on this tradition, but he becomes increasingly aware of its limitations, finally rejecting economic *laissez-faire* in favour of government planning, but retaining *laissez-faire* in the world of the spirit.

The optimistic philosophy of mid-Victorian England was typical of an age of growing prosperity and imperial expansion. But doubts developed, not only about God, but about the inevitability of progress and the effects of the principle of *laissez-faire*, of 'doing what one likes'. The latter is the main object of Matthew Arnold's attack in that great work of social criticism *Culture and Anarchy* (1869); in it Arnold analyses the causes of social fragmentation and prescribes culture (the pursuit of 'sweetness and light') as its cure. Coming at the end of a long tradition, Forster's *Howards End* offers a union of culture and commerce, together with a return to the natural rhythms of the earth. A comparison of Forster's novel with Matthew Arnold's work and also with such critiques of machine culture as Edward Carpenter's *Civilisation: its Cause and Cure* (1889) and Veblen's radical *Theory of the Leisure Class*, as well as with C. F. G. Masterman's *Condition of England* (1909) and T. S. Eliot's two conservative analyses of English culture, *The Idea of a Christian Society* (1939) and *Notes Towards the Definition of Culture* (1949) reveals the central importance of *Howards End* in the great nineteenth- and twentieth-century debate on culture and society.

Towards the end of the nineteenth century, some of the practical effects of political *laissez-faire* strained the optimism of Victorian political liberalism. First, the effects of *laissez-faire* economics in creating large-scale hardship among the working class became so obvious that they could no longer be ignored, particularly after the formation of the Independent Labour Party and the election of the first Labour Member of Parliament, Keir Hardie, in 1893. Second, the Boer War (1899–1902) brought home to people the fact that the Imperial ideal of bringing freedom to the other peoples of the world had its darker economic side. 'We began the century with a false start – Jingoism and the Boer War – and soon became ashamed of it', Forster writes in retrospect.

> We began by thinking we should paint the world red, red being in those days a most respectable colour, and indicating the British Empire. Kipling, the tribes without the law, the white man's burden, these things were genuinely believed in for a few years by thoughtful people, but only for a few years . . . It was no good talking about the tribes without the law when tribes said they had laws. It was no good taking up the white man's burden when it didn't want to be taken up. Many of us soon saw that this crude imperialism had an economic side and we were put off ('In the Early Years of this Century', KCL).

It is not surprising that Forster should have hailed the first number of the *Independent Review* as marking a new era, since the *Independent*, under an editorial board that included Wedd, Dickinson, and C. F. G. Masterman, came into existence to counter Joseph Chamberlain's strident policy of economic and political imperialism.

But it was not only the cruder forms of Imperialism that Forster came to see through. He saw through the liberal tradition's naïve faith in progress: its simple oppositions of good and evil, its failure to recognize 'good-and-evil' in man. With an acute sense of the daemonic as the source of both good and evil in man, a sense he shared with the Romantics and the writers of the *fin de siècle*, he could not accept so simple a view of human nature. In his novels, although 'the plot speaks of clear certainties, the manner insists that nothing can be so simple' (Trilling, 1944, p. 13). He came to recognize that things would not get better and better as liberalism promised, that it was blind to the horrors that science had in store for the human race and that it had tragically 'failed to foresee the future'. As a beneficiary, intellectual and financial, of this whole tradition, Forster criticizes it from within. This gives his work a special authority. But, in spite of his dissatisfaction with the weaknesses of the liberal tradition, his writings affirm its central creed: the importance of the individual and the sanctity of personal relations. Writing in the 1930s, after *A Passage to India* (1924), with its chastening vision of the difficulties that beset men of goodwill but of different cultural backgrounds, Forster recalled Helen Schlegel's statement in *Howards End* that 'personal relations are the only things that matter for ever and ever', and confirmed his earlier faith by saying, 'I still believe this as regards the private life.'

The attempt to reconcile contradictory elements within the self and within society is not only typical of Forster's liberal humanist inheritance, an inheritance he puts to the ultimate test in *A Passage to India*, it is also typical of his great debt to Romanticism. As John Beer has remarked, 'to understand Forster fully, one has to see him at the end of that earlier phase, the spiritual heir of Blake, Coleridge and Shelley, of Beethoven and Wagner' (Beer, 1962, p. 15). Forster shares with these artists a common ideal of man's heroic potential. With the English Romantic poets he constantly emphasizes the need to combine 'head' and 'heart'; like them he celebrates the wisdom of the body, and the regenerative power of love; like them he believes that the imagination has the power to seize on symbolic moments of truth (Wordsworth's 'spots of time'; Pater's 'present moment' which 'alone really is'): such moments, treasured in the memory, become 'the master light of all our seeing'. The visionary element, it is true, is constantly held in check and modified by irony, but it alone provides the author and his characters with their visions of harmony, their insights into ultimate reality, earthbound and untranscendental as these are. In *The Longest Journey*, through the character of Rickie, Forster writes of the symbolic moment:

> It's nothing in itself, yet for the moment it stands for some eternal principle. We accept it, at whatever cost, and we have accepted life. But if we are frightened and reject it, the moment, so to speak passes; the symbol is never offered again (ch. 14).

One article of the Romantic aesthetic here receives a severe ethical (not to say Calvinistic) emphasis.

Like the major Romantics, Forster sought a harmony between man and the earth, but he lived in a post-Darwinian age. In this period, when men could no longer find spiritual ecstasy in union with God, nor sense of divine purpose in nature, many writers seized on the eternal moment and the ecstasy discovered in man's kinship with the earth as experiences that alone gave meaning to life. In *Howards End*, Leonard Bast, like Meredith's Richard Feverel, longs to 'get back to the Earth'; so, too, does Rickie Elliot in *The Longest Journey*. Writers as various as Meredith, Robert Louis Stevenson, George Borrow, Havelock Ellis, Richard Jefferies, W. H. Hudson, George Gissing and Edward Carpenter celebrated the joy of man's return to the earth, as the source of dynamic rhythm, vitality, mystery, and as an antidote to the machine age. Of these, Carpenter offers the closest parallel to

Forster, although his writing differs considerably in form and tone. His works combine a passionate love of the working man with a celebration of the earth; they also express bitter hostility to the materialism of modern civilization. Although Sidney and Beatrice Webb jeered when Carpenter read *Civilisation: its Cause and Cure* to the Fabian Society, Carpenter was right to point out that 'civilization' could no longer retain its 'old optimistic mid-Victorian sense'; and he possessed a prophetic vision of the corrupting influences of twentieth-century materialism, a vision that proved an inspiration to D. H. Lawrence. Forster wrote two appreciative essays on Carpenter, knew him well, and, in 1965, said that Carpenter had much influenced him. His debt to this particular form of late-nineteenth-century Romanticism has not received the notice it deserves.

One further debt that Forster owes to the Romantic tradition is more closely related to the literary form of his works than to the spirit of his vision. Inspiring his work as a novelist and as a critic, is the ideal of art as an autonomous order, one that achieves a balance and reconciliation of opposite or discordant qualities, a unique order that possesses strict internal coherence. 'When we are reading the *Ancient Mariner*', he remarks, 'we have entered a universe that only answers to its own laws, supports itself, internally coheres, and has a new standard of truth.' It is this concept that lies behind his own ideal of a novel that is 'stitched internally', an ideal expounded in the chapter on 'Rhythm' in *Aspects of the Novel* and exemplified in all his novels but especially in *Howards End* and *A Passage to India*.

It has been suggested that Forster's ideas on art and life sprang largely from the Bloomsbury Group (Johnstone, 1954), but the Bloomsbury Group as a literary movement is something of a popular myth, kept alive by nostalgic memoir and good publicity. It was never a cohesive school with common aesthetic aims, but an informal association of friends, who were linked by Cambridge and family ties and who visited each other in Bloomsbury, where they lived conveniently close to the British Museum for their writing and research. At the centre of the circle were the two Stephen sisters, Virginia (Woolf) and Vanessa (Bell), daughters of Sir Leslie Stephen; also prominent were the biographer and essayist Lytton Strachey, the art critic Roger Fry, the artists and critics Duncan Grant and Clive Bell, the economist Maynard Keynes and the former Colonial servant turned political theorist and essayist, Leonard Woolf. Even those who were indisputably part of the circle disagree about whether the group came into being as early as 1907 or as late as 1912, after Woolf's return from Ceylon, and who actually belonged; but on one thing they all seem to agree: that Forster moved only 'on the periphery' (Stallybrass, 1969, p. 31). Leonard Woolf nicknamed him the Taupe, 'partly because of his faint physical resemblance to a mole, but principally because he seemed intellectually and emotionally to travel unseen underground' (Woolf, 1960, p. 171); others noted that he was a great slipper away, like his fictional creations, Mrs Moore and Professor Godbole. His introduction came through Arthur Cole; he himself says that he 'didn't belong automatically'; and, after 1916, the gulf between his Bloomsbury friends and himself widened and he felt that 'he couldn't go there for any sort of comfort or sympathy' (CB and 'Bloomsbury', KCL). He found antipathetic their tendency to treat everything outside their civilized circle as a 'screaming farce'. But he considered Bloomsbury 'the only genuine movement in English civilisation'. He denied the often repeated charges of exclusiveness – 'its contempt for the outsider plays a very small part of its actuality' – and summed it up humorously as 'Essentially *gentlefolks* – would open other people's letters, but wouldn't steal, bully, slander or blackmail like many of their critics, and have acquired a culture in harmony with their social position.' The voice of Bloomsbury was the voice of the Cambridge Apostles translated to London, become more cliquish, more combative, and a little shrill. The notions of aesthetic form that Forster is supposed to have taken from Bloomsbury, he first heard in Roger Fry's lectures at Cambridge. The idea that the enjoyment of beauty and personal relations were the highest goods, the habit of questioning received opinion, the frank treatment of sex, the mixture of seriousness and jest, the sheer value of good talk, all these characteristics of the Bloomsbury circle he had first come across at Cambridge. And the 'strong suspicion of the worldly wise, an unalterable emphasis on personal salvation and a penchant for meditation among intimate friends', was a fourth-generation inheritance from the Clapham Sect (Annan, 1951, p. 195). It was this general body of civilized values that Forster and his Bloomsbury friends upheld and celebrated in their writings. To later generations they appear evangelists of the New Morality.

While much may be gained from seeing Forster's works in relation to nineteenth-century liberalism, Romanticism, the Cambridge Apostles, and Bloomsbury, much too may be gained from relating them to the social conditions of the age. 'The outside square' of Forster's novels 'is the conditions of contemporary history', says Stephen Spender, alluding to the image of reality depicted by Stewart Ansell, in *The Longest Journey*, 'within the square a circle, and within the circle a square' (Spender, 1970, p. 4). The outside square of Forster's early life was late-Victorian society. Forster reached his majority in 1900, a year before the death of Queen Victoria. He was brought up, he says, thinking of the best side of the liberal intellectual tradition, in an age that 'practised benevolence and philanthropy, was humane and intellectually curious, upheld free speech, had little colour prejudice, believed that individuals are and should be different, and entertained a sincere faith in the progress of society' ('The Challenge of Our Time', TCD). But, at the end of this prosperous British Century, cracks began to appear. When men stopped to think, the two great questions they asked themselves were: was the Empire about to fall into ruins? was the national life degenerating? As an answer to the first, in 1903, Joseph Chamberlain launched his policy of Tariff Reform to retain the loyalty of the Empire through a system of Imperial preference. This struck at the heart of the Liberal faith in Free Trade; but the country's attachment to this deep-seated faith was not broken until the political and economic upheavals of the First World War. There are obvious echoes of this great debate on Free Trade, Tariff Reform and Empire in *Howards End*; in *Maurice* the hero finds himself booked to canvass support for Tariff Reform at Clive's country house, Penge. The second great question, relating to the threatened decline of national culture, is also thoroughly aired in *Howards End*. It was mainly prompted by the growth of great cities, with the accompanying breakdown of traditional values, the increase of violence, and social unrest. The horror these evoked and the growing sense of impotence appear in numerous works published between 1900 and 1910, some of which are discussed in chapter 5. The deep vein of pessimism in the literature of the last two decades of the nineteenth century arises as much from the challenge of the city as from any *fin de siècle* weariness or that 'sense of an ending' common at the end of most centuries.

Forster's first four novels were published in the Edwardian period, 1901–10. The first three, *Where Angels Fear to Tread*, *The Longest Journey*, and *A Room with a View*, on a superficial reading, tend to confirm the popular image of the Edwardian age as an age of untroubled peace, an image now thoroughly discredited by historians, who point to the acute social unrest in England. Neither political nor economic questions enter these domestic comedies, yet they are as critical of the deadness of the middle class as the more socially oriented novels by Galsworthy or the more didactic plays by Shaw. Through the character of Philip Herriton, in *Where Angels Fear to Tread*, Forster establishes connections between deadness in art and in life that lie outside the range of most other Edwardian writers. By means of a deft social shorthand, he evokes the Edwardian world with all its minute particularities and social shibboleths, thus avoiding the laboured documentation of the Edwardian realists, Galsworthy, Bennett, and Wells. He also gives to people, places, institutions, and social behaviour in his novels a representative quality that makes further analysis or commentary unnecessary. And he does this, unlike James and Ford Madox Ford, without a lot of theoretical fuss about 'rendering' his world.

Although it was a period of rapid social change, the basic structure of society remained largely unchanged: class distinctions and social conventions were rigid and remained so until the First World War. What all Forster's early novels exhibit is not the injustice of the class system, but the stultifying effect of outmoded codes of behaviour on the free spirit of man, their constraining effect on his desire not to be fenced in by society. Consequently images of fences and hedges recur frequently. On one occasion the idea of a hedge provides the title of a story, 'The Other Side of the Hedge'; and in *A Room with a View* Cecil Vyse shows off his cleverness on the subject of 'whether we fence ourselves in or whether we are fenced out by the barriers of others' (RWV, ch. 9). His comedy like Jane Austen's, which he admired and imitated, operates within a rigid set of social conventions. For modern readers these details may have a period charm or they may positively repel. But the main point is that Forster's social comedy works through these conventions; it neither endorses them nor approves. All comedy works through exposing the inflexibility of codes of behaviour, whether personal or social, and is based on a perception of structures underlying external actions, words and gestures. Forster penetrates the structure of Edwardian society more deeply than most of his more politically minded contemporaries. As J. B. Priestley shrewdly remarked, 'he is in these novels anti-Edwardian while yet remaining Edwardian, further proof of this age's extraordinary variety' (Priestley, 1970, p. 129).

H. G. Wells called the Edwardian period an age of 'strained optimism'. Most of the serious novelists were conscious of this element of strain and sought to explore some of its causes and consequences. There was peace abroad, as the result of Edward VII's diplomacy, but unrest at home. The Socialists claimed that the rich were getting richer and the poor poorer; but, in fact, 'income seems to have been distributed in much the same proportions as in mid-Victorian times' (Read, 1972, p. 48). The real causes of discontent were the levelling off of wages after a period of steady growth and the ostentatious display of wealth by the new Edwardian plutocracy. Wells gives a memorable account of this in Ponderevo's meteoric career in *Tono Bungay* (1909). The new generation of novelists, mostly from the lower middle class, were more interested in the social and cultural aspirations of the Edwardian 'little man', Mr Kipps, than in recording the lives of the poor, of whom they knew little. From 1906 onwards, the Liberal Government sought to improve the lot of the poor by introducing social services and some measure of public ownership and control of industry. But its attempt to mediate between the extremes of Socialism and Conservatism failed. Lloyd George's 'People's Budget' of 1909 nearly led to the abolition of the House of Lords but not to the alleviation of poverty. Throughout this period the Fabian Society, founded at the end of the last century, popularized the idea of gradual Socialism; its main influence was in the intellectual circles in which Forster moved. From 1905 onwards, there was a militant campaign for Votes for Women. However, it is impossible to imagine Forster's Margaret Schlegel attacking policemen and politicians, as Ford Madox Ford's Valentine Wannop does in *Some Do Not* (1924). But like many of her class in Edwardian England, Miss Schlegel believed that women should work; and her private discussion club reflects accurately the new interest women were taking in social questions, especially the relief of poverty. Although Forster never writes about the poor, his vision of the 'abyss' into which they may fall is as compelling as Gissing's in *Workers in the Dawn* (1880), or Masterman's in *From the Abyss* (1903). In an unpublished essay describing an early meeting with Clive Bell in the gallery of Covent Garden Theatre, Forster makes it clear that it was a difference in their respective attitudes to the poor that kept them apart, 'for I felt it a duty to be unhappy without reserves whenever the poor entered my mind'.

Forster is something of a dark horse in English letters; it is impossible to place him in any group or school. Certainly he stands midway between the Edwardians, Galsworthy, Bennett, and Wells (who seem not quite the realists they were once thought to be), and the Georgian symbolists, James Joyce and Virginia Woolf. Forster combines much that is best in both traditions of fiction. Indeed, how to be just to the

realist and the symbolist sides of his art is still the central task of criticism, as it was for such early critics as Virginia Woolf. For F. R. Leavis
the essential Forster is a realist, for Frank Kermode he is a symbolist,
while John Beer sees the subtle interpenetration of the two modes. The
writer with whom Forster has most in common is D. H. Lawrence.
He visited Lawrence, they corresponded on intimate terms, they criti-
cized each other's works with great frankness, and Forster at an early
stage heralded Lawrence as the greatest creative writer of his generation. Both, as Wilfred Stone has pointed out, were prophetic vitalists,
opposed to the machine age; both were 'pagans haunted by Christianity, trying to rediscover in the forms of the creative imagination a new
vision of the whole'; they both stressed spontaneity in sexual and
personal relations and created their fictional worlds on a contrast
between the natural and the social world. Yet, for all these similarities,
there is a striking difference in the tone and texture of their writing.
And even when they seem most alike, they themselves were aware of
difference. For example, Lawrence wrote a passionate denunciation of
Forster's primitivism and Pan worship, pointing out that his own
'Angels' and 'Devils' were 'symbols for the flower into which we strive
to burst', while Forster's Pan was 'a stooping back to the well-head, a
perverse pushing back the waters to their source', which he thought
was 'stupid & an annihilation' (letter to Forster, 3 February 1915, KCL).

Jane Austen 'whose novels continue to live their own wonderful
internal life', Meredith, and Samuel Butler were Forster's acknowledged mentors. From Jane Austen, he learned 'the possibilities of
domestic comedy', but 'I was more ambitious', he adds, 'and tried to
hitch it onto something else', to prophecy and visionary symbolism,
in fact. From Meredith, he took the 'romantic possibilities of scenery'
and the 'Comic Spirit'; but he found that the first led to falsity and the
second to mannered archness and soon moved away from Meredith;
this is clear from his decision to discard an overwritten account of
Stephen Wonham's encounter with nature from The Longest Journey,
and also from his disparaging remarks on Meredith in Aspects of the
Novel. From Butler, the author of Erewhon and The Way of All Flesh,
he took a great deal. Butler woke him up, he taught him how to deal
with money, offered him an original example of fantasy in Erewhon
and showed 'that the majority of men are kept straight – not by
principle – but instinct'. Butler also revealed the importance of the
unconscious, an importance reinforced later by a reading of Proust.

Forster's admiration for Proust is a reminder that he is one of the least provincial English novelists. Once Wedd had put him on to Zola and Ibsen he began to read widely in European literature; something of the breadth and catholicity of his taste and his capacity to seize on significant new writers will emerge in later chapters. Here it is sufficient to draw attention to two European figures who profoundly influenced his early development: Ibsen and Wagner. The choice is typical of the man and of the age. Not only was there a temperamental affinity, but also both continental artists enjoyed a great vogue in England at the turn of the century, especially in advanced circles, although both were thought to be difficult and to require explanation, as Shaw recognized when he wrote *The Quintessence of Ibsenism*. George Moore's novel *Evelyn Innes* (1898) accurately reflects Wagner's influence in England at the turn of the century. Forster was attracted by the romantic lyric strain and the dark elemental quality in Wagner and Ibsen, the strange fusion of the seen and the unseen. He identified himself with the hero of Ibsen's *Peer Gynt*, who is the embodiment of youthful indecision, used the pseudonym 'Peer Gynt' for his university essays and first published pieces, and defined the main theme of the play as 'that of *salvation by being loved*' (CB, KCL). Wagnerian leit-motifs, or recurrent themes, are the very life-blood of Forster's fictional art, seen in the wisp of hay motif in *Howards End*, and the wasp, echo, and over-arching sky in *A Passage to India*. But in considering all these questions of debts and influences – a word incidentally that Forster disliked – it is worth remembering the novelist's insistence 'that a writer's development is internal.'

Forster lived a long and relatively uneventful life. A late Victorian by birth, he survived both world wars and finally died in June 1970, aged ninety-one. His career as a writer began and ended at Cambridge, where he spent the last twenty-five years of his life. It was fortunate for someone who believed so passionately in personal relations that a private income, together with growing success as a novelist, made it unnecessary for him to adopt a profession or to accept any permanent appointment. Although he proclaimed the importance of work through Margaret Schlegel in *Howards End*, he himself found personal fulfilment in living rather than in work. Free to travel as soon as he came down from Cambridge in 1901, his first two visits to Europe made him a writer. After the publication of *Where Angels Fear to Tread* (1905), *The Longest Journey* (1907), *A Room with a View* (1908), and *Howards End* (1910), he once again travelled extensively abroad.

He visited India in 1912–13, and again in 1921, when he acted as private Secretary to the Maharajah of Dewas Senior, visits that provided the material for his best-known novel, *A Passage to India* (1924). During part of the war years, 1915–19, he served with the Red Cross in Alexandria. This experience, as will be seen in chapter 7, undoubtedly deepened his insight into human nature and extended his range of knowledge and sympathies, in preparation for writing his masterpiece, *A Passage to India*. It also inspired three minor works: *The Government of Egypt* (1920), *Alexandria: A History and a Guide* (1922), and *Pharos and Pharillon* (1923).

The First World War effectively destroyed Forster's faith in old-fashioned political Liberalism. In 'Literature and the War', a paper read to the Weybridge Literary Society, he spoke of the indirect power of books to counteract the vast forces of fear and hatred unleashed, through establishing links with a nobler past. But it is clear that he ceased to believe in the possibility of returning to the comfortable and expansive idealism of the pre-war era. 'The nations are at War, with misery certain for the lower classes in all of them, whoever wins: the young men who ought to be the fathers of the next generation are killing one another all over Europe.' It seemed that there never had been a time 'when one's own little life and one's own little income' had been of less importance. In the post-war world, a 'civilization of disillusioned people', one could no longer believe that 'all problems would be solved and God's great Q.E.D. peal out', nor ever again 'hold the Victorian sentimental view of personal relationship, which deified and obscured the reproductive instincts and pretended that marriages were made in Heaven' ('English Literature since the War 1914–1918', KCL). The war enforced a radical reassessment of all the values Forster had inherited from nineteenth-century liberalism and awoke feelings of fear and anguish for the future. Leonard Woolf spoke for Forster and a whole generation when he wrote:

In 1914, in the background of one's life and one's mind there were light and hope; by 1918 one had unconsciously accepted a perpetual public menace and darkness and had admitted into the privacy of one's mind or soul an iron fatalistic acquiescence in insecurity and barbarism (Woolf, 1967, p. 9).

Against this menacing darkness Forster made a stand that proved a source of quiet inspiration to several generations of writers.

The war increased Forster's hostility to the complacency and arrogance of the English middle classes and to the gross inequalities of society, so that it was natural for him to turn from Liberalism to Socialism in the 1920s. For a brief period after his return from Alexandria he was literary editor of the Socialist *Daily Herald*, and many of his essays and reviews appeared in left-wing newspapers and magazines. Leonard Woolf has described how his own dual connection with the Hogarth Press and the *Nation*, of which he was editor, was partly instrumental in bringing Forster and others to write for the *Nation*. Undoubtedly had Forster wished, he could have enjoyed a highly successful career as a literary journalist; but he preferred to write only occasionally and on subjects that interested him. As he remarked to an American friend, he also preferred to remain faithful to his two mistresses, 'procrastination and sloth'.

In 1927, Forster was elected a Supernumerary Fellow at his old college, King's College, Cambridge, and remained one until 1933. The stimulating quality of the Clark Lectures, *Aspects of the Novel*, delivered at Trinity College in 1927, and the originality of numerous essays and talks, including those given for radio, suggest that, had he been able to overcome his innate shyness, he could have been a brilliant university teacher, like his friend, Goldsworthy Lowes Dickinson. Although all his close friends and contemporaries stress his genius for self-effacement and understatement, he was always willing to speak out on vital issues, such as censorship, conservation, and international relations. He became an active member of numerous societies and protest groups, yet he had greater faith in a well-worded letter to a paper or public authority than in such organized activities. Quentin Bell quotes Virginia Woolf's lively account of a visit from Forster in May 1928, when they got drunk and 'talked sodomy and sapphism'. During the weekend, they wrote articles for the *Nation* and got up petitions to oppose the censorship of Radclyffe Hall's *The Well of Loneliness* (Bell, 1972, II, p. 138). In 1934, he became the first President of the National Council for Civil Liberties and held the same office again in 1942. He attended many international conferences of writers and addressed the Paris Conference in 1935 on the subject of Liberty in England. He was a prominent member of the Humanist Society; and his Presidential Address in 1960 provides a frank and revealing account of his early emancipation from orthodox Christianity. He was often invited to give public lectures; the best known of these are his Rede Lecture on Virginia Woolf (1941) and the Ker Lecture in 1945, on 'The Development of English Prose between 1918 and 1939'.

In later life, Forster retained his interest in India and continued to keep in touch in a variety of ways. He wrote frequent book reviews on Indian topics, he gave regular monthly talks on the BBC Eastern Service from 1940 onwards, he received a steady stream of Indian visitors at Cambridge; and, in 1945, he paid his third visit to India. On this occasion, he recorded his impressions of all the many changes that had taken place since his first two visits in 1912–13 and' 1921. About the development of some of the arts, especially the cinema, he was enthusiastic; but he could see no permanent solution to 'the tragic problem of India's future'.

> The only thing that cuts a little ice is affection or the possibility
> of affection . . . But it must be genuine affection and liking. It
> must not be exercised with any ulterior motive. It must be an
> expression of the common humanity which in India and England
> and all the world over has been so thwarted of late, and so despised.

Twenty years later and a world war between, the message was much the same as that in *A Passage to India*.

During the Second World War and afterwards, Forster's novels became better known in America and reached a new public in England, especially among young readers who were facing ultimate questions with a peculiar sense of urgency as the result of the war. Lionel Trilling's brilliant and committed book, *E. M. Forster: A Study*, first published in America in 1943, and in England a year later, helped to establish Forster's status as a major writer, and to extend his fame. But the wider readership had much to do with the whole ethos of the period. People were searching for valid alternatives to the slogans and second-hand values of the day, and they found them in Forster's novels. The republication of the Pocket Edition in 1947 was timely; later paperback editions have made him one of the most widely read modern novelists.

Greater recognition in America inevitably led to invitations to lecture there. In 1947, Forster's actor friend, William Roerich, succeeded in persuading him to overcome his modesty on musical matters and accept the invitation to deliver a paper at a Symposium on Musical Criticism at Harvard. The paper, although full of good things, was still somewhat disorderly when Forster arrived, and so Roerich asked if he might cut it up and paste it together in a different order. Forster agreed, but added: 'Just be sure it says "Love" at the beginning, the middle and at the end' (Stallybrass, 1969, p. 65). The paper, 'The

Raison d'Être of Criticism in the Arts', was given and proved a great success in America and in Britain, where it was broadcast and subsequently printed in *Two Cheers for Democracy*. On this first visit to America, the novelist took in most of the obvious tourist attractions, but he also included visits to small cottages and out of the way places. And he made a point of seeing old friends who had settled in America, including Gerald Heard, Christopher Isherwood, and Christopher Wood. Two years later, in 1949, he returned to address the American Academy of Arts and Letters, on 'Art for Art's Sake', a deliberately provocative title for the time. On his visits, his friends did their best to protect his privacy from invasion, but after one determined woman had broken through and demanded something for publication, Forster remarked:

> I have been meeting that lady for years. When I was a very small frog in a very small pond she came out from Dorking to get me to write little pieces for the local newspaper. Now that I am a rather large frog in a very large pond she comes from New York. She is always the same lady (Stallybrass, 1969, pp. 68–9).

In later years, when an urgent transatlantic telephone call came at the porter's lodge at King's offering thousands of dollars for the film rights of *A Passage to India*, Forster turned a deaf ear. He enjoyed, but was never corrupted by, success.

Although *Howards End* is one of the great novels about London, Forster was never a metropolitan writer. His heart was in the country; it was there and at Cambridge that he felt most at home. When, therefore the small East Anglian town of Aldeburgh held its first Festival in 1948, he gave it his enthusiastic support. In a radio talk, he rightly insisted that a festival must have a distinguishing character to justify its existence and opposed proposals to solve the Aldeburgh Festival's financial problems through permanent orchestral and opera groups based in London. 'As soon as you start by being central you centralise. You obliterate distinction. You amuse the provinces from the metropolis.' Close association with Aldeburgh was a source of great happiness in Forster's later life. At the first Festival, he gave a talk on 'Crabbe and *Peter Grimes*', and in 1950 on John Skelton. He also read extracts from his unpublished novel *Arctic Summer*, in the following year. But what created a completely new dimension in his life was his collaboration with Eric Crozier on a libretto for Benjamin Britten's opera *Billy Budd*, which was first produced at Covent Garden in December 1951.

One interesting extension of Forster's fame came through dramatic versions of his novels made for stage and radio. Stephen Tait and Kenneth Allott produced a dramatized version of *A Room with a View* in 1950 and Santha Rama Rao a successful stage version of *A Passage to India*, first produced at the Oxford Playhouse in 1960 and subsequently in London and New York, where it ran from 9 July 1963 until 25 January 1964. Three years later a dramatization of *Howards End* by Lance Sieveking and Richard Cotrell ran in London from 28 February to 1 April 1967. Apart from helping to popularize his novels, these stage versions drew attention to the dramatic nature of much of Forster's writing and to the superb quality of the dialogue. A further indication of the wider recognition Forster won in the last years of his life was the award of the Companion of Honour in 1953 and the Order of Merit in 1969.

A pattern can be discerned in the second half of Forster's life. When, for a variety of reasons that will emerge later, he gave up publishing, but not writing, fiction, he turned to criticism, biography, and essays on public affairs. Having already exposed the evils of uniformity and authority in his novels, whether in public schools or in the rulers of India, he was well equipped to analyse the structures of power and self-delusion, underlying the totalitarian regimes in Europe. In the 1920s and 1930s, although he wrote comparatively little, he attained a symbolic importance for such left-wing writers as W. H. Auden, Christopher Isherwood, and Stephen Spender. He became a symbol of the liberal conscience of England. In 1940, when a wholly new phase of his career began, that of a brilliant broadcaster on public affairs, he spoke to a nation of the twilight that would darken Europe if Hitler's Germany triumphed. Without bluster or over-emphasis, he spoke of the things worth fighting for. In war-time, few speakers remain untouched by hysteria or official propaganda; Forster proved an exception.

Forster's later essays, published in *Two Cheers for Democracy*, exhibit the toughness and flexibility of the liberal humanist tradition, its capacity to survive and make its truths heard, through the 'slighter voices of dissent', a phrase Forster first used of the early Eliot. Whether Forster speaks as a novelist or as a publicist, we have faith in his voice, not because it is infallible, but because it never claims too much. It can be said of him what has been said of W. B. Yeats, 'we may not agree with the voice but we can trust it', because we know 'it is speaking what it knows to be true.'

2

Short Stories

When Forster came down from Cambridge in 1901 he travelled extensively in Europe, thus conforming to the fashionable custom, established from the Renaissance onwards, for a young gentleman to complete his education by making the Grand Tour. But whereas, in earlier generations, the young man escaped from his family and accustomed environment, taking only an older man as tutor or friend (as Horace Walpole took the poet Gray), by the time Forster travelled, the tradition had seen many changes: Forster's travelling companion was his mother, and he exchanged the free society of Cambridge for the restricted society of the English pension. After Byron and the other Romantic poets had invested the continent with fresh glamour and familiarized a wide public with its beauty and historical associations, the stream of visitors to Europe became a flood; permanent colonies grew up on the Riviera and in the ancient Italian cities; hotels and pensions sprang up to provide suitable accommodation for those who came; and the habit of completing one's education abroad, previously restricted to the wealthy aristocracy, now included far more of the middle class, many of whom carried their conventional English standards wherever they went, remaining untouched by the spirit of the countries they visited: Forster's short stories expose the vulgarity and limitations of such people. The early fiction also expresses the strong desire to escape from a limited English-oriented society, from family bonds, from the society of women also.

After about the 1850s there was a vast increase in the literature of travel. By 1864, Trollope – always a good index of current taste – declined to describe the Vavasor's Swiss tour, because he felt that the market was already saturated with accounts of Switzerland (*Can You Forgive Her?*, ch. 5). Out of this vast literature of travel, which came into being to instruct, to inform and to entertain, two items are specially relevant to Forster. The first is the series of *Guides* produced by Baedeker from the 1860s onwards, which told the foreign visitor what to see and what to admire: it was from Baedeker as an authoritative guide to taste that Mr Emerson seeks to emancipate Lucy Honeychurch in *A Room with a View*; similar liberations await other Forsterian characters as they learn to discard their English prejudices as well as their Baedeker prop and to respond to the *genius loci*, or spirit of place. The second item, the various volumes of *Sketches* by John Addington Symonds, notably *Sketches in Italy and Greece* (Smith, Elder, London, 1874 and 3 vols, 1898), helped to popularize an approach to the Italian people and landscape that stressed the importance of the *genius loci* and the eternal moment, both of which play vital roles in Forster's short stories and early novels. Symonds's description of how, in 'May in Umbria', 'it is sometimes the traveller's good fortune in some remote place to meet with an inhabitant who incarnates and interprets for him the *genius loci* as he has conceived it' (*Sketches*, 1898, II, 39) might almost be a gloss on Forster's early fiction. The stranger will henceforth, Symonds adds, 'become the meeting-point of many memories, the central figure in a composition which derives from him its vividness'. And his insistence that what was lacking in the modern artist was 'the mythopoeic sense' encouraged travellers to revive a way of apprehending the world that found 'archetypes and everlasting patterns of man's deepest sense of what is wonderful in nature'. For Symonds, as later for Forster, the raising of a single man to mythopoeic stature disguised and sublimated his homosexual passions.

Travel and the response to the spirit of place played a crucial role in making Forster a writer. His two early visits to Europe, the first to Italy, among other countries, between October 1901 and September 1902, and the second, which included Greece, from March to August 1903, provided him with much of the inspiration and material for his early writings, as may be seen from short stories such as 'The Story of a Panic' and 'The Road from Colonus', and also the two Italian novels, *Where Angels Fear to Tread* (1905) and *A Room with a View* (1908). Travel also provided the material and inspiration for the essays 'Macolnia Shops', 'Cnidus', 'Gemistus Pletho', and 'Cardan', all published between November 1903 and April 1905 in the *Independent Review*, and later reprinted in *Abinger Harvest* (1936). The visits to Italy and Greece made the past come more vividly alive than the formal study of history and the classics at Cambridge. In an illuminating piece of reminiscence, called 'Three Countries', written around

1950, Forster defines the influence that Italy, England and India had on his writing: of these Italy made the strongest and most indelible impression and provided him with the necessary inspiration. He recounts as an example of the inspiration of the spirit of place how the idea of 'The Story of a Panic' suddenly came to him in a valley a few miles north of Ravello, called Vallone Fontana Carosa and how the novel *Where Angels Fear to Tread* was based on 'a piece of effrontery', the taking up of an overheard hotel conversation about 'an English lady who had married an Italian far beneath her socially'. He then tells how he was able to create Gino and place him in Italian society (of which he knew nothing), by guessing 'at his relatives, his daily life, his habits, his house, and his sketchy conception of housekeeping'. In considering the influence of travel on Forster, it is worth remembering that there is no strict equivalence between geographical realities and the countries of the mind. In his Commonplace Book, Forster remarks 'Map-geography is a convention which is useful for practical purposes but has nothing to do with experience.' What he found abroad was a completely new mental and emotional landscape.

In many ways the short stories form an ideal introduction to Forster's fictional universe, since they represent some of his earliest writing and introduce us to his characteristic blend of poetry and realism. They also explore themes that are more amply developed in the novels, such themes as salvation, the 'rescue party', the past, personal relations, getting in touch with nature, money, and the attack on conventional ideas of good form. There are four collections of short stories: *The Celestial Omnibus* (1911), *The Eternal Moment* (1928), *Collected Short Stories* (1947) – combining the earlier two collections – and the posthumous *The Life to Come, and Other Stories* (1972). From the dates of publication, it might seem that the stories belong to the latter part of Forster's career, that is, to the period after the publication of *Howards End* in 1910, a mistake made by some contemporary reviewers. In fact, many were written very early and published in various magazines before the publication of his first novel *Where Angels Fear to Tread* in 1905, although their composition must have been roughly contemporary with the writing of this novel and with the two early versions of *A Room with a View* (see below, pp. 42–3). So, for example, 'Albergo Empedocle', in *The Life to Come* collection of 1972, was Forster's first printed story, appearing in the magazine *Temple Bar* in December 1903. 'The Eternal Moment', the title story of the 1928 collection, first appeared in the *Independent Review* as early as June 1905, the same journal having already published three of Forster's short stories in the preceding year: 'The Road from Colonus', 'The Story of a Panic', and 'The Other Side of the Hedge'.

In the Introduction to *Collected Short Stories* Forster calls his tales 'fantasies'. They are certainly not to be judged by standards appropriate to realism. Some, such as 'The Other Side of the Hedge' and 'Mr Andrews', are pure fantasy; others, such as 'The Story of a Panic' and the 'Other Kingdom', combine fantasy and social realism. The supernatural irrupts and shatters the surface of polite society, the infinite invades the finite world of picnics and civilized chatter. One story, 'The Eternal Moment', is not really a fantasy at all. In an essay on Butler's *Erewhon*, written in 1944 (TCD), Forster remarked: 'I like that idea of fantasy, of muddling up the actual and the impossible until the reader isn't sure which is which, and I have sometimes tried to do it when writing myself'. It is the only 'muddle' he condones. The mode suits his preference for obliquity, surprise, and understatement.

Fantasy occupies a curious middle ground between allegory and symbolism. It establishes its own laws, revels in swift flights of fancy, is playful, often witty, makes great demands on its readers – it 'makes us pay more', says Forster in his chapter on Fantasy in *Aspects of the Novel* (1927). Below it however lies the bottomless pit of English whimsy. It is into this pit that some of Forster's stories fall when he indulges in facetious make-believe, donnish asides, and the humour of the schoolroom. But the short story is the ideal form for fantasy, since what it normally offers is a poetic image of life, not a realistic chronicle. Essentially, Forster's short stories offer us the truths of poetry not the facts of prose fiction; yet even in the comedy of manners, the genre of his novels, the poetic or visionary element plays a crucial role. How well does he fuse these two elements, poetry and realism? This is the central critical question to be asked about Forster; and the short stories are the first of his works to pose it.

Forster turned to the short story for a variety of reasons connected with his temperament and the spirit of his age. It seemed the right form to contain his personal blend of poetry and deft social comedy; moreover it offered itself as the first obvious step in authorship. The years 1880–1920 mark the great period of the short story. In Europe, the masters were Maupassant and Chekov; in England, they were Henry James, Kipling and Conrad. There were probably more magazines publishing short stories then than at any other period and Forster had several friends on the board of one of the magazines, the *Independent Review*. Many of the major English novelists produced some of their most distinguished work in this form; it had a peculiar fascination for writers who wished to combine realism and fantasy, the natural and the supernatural. Thus, in writing stories about Pan and the intervention of the supernatural, Forster was in part conforming to a current literary fashion; but he was also responding to the direct challenge and inspiration of the Italian landscape.

At the time he had not read Arthur Machen's 'The Great God Pan' and even if he had, it is doubtful whether such a contrived piece of *fin de siècle* evil and horror would have made much appeal. But it was not necessary to have read Machen. The theme of Pan was 'in the air', as Forster recalled many years later in a radio talk on Machen; in fact, it was all pervasive. It may be found in Yeats's poetry of the 1890s, in Meredith's novels (much admired by Forster when he first began to write), in the nature writing of Richard Jefferies (who also celebrates the spirit of place and the eternal moment), and, at a much more popular level, in Saki and in Kenneth Grahame's *The Wind in the Willows*. The cult had two sides: satanic and benevolent, the latter being part of the Romantic heritage, with its worship of nature, and consoling pantheism, the former an expression of late-nineteenth-century decadence.

Almost as pervasive was the related cult of the supernatural. Arthur Machen, Algernon Blackwood, and M. R. James were the acknowledged masters of this form of entertainment. But Henry James in *The Turn of the Screw* showed that it was possible to adapt the ghost story to serious artistic ends; this is, in part, what Forster too attempted. However, in January 1905, he wrote to his friend R. C. Trevelyan, 'I somehow think I am too refined to write a ghost story.' It seems likely that he may have received the same advice from an editor as his fictional creation, Rickie Elliott: 'Write a really good ghost story and we'd take it at once' (LJ, ch. 15). Forster's own attempt to write such a story, however, 'The Purple Envelope', was rejected by the editor of the *Temple Bar* and much later by the publishers of the collection *The Celestial Omnibus*, in 1911. 'The Purple Envelope' is a confused story about mysterious words that appear in a shaving glass; it includes sleep-walking, sudden death, and a hidden will. In spite of such ingredients, it causes no frisson; and the mystery has to be awkwardly explained at the end.

By the time Forster's stories first appeared in book form in 1911 and 1928, he was an established novelist with four novels to his credit, including the best-seller *Howards End*. Readers and reviewers were therefore puzzled by his choice of theme in the short stories, the combination of poetry and realism, the occasional immaturity, the thinness of the social documentation. Few related the tales to their early origin and their appropriate literary context. To do this is the first step in a just appreciation of these stories that are simultaneously characteristic products of the turn of the century and of the author's early vision of life.

'The Story of a Panic' (IR, August 1904) illustrates many of the characteristic features of Forster's short stories: the use of an obtuse narrator, the sudden irruption of the supernatural, the contrast between the instinctive and the conventional life, the related themes of salvation and brotherhood. Like 'The Road from Colonus' and the less successful 'The Rock' (first published in LTC in 1972), 'The Story of a Panic' was inspired by the *genius loci*. In the Introduction to the *Collected Short Stories*, Forster explains how it came to be written. It originated in a walk near Ravello in May 1902.

> I sat down in a valley, a few miles above the town, and suddenly
> the first chapter of the story rushed into my mind as if it had
> waited for me there. I received it as an entity and wrote it out
> as soon as I returned to the hotel But it seemed unfinished and a
> few days later I added some more until it was three times as long;
> as now printed (CSS, p. v).

Even though this experience of 'sitting down on the theme as if it were an anthill' may have been rare, the spirit of place, if not necessarily the immediate inspiration of place, plays almost as important a part in Forster's writing as it does in that of D. H. Lawrence.

The narrator of 'The Story of a Panic' is an insensitive, conventionally minded Englishman – a convenient device for dramatizing contrasting scales of value. Together with his two daughters, he is staying in a hotel at Ravello. Also staying there are the Miss Robinsons and their nephew, Eustace, who resists the narrator's attempts to make him conform to the respectable stereotype of an athletic public schoolboy. Completing the company are Mr Sandbach, who is a retired clergyman, and Mr Leyland, an artist. The English visitors picnic in the chestnut woods above Ravello. While the adults talk about picturesque beauty, Eustace cuts a piece of wood to make a whistle (a Pan pipe, we later realize). Leyland's complaint that 'the woods no longer give shelter to Pan', provides Mr Sandbach with his cue for an informal sermon and the reader with the essential donnée of the story.

> 'Pan!' cried Mr Sandbach, his mellow voice filling the valley as
> if it had been a great green church, 'Pan is dead. That is why the
> woods do not shelter him.' And he began to tell the striking
> story of the mariners who were sailing near the coast at the time
> of the birth of Christ, and three times heard a loud voice saying:
> 'The Great God Pan is dead' (CSS, p. 6).

This 'striking story', originally told by Plutarch (*Moralia*, 'De Defectu Oraculorum', XVII), had been put in a Christian framework by Eusebius, and it is this version Mr Sandbach, as a good Christian, recounts. Disproof follows. A few minutes later, all experience a moment of panic, even the stolid narrator, and they run away.

> It was not the spiritual fear that one has known at other times,
> but brutal overmastering physical fear, stopping up the ears, and
> dropping clouds before the eyes, and filling the mouth with foul
> tastes. And it was no ordinary humiliation that survived; for I
> had been afraid, not as a man, but as a beast (CSS, p. 8).

The testimony wrung from the commonplace narrator about this extraordinary event imparts the necessary dramatic conviction to this part of the story.

When the frightened English visitors recover, they find that Eustace is missing. They discover him in the chestnut woods, lying on his back, blissfully happy, but with the unmistakable traces of Pan, of goat hooves near by. Mr Sandbach performs an impromptu exorcism of 'The Evil One'. All agree to say nothing about the event. But the boy Eustace takes no part in the conversation or the agreement. He shows a sudden eagerness to know where Gennaro 'the stop-gap waiter, a clumsy impertinent fisherlad' is (clearly the Italian counterpart of Forster's childhood playmate, Ansell, the garden-boy). Eustace races about the wood and reappears with a poor dazed hare on his arm. A little later, he spontaneously kisses an old Italian woman and offers her flowers. Returning to the hotel, he runs to embrace Gennaro. The adults decide that he is mad and requires careful watching. The narrator officiously reproves Gennaro for using the familiar second personal singular 'tu' in addressing Eustace. But clearly Eustace and Gennaro are now brothers, an early affirmation of the connection between the instinctive response to nature and human brotherhood, more fully explored in *The Longest Journey* and *Maurice*.

The last section of the story explores a typical complex of Forsterian themes: the misguided rescue party, the theme of salvation, money as an agent of corruption and death. At night, the narrator wakes to discover Eustace performing extraordinary antics outside the hotel. 'Eustace Robinson, aged fourteen, was standing in his nightshirt saluting, praising, and blessing, the great forces and manifestations of Nature.' The narrator, at the instigation of his daughter, who recognizes the bond between Gennaro and Eustace which her father is too obtuse to understand, suborns Gennaro to help catch Eustace. The scene between the tempter and the poor Italian boy is filled with astute irony. The two boys, brothers in nature, now meet. At the very moment that Eustace's love of nature recreates the bond of brotherhood, the narrator crackles a new ten lira note. Gennaro sticks out his hand with a jerk, but the unsuspecting Eustace grips it in his own. As he shares confidences with his Italian brother, the watching adults pounce. 'He gave a shrill heart piercing scream; and the white roses, which were falling that year, descended in showers on him as we dragged him to the house.' But the rescue party fails. Both boys leap out of a window and 'land with a heavy thud on the asphalt path'. Eustace escapes and never returns. Gennaro, the unwilling accomplice in the plot, recognizes instinctively that Eustace has gone in answer to the call of the Great God Pan, and cries out: 'He has understood and he is saved . . . Now, instead of dying he will live!' Overcome himself with remorse for selling his friend, he grasps the ten lira note, and dies. The tale ends with the narrator's remark that the leap from the window would never have killed an Englishman, and the sounds of happiness far down the valley, where 'still resounded the shouts and laughter of the escaping boy.'

Two other stories are inspired immediately by a particular place, 'The Road from Colonus', the story of a modern Oedipus who in saving his life loses his soul, and 'The Rock'. Both are also centrally concerned with the theme of salvation. The first is a success, the second a comparative failure – a 'complete flop', according to its author, even though the original inspiration at Gurnard's Head in Cornwall had been genuine. Several qualities go to make 'The Road from Colonus' the fine story that it is. To begin with, the themes of true and false salvation, the symbolic moment of choice, and the transfiguration of the ordinary world of a Greek inn and a votive tree, are firmly embedded in fully realized character, scene and action; the themes are not external or over-obtrusive as they are in 'The Rock'. In the story set in Greece, Forster exploits to the full 'the romantic possibilities of scenery'.

'I never saw anything so marvellous before,' said Mr Lucas. 'I could even step inside the trunk and see where the water comes from.'

For a moment he hesitated to violate the shrine. Then he remembered with a smile his own thought – 'the place shall be mine; I will enter it and possess it' – and leapt almost aggressively on to a stone within.

The water pressed up steadily and noiselessly from the hollow roots and hidden crevices of the plane, forming a wonderful amber pool ere it spilt over the lip of bark on to the earth outside. Mr Lucas tasted it and it was sweet, and when he looked up the black funnel of the trunk he saw sky which was blue, and some leaves which were green; and he remembered, without smiling, another of his thoughts.

Others had been before him – indeed he had a curious sense of companionship. Little votive offerings to the presiding Power were fastened on to the bark – tiny arms and legs and eyes in tin, grotesque models of the brain or the heart – all tokens of some recovery of strength or wisdom or love. There was no such thing as the solitude of nature, for the sorrows and joys of humanity had pressed even into the bosom of a tree. He spread out his arms and steadied himself against the soft charred wood, and then slowly leant back, till his body was resting on the trunk behind. His eyes closed, and he had the strange feeling of one who is moving, yet at peace – the feeling of the swimmer, who, after long struggling with chopping seas, finds that after all the tide will sweep him to his goal.

So he lay motionless, conscious only of the stream below his feet, and that all things were a stream, in which he was moving (CSS, pp. 103–4).

The irony that plays on the two different senses in which one may save one's life is more deft in 'The Road from Colonus' than in 'The Rock', in which the actual saving of the hero from drowning leads explicitly to the question: what is a life worth and how much should the hero give to his rescuers. Again the dialogue in 'The Road from

Colonus', although it develops potent symbolic overtones, is more natural. In 'The Rock', the wife spells out too obviously the meaning to the narrator when she says that 'there are no such things as purely practical questions. Every question springs straight out of the infinite, and until you acknowledge that you will never answer it.' Moreover, when the narrator hears that the hero has finally decided, one day when the sun 'was flaming under the wych elm', to reward his rescuers with nothing, but to go and live with them, the comment, this taught him 'that some of us can meet reality on this side of the grave', sticks out awkwardly in the story. He was to embody the sentiment more subtly in his novels. And the wych elm turns up again in *Howards End*. Finally, where the climax of 'The Road from Colonus' rests on the sober irony that Mr Lucas, who was granted a vision of the waters of salvation in Greece, ends his days in London complaining of the noise of children and 'running water', 'The Rock' ends with a sentimental and unrealized vision of the possibility of combining passion and self-denial. Although 'The Rock' is shot through with Forster's favourite and private images, it proves that something more than the inspiration of place and a symbolic situation are necessary to produce a good short story. What it lacks is the art of suggestion and ironic control.

Much of Forster's irony in the short stories is directed at those who substitute second-hand literary notions and ideas of good form for a genuine insight into reality. 'The Celestial Omnibus' provides a typical example. In this story, the respectable and pompous Mr Bons, whose name is 'snob' reversed, talks knowledgeably about literature and art, but is aghast when he meets the heroes of literature and the great writers of the past, as he accompanies the boy on his journey in 'The Celestial Omnibus'. In terror, he screams to be saved. To the driver of the Omnibus, he says, 'I have honoured you. I have quoted you. I have bound you in vellum. Take me back to my world.' To which Dante replies:

> I am the means and not the end. I am the food and not the life. Stand by yourself, as that boy has stood. I cannot save you. For poetry is a spirit; and they that would worship it must worship in spirit and in truth (CSS, pp. 57–8).

Both the 'Other Kingdom' and 'Albergo Empedocle' also contrast conventional respect for the classics with a natural response to the spirit of pagan mythology. In the 'Other Kingdom', it is the 'crude unsophisticated person', Miss Beaumont, who establishes her kinship with ancient myths; she escapes from the possessiveness of her suitor by becoming a tree. And in 'Albergo Empedocle', it is not the young lady who knows all about the transmigration of souls who becomes a natural Greek, but Harold whose 'character was so simple; it consisted of little more than two things, the power to love and the desire for truth'. 'It is imagination,' Mildred declares, 'that makes the past live.' But the story asks us to accept that the only true access to the past is through a simple love of beauty and truth: and this Harold possesses. Already we encounter that over-valuation of the untutored instinct that recurs in Forster's athletic primitives and so disturbs the balance of his moral vision.

Two stories that have similar descriptions of academic notes floating downward through water also develop a strong contrast between the world of learning and the world of the passions. These are 'Ansell' and 'The Story of the Siren'. The first is a slight piece, written as early as 1902 or 1903, but not published until 1972; its chief interest is auto-biographical, for it clearly relates to Forster's own friendship with Ansell, the garden-boy. This experience liberated Forster into a freer, more natural world. The story is a subsequent tribute to that liberation. 'Whenever we pass the place Ansell looks over and says "Them Books" and laughs, and I laugh too as heartily as he.' 'The Story of the Siren', a tale that contrasts the repressive force of Christianity with a pagan spirit capable of destroying silence and saving the world, is the tribute of a gentle civilized writer to the unconscious and violent energies expressed by simple peasant people. Rebecca West, who reviewed it in 1920, noted how Forster's attempt to bring back paganism, a religion beyond recall, gave this story an 'atmosphere of the ghostly hour before twilight' (Gardner, 1973, p. 189). The simple evocative quality of the prose raises this story of violence and superstition to the status of a powerful myth.

> 'Save the world?' I cried. 'Did the prophecy end like that?' He leaned back against the rock, breathing deep. Through all the blue-green reflections I saw him colour. I heard him say: 'Silence and loneliness cannot last for ever. It may be a hundred or a thousand years, but the sea lasts longer, and she shall come out of it and sing.' I would have asked him more, but at that moment the whole cave darkened, and there rode in through its narrow entrance the returning boat (CSS, p. 206).

'The Story of the Siren' is one of Forster's few successful attempts to present violence as the corrective to the values of Christian civilization without appearing to condone brutality, as he sometimes seems to do in *The Longest Journey*, *Where Angels Fear to Tread*, and *Maurice*.

Most of the stories focus on the importance of the past, either the spirit of the classical past or a past moment in the life of one of the characters, a moment of heightened consciousness, instinctive joy or vision that momentarily transfigures the ordinary world but which is either rejected or forgotten. Especially notable in this second category is 'The Eternal Moment', which, unlike the rest of the stories, contains no element of fantasy. It recounts the return of a female novelist to a small Italian town that her novel had helped to put on the literary map and thus spoil (had not Forster himself put San Gimignano into *Where Angels Fear to Tread* under the thinly disguised name of Monteriano?) The past experience that constitutes Miss Raby's eternal moment is a kiss from a young Italian guide, 'a presumptuous boy' who had taken her 'to the gates of heaven'. On her return, years later, she discovers that her former guide has become as hopelessly vulgarized as the town itself; and she is forced to recognize that she is no longer in love with him, that although the 'incident upon the mountain had been one of the great moments of her life – perhaps the greatest, certainly the most enduring', it belonged to the past. Yet the past moment remains eternal because it has been deeply felt. It constitutes the index of reality by which Miss Raby understands and judges the present. But because it exists only in memory it is neither recoverable nor repeatable. And the moment was never consummated except in the fleeting kiss. Her exposure of 'her thoughts and desires to a man of another class' is for Colonel Leyland, her companion and typical representative of the undeveloped heart in English society, unpardonable, because she has revealed the 'nakedness' of the middle-class 'to the alien'.

The idea of the eternal moment occurs frequently in Forster's fiction, for example in Lucy's kiss on the violet slopes at Fiesole in *A Room with a View* and Rickie's vision of Agnes's and Gerald's love in *The Longest Journey*. The short story 'The Eternal Moment', taken in conjunction with the homosexual stories in *The Life to Come* volume, suggests that at the personal level the idea may have been a convenient imaginative transfiguration of chance homosexual encounters, which, given the inhibitions of Forster's temperament and the moral and literary taboos of society, must remain unfulfilled and be expressed only indirectly. A manuscript passage, never incorporated into *Where*

Angels Fear to Tread, which contains Philip Herriton's tribute to the friends he made through casual encounters, reflects Forster's own experiences and feelings

> O friends, dear friends of mine whom I have made in Italy!
> cabmen, waiters, sacristans, shop assistants, soldiers. . . . We have
> been friends for years, I think when we first met. . . . You told
> me everything, and I told you more than I shall ever tell my true
> and tried acquaintance here. Then we parted with warm hand
> grasp, wondering why we had been kept apart so long. And
> thank goodness, I shall never see one of you again (Ellem, 1971,
> p. 623).

There can be no doubt of the relevance of this to Forster himself, since he adds: 'So it was with Philip, my tried and true acquaintance: who on this occasion, as on many others, feels and behaves as I do.'

The notion of imaginative transposition of homosexual into heterosexual relations also throws light on the sense of guilt and remorse that so frequently accompanies the eternal moment in Forster's fiction, previously so puzzling to most readers. However, the idea of the eternal moment has deep roots in the literary tradition as well as in the author's psyche: it represents one of Forster's most obvious debts to nineteenth-century Romanticism. In *The Prelude*, Wordsworth celebrates the importance of certain 'spots of time' and shows they possess a 'vivifying virtue'. Pater's Marius experiences such moments of heightened consciousness; but for him they 'only left the actual world more lonely than ever'. The same *fin de siècle* sense of loss occasionally casts a melancholy light over Forster's eternal moments, as it does too over Joyce's 'epiphanies' in the *Dubliners* (1914). In general, however, Forster assimilates the visionary moments of high Romanticism into the more decorous world of domestic comedy, but not without some incongruity, not without creating the impression that joy always lives in the past, as such dissimilar characters as Miss Abbott, Rickie, Helen Schlegel, and Maurice affirm. For someone who was forced by convention to celebrate heterosexual love when his chief insight lay elsewhere, the idea of the eternal moment was specially attractive. It was easier to render the past symbolic moment than the passionate present. The result is, however, that for all the beauty, the high intelligence and sparkling wit of Forster's fiction, the emphasis placed on the past creates a sadness, an emptiness, a withdrawal of living energies from the present that is damaging to his art. Most damaging of all, Forster's fantasies invite the charge of sentimentality, since the actual rendering of the moment does not always justify the peculiar value placed upon it.

Several stories are more concerned with the visionary future than with the visionary past. 'Mr Andrews' for example, is a brief fantasy that presents the souls of the dead ascending towards the Judgment Seat at the Gate of Heaven, among them the soul of a respectable English Christian, Mr Andrews, and the soul of a Turk, who has pillaged the villages of the infidel and married three times. They enter as brothers, each praying that the other be admitted, but they soon decide to leave, having tired of their limited visions of perfection. '"I am going," said Mr Andrews at last. "We desire infinity and we cannot imagine it. How can we expect it to be granted? I have never imagined anything infinitely good or beautiful excepting in my dreams."' They therefore depart from the unsatisfactory heaven of their own devising and expectations and join the World Soul, but 'with all the experiences they had gained, and all the love and wisdom they had generated', which somehow pass into the World Soul and make it better. In its limited way this brief fantasy foreshadows *A Passage to India*, partly in its theme of interracial brotherhood, and partly in its concern with man's inability to comprehend the infinite: the simultaneously humanizing and yet dwarfing effect of the infinite, rendered with such reverberating power in the last scene between Fielding and Adela in *A Passage to India*, where 'a friendliness, as of dwarfs shaking hands, was in the air.'

A strange little story called 'The Point of It', which puzzled reviewers but delighted Edith Sitwell, who thought it wonderful, also projects its moment of ultimate revelation into the life beyond the grave. The chief interest of this story is that Micky, who has not so much rejected as failed to understand the symbolic moment of his friend Harold's death, is given what Henry James called a 'second go', a second chance of salvation. He does not, like so many of Forster's other heroes, join the ranks of the benighted irredeemably, although indeed his second chance does not come until he is dead.

> Hell made her last effort, and all that is evil in creation, all the distortions of love and truth by which we are vexed, came surging down the estuary, and the boat hung motionless. Micky heard the pant of breath through the roaring, the crack of muscles; then he heard a voice say, 'The point of it . . .' and a weight fell off his body and he crossed mid-stream (CSS, p. 179).

Unique among the stories that focus upon the visionary future is 'The Machine Stops', an anti-Wellsian fantasy published in 1909, which presents a horrifying picture of what may happen when machinery comes to control our lives and man ceases to be the measure of all things. Edwin Muir, himself a distinguished exponent of fantasy, complained that Forster gave no reason why humanity in its last stages should 'live in cells under the ground, shut off from the outer air, the surface of the earth, the sea, the sky, and one another' and that therefore the story became 'unreal' (Gardner, 1973, p. 352). Compared with such other writers of utopian or anti-utopian fiction as Zamyatin, Wells, Huxley, and Orwell, it is true that Forster spends little time in demonstrating that the fantasy future is a logical development from the present, or in establishing its origin and precise psychological and scientific basis. Even Morris's *News from Nowhere* (1891) and Butler's *Erewhon* (1872), which Forster admired, break off to explain how their fantasy worlds came into existence. But Muir is mistaken in suggesting that Forster provides no explanation: he does. The world of 'The Machine Stops' is made to seem a perfectly logical extension of our own. And the critique it offers is in complete harmony with Forster's whole vision of life. He sees that man no longer lives in direct contact with the earth, that he no longer experiences life through the senses, the five portals of the soul, but takes his knowledge second-hand from lectures, newspapers, books, and screens, and is therefore gradually becoming subservient to the machinery and technology of which he was once the master. As soon as the Machine has annihilated space and made every country alike there is no point in travel. As he remarked in an essay on Auden's *The Enchafèd Flood* in 1951, 'we have annihilated time and space, we have furrowed the desert, and spanned the sea, only to find at the end of every vista our own unattractive features' (TCD). In the world of 'The Machine Stops', men therefore naturally retreat into their air-conditioned cells to enjoy the illusory joys of machine culture.

Most original of all is Forster's insight into the possibility that man will become so uncritically dependent on the machine that he will not notice its gradual deterioration: he will accept the jarring sounds as part of the harmony, the foul air and diminished light as natural. The relevance of this to modern-day world-pollution and the break-down in basic social services is obvious. The people in the world of the machines have never known silence. When the machine stops and there is silence, thousands of people are killed outright. Ultimately only Vashti and her son Kuni escape – escape in spirit, if not in body.

> They wept for humanity, those two, not for themselves. They could not bear that this should be the end. Ere silence was completed their hearts were opened, and they knew what had been important on earth. Man, the flower of all flesh, the noblest of all creatures visible, man who had once made god in his image, and had mirrored his strength on the constellations, beautiful naked man was dying, strangled in the garments he had woven . . . The sin against the body – it was for that they wept in chief; the centuries of wrong against the muscles and the nerves, and those five portals by which we apprehend (CSS, p. 157).

An airship crashes down through one of the vomitories and explodes. 'For a moment they saw the nations of the dead, and, before they joined them, scraps of the untainted sky.' Edith Sitwell wrote to the author that this story made her feel as though she came 'out of a dark tunnel' in which she had always lived into an immense open space and was 'seeing things living for the first time' (letter, 30 March 1928, KCL). 'The Machine Stops', so unlike Forster's other writing in its science fiction framework, expresses the essence of Forster's humanist faith, with its message that man is the measure of all things, that the body is holy, and that our lives are only complete within a perspective that includes the infinite. In this story the infinite is imaged in the 'untainted sky', in *A Passage to India* in the 'overarching sky'.

'"When real things are so wonderful, what is the point of pretending?"', reflects Rickie as he compares one of his little stories about Pan with the reality of the love between Agnes and Gerald (LJ, ch. 5). For Rickie's creator, fantasy offered a means of focusing simultaneously on the finite and the infinite, of relating the unseen to the seen, and thus of achieving the 'double vision', but it is questionable whether he succeeded in fusing the two perspectives in his short stories as well as in his novels. In the short stories, the unseen too often assumes the fashionable guise of Pan, and this leads either to learned evasion or – as Lawrence saw – to a meaningless primitivism, 'saying the source is everything'. Years later, in 1928, Forster wrote in his Commonplace Book: 'What a pity the poetry in me has got mixed up with Pan.' In the novels, the unseen assumes more varied guises. To brood too much on the 'superiority of the unseen to the seen' is medieval,

Margaret Schlegel warns her sister in *Howards End* (ch. 12). '"Our business is not to contrast the two, but to reconcile them."' The characters in Forster's novels are haunted by the unseen; infinity attends them and the world they inhabit. But the effect in the novels, as opposed to the short stories, comes through such original inventions as Helen's vision of panic and emptiness as she hears the goblin footfalls in Beethoven's Fifth Symphony and Mrs Moore's vision of an echoing universe; it comes through the hauntingly evocative quality of Forster's prose: it does not come from exploring fantasy or following the cloven hoof of Pan.

3
Italian Novels

'Lucy', 'New Lucy', *A Room with a View*

From the Society of the Cambridge Apostles, Forster had acquired the habit of questioning all conventional ideas about beauty and truth, but when he travelled abroad in October 1901 to see the lands whose ancient literature he had studied at Cambridge, the circles he entered, in the little pensions where he and his mother stayed, were dominated by rigid middle-class English codes: moral, social and aesthetic. Irritating as these codes seemed at the time, they not only yielded the material on which to exercise his ironic spirit in short stories, but also provided a framework of contrasting values ideally suited to novels of domestic comedy in the Jane Austen manner. 'But oh what a viewpoint is the English hotel or Pension!' he exclaimed in March 1902; and, earlier in the same month, wrote to his friend Goldsworthy Lowes Dickinson, 'I wish I didn't see everything with this horrible foreground of enthusiastic ladies, but it is impossible to get away from it' (Ellem, 1971, p. 624). In the two Italian novels, *A Room with a View* and *Where Angels Fear to Tread*, he rises above the limited viewpoint of the pension and adjusts foreground and background to suit his comic purpose. But the achievement did not come without a struggle.

The evidence of this struggle lies in the two earlier versions of *A Room with a View*, parts of which survive in manuscript in King's College Library, Cambridge (Ellem, 1971, pp. 623–5). The first, 'Lucy', took its origin from Forster's stay in Florence in October 1901, and was written on his return to England, between October 1902 and December 1903. The whole action takes place in Italy and centres on the residents of the Pension Bertolini, who are putting on a benefit-concert for charity: the concert was to be the main episode. The characters in this version are too close to their real life counterparts; and the high-minded dialogues on the antithesis between life and art are transpositions of typical Cambridge Apostolic discussions into another context. Because of its excessive concern with the art, architecture and local colour of Italy, this might almost be labelled a Baedeker novel. The second version, the 'New Lucy', begun in December 1903, is altogether more ambitious. Forster now added the contrasted Italian/ English two-part structure, which is retained in the published novel, *A Room with a View*. He also worked out the conflict between spontaneous love and conventional codes at a deeper, more passionate level; and he made the ending tragic, as in *The Longest Journey*. Although there is some confusion in the structure and characterization, this version marks a great step forward. But then Forster laid it aside to write *Where Angels Fear to Tread* (1905) and *The Longest Journey* (1907). When he returned to the 'New Lucy' in June 1907, he had achieved greater detachment from his material and was a more experienced writer. Discarding Lucy's and George's plan to elope (on bicycles) and George's improbable sudden death, 'he died at once. No pain . . . No disfigurement either', he recast and rewrote the story of Lucy Honeychurch's education of the heart in the spirit of high comedy. *A Room with a View*, by common consent, is Forster's sunniest novel, the one in which he comes closest in spirit to Jane Austen. It celebrates the victory of Love and Truth over 'Muddle', a word of rich and varied connotation in Forster's fiction that normally signifies some fatal obscuring of inner vision by the falsifying conventions of society. 'One of Morgan's greatest virtues', William Plomer remarked, 'was his life long struggle to get at and formulate exact truths and the relations between different truths, and so to do away with "muddle" (one of his favourite words).' The theme is all-pervasive in his fiction.

The opening chapter, in characteristic Forsterian manner, bounces us into the middle of a conversation between Lucy Honeychurch and her elderly chaperone Miss Bartlett: they are talking about the failure of the Pension Bertolini to come up to expectations. For one thing their rooms have no view and for another, the cockney-run pension, with its 'portraits of the late Queen' and its typical English residents, makes them think that they might just as well have remained in London. Mr Emerson, an old man with unorthodox views and manners of behaviour at odds with the cautious gentility that prevails in the pension, offers his room and his son's, both of which have views. The offer, instead of giving immediate pleasure, causes embarrassment all round; and even when it is accepted, Miss Bartlett takes the larger room so that her tender young charge should not sleep in the room previously occupied by the young man, George Emerson. Here, in this trivial incident, which gives duty the 'sensation of a fog' from which Lucy must escape to the clear night air, we have the first dramatic confrontation between the two worlds and the two sets of values: the foggy world of genteel propriety, and the clear world of reason, spontaneity, and naturalness. To the modern reader all the fuss about the rules of propriety relating to offers of rooms, proper topics of conversation, chaperonage, and a stolen kiss, may seem excessive – as indeed it did to a contemporary reviewer, R. A. Scott-James in 1908 – but it is artistically justified as the dramatization of two different attitudes towards life. The sharply observed details establish the need for 'a view', that is the need to cultivate a wider perspective than social propriety, the need to relate the finite and the infinite. From the confusion of values in Lucy's mind, Forster develops high comedy and serious moral discriminations, maintaining a perfect balance between the two.

Lucy's visit to Santa Croce, on the morning following the exchange of rooms, further illustrates the conflict between naturalness and conventionality, the conflict between the inward promptings of the self and conformity to external codes of behaviour. The structure of the incidents and the structure of the language constantly reinforce these distinctions. On this occasion, Lucy's guide is Miss Lavish, a gushing English novelist, who sets up her own emancipated and unorthodox views as a kind of orthodoxy to be admired and adopted, affecting scorn for Baedeker while obviously writing Baedeker novels as she moves from one Italian town to another in search of inspiration. Forster's prose artfully mimics the bright shrill discontinuities of her speech and movement, her patronizing attitude to Italians: '"Look at that adorable wine-cart! How the driver stares at us, dear, simple soul."' But for Lucy, the inexperienced traveller, it 'was a treat . . . to be with anyone so clever and so cheerful.' Miss Lavish disappears down a side street and Lucy finds herself 'jilted' by her brilliant companion and deprived of her Baedeker. So she enters the church on her own.

Immediately Lucy's reflections make it apparent how difficult it is to respond honestly to unfamiliar sights abroad.

Of course, it must be a wonderful building. But how like a barn! And how very cold! Of course, it contained frescoes by Giotto, in the presence of whose tactile values she was capable of feeling what was proper. But who was to tell her which they were? (RWV, ch. 2).

Lucy is torn between what she genuinely feels and what she thinks she ought to feel. Young, inexperienced, she has at least heard of Bernard Berenson's, or perhaps Roger Fry's, praise of Giotto's 'tactile' values, but she cannot really connect such bookish ideas with her own experience. She now receives a second education in naturalness, the first being Mr Emerson's offer of the rooms. The 'pernicious charm of Italy' begins to work on her. She becomes aware of the discrepancy between the lively confused spirit of the church and the earnest mood of the tourists, 'their noses were as red as their Baedekers', admiring only what they are told to admire. An act of spontaneous humanity – the attempt to save a child from falling heavily on a stone prelate's upturned toes – brings Lucy and the Emersons together once more. '"Hateful bishop!" exclaimed the voice of old Mr Emerson, who had darted forward also.' When Lucy primly refuses Mr Emerson's invitation to join their tour of the church, Mr Emerson's reproof underlines the thematic contrast between naturalness and convention.

> 'My dear,' said the old man gently, 'I think that you are repeating what you have heard older people say. You are pretending to be touchy; but you are not really. Stop being so tiresome, and tell me instead what part of the church you want to see.'

During their tour, Mr Emerson hears an Anglican clergyman telling his party of tourists to remember that the church was built by faith. '"Remember nothing of the sort!"', the old man interjects loudly, '"That simply means the workmen weren't paid properly."' This is yet another incident to dramatize the conflict between orthodox and unorthodox responses to Italy, convention and spontaneity. But, most important of all, is Mr Emerson's appeal to Lucy to understand his son George and not allow herself to become muddled by listening to others. '"Let yourself go. Pull out from the depths those thoughts that you do not understand, and spread them out in the sunlight and know the meaning of them. By understanding George you may learn to understand yourself."' Lucy's education in naturalness and truth to the self – which she strongly resists, since she regards Mr Emerson as a foolish and irreligious old man – ends abruptly with the arrival of her chaperone, Miss Bartlett. '"Oh, good gracious me!" said Lucy, suddenly collapsing and again seeing the whole of life in a new perspective.' After momentary glimpses into Mr Emerson's frank way of seeing the world and odd flashes of spontaneity in her own right, she resumes her orthodox social self and bids her guides a polite farewell.

The offer of the rooms with a view and the encounter with old Mr Emerson and his naturally responsive but unfulfilled son in Santa Croce prepare the way for the two main dramatic scenes in the first half of the novel. The first is the scene in which Lucy sees an Italian murdered in the Piazza Signoria and faints in George's arms – ironically this part of the book is simply called 'Fourth Chapter', whereas the less eventful sections all have whimsical Meredithian titles. The second is the scene in which George kisses her at Fiesole. Both reveal Forster's gift for investing a particular moment with potent significance, although each to some extent remains mysterious. Enigmatic as the Piazza episode undoubtedly is, it serves to suggest Lucy's initiation into a sphere of reality from which her sheltered upbringing has previously protected her. Forster deliberately underplays the Italians' quarrel in order to reduce the element of melodrama, to suggest how suddenly violence (so often equated with reality in Forster) may irrupt in any society. In a strangely moving fashion the incident brings Lucy and George so close together that 'identity of position' suggests 'eternal comradeship'.

> Two Italians by the Loggia had been bickering about a debt. 'Cinque lire,' they had cried, 'cinque lire!' They sparred at each other, and one of them was hit lightly upon the chest. He frowned; he bent towards Lucy with a look of interest, as if he had an important message for her. He opened his lips to deliver it, and a stream of red came out between them and trickled down his unshaven chin (RWV, ch. 4).

The incident not only throws Lucy into George's arms and stains her 'dead' art-prints with 'live' blood; it also suggests some deep connection between the instinctive energies released in the quarrel and those displayed by George. The spilling of blood appears to be specially connected with initiation into reality for Forster. Worters returns to reality when he cuts his hand in 'Other Kingdom', Kuno's 'blood spurts over his mother's hands when they regain a vision of reality' in 'The Machine Stops', Gerald kisses the blood on Agnes's handkerchief in *The Longest Journey*. But the coexistence of love and violence is too complex for Lucy to grasp: '"And the murderer tried to kiss him, you say – how very odd Italians are!"' Yet this incident clearly forms her initiation into the complexity of reality. 'To behave wildly at the sight of death is pardonable. But to discuss it afterwards, to pass from discussion into silence, and through silence into sympathy, that is an error, not of a startled emotion, but the whole fabric' (RWV, ch. 6). From now on, the opposition between true complexity and untruthful muddle becomes a major structural principle, embodied in characters, plot, image.

The second major dramatic scene, the picnic at Fiesole, is reminiscent of 'The Story of a Panic', but is more firmly integrated into the world of domestic comedy. The action is set within a framework of classical mythology, with the young Italian coachman as Phaeton and his girl as Persephone. The party of visitors scatters as if Pan had been amongst them, not, Forster adds 'the great God Pan', but the 'little god Pan, who presides over social contretemps and unsuccessful picnics' (ch. 7). On the actual drive to Fiesole, the young coachman and his girl provide an example of uninhibited naturalness by kissing. They are duly rebuked by the resident Anglican clergyman, Mr Eager, much to old Mr Emerson's annoyance. '"Do we find happiness so often that we should turn it off the box when it happens to sit there? To be driven by lovers – A king might envy us . . ."' The classical allusions to the young lovers throughout, as Phaeton, the driver of the sun chariot, and Persephone the embodiment of returning spring, might at first glance appear to be mannered whimsy, but it is assimilated into the mixed serio-comic texture of the writing. Moreover, by suggesting how ordinary mortals may be transfigured by love, it foreshadows the transfiguration scene that follows and the conclusion of the novel, where George and Lucy become part of a mythopoeic world. Lucy, in pursuit of that 'good man' Mr Beebe, the clergyman, comes upon that other good man, George Emerson, as she stands on the violet-clad hill.

> Standing at its brink, like a swimmer who prepares, was the good man. But he was not the good man that she had expected, and he was alone.
>
> George had turned at the sound of her arrival. For a moment he contemplated her, as one who had fallen out of heaven. He saw radiant joy in her face, he saw the flowers beat against her dress in blue waves. The bushes above them closed. He stepped quickly forward and kissed her.
>
> Before she could speak, almost before she could feel, a voice called, 'Lucy! Lucy! Lucy!' The silence of life had been broken by Miss Bartlett, who stood brown against the view (RWV, ch. 6).

47

Once again, as in the church of Santa Croce, Miss Bartlett stands between Lucy and the view, that is, between Lucy and her extended insight into reality.

As soon as the party packs up, leaving George to make his own way home, Lucy's new sense of reality is put to the test. Frightened by the storm, a symbol of the unknown, she looks to Charlotte Bartlett for comfort, confessing that she has been foolish just when she thought she was developing. Before she surrenders to her chaperone's coarse, prudential arguments, she struggles to retain the moment of truth, anxious not to allow it to become distorted or submerged.

> I think he was taken by surprise, just as I was before. But this time I'm not to blame; I do want you to believe that. I simply slipped into those violets. No, I want to be really truthful. I am a little to blame. I had silly thoughts. The sky, you know, was gold, and the ground all blue, and for a moment he looked like some one in a book (ch. 7).

By devious means, Miss Bartlett manoeuvres Lucy into accepting a policy of escape. The novelist, perhaps a trifle over-solemnly, comments that Lucy 'was suffering from the most grievous wrong which this world has yet discovered: diplomatic advantage had been taken of her sincerity, of her craving for sympathy and love'. From this moment 'she disliked confidences, for they might lead to self-knowledge and to that king of terrors – Light' (ch. 19). In effect, the second half of *A Room with a View* asks the question: Can Lucy recover from such wrong? Can she be true to the new view of reality granted her on the slopes of Fiesole and thus triumph over the spirit of muddle that threatens to dominate her life?

In the second half of the novel set in England, we witness the conflicting claims of Cecil Vyse and George Emerson for Lucy's heart, a conflict between civilized artifice and good nature. Cecil's introduction in the chapter entitled 'Medieval' establishes that he is medieval only in the sense that, 'an ascetic at heart', he has failed to connect body and spirit. Conscious of his superior London background, he patronizes Lucy and her charming country circle. In fact, his metropolitan culture is stuffy and pretentious and Windy Corner is quite free from the characteristic limitations of either country or suburban society; like Fiesole, it has a view; in comparison with the expensively built architect-designed houses with their look of impermanence and not belonging, Windy Corner seems 'as inevitable as an ugliness of Nature's own creation'. It is from this healthy natural society that Cecil proposes to rescue Lucy – the rescue party is Forster's favourite device for contrasting true and false forms of salvation. But Cecil lacks George's instinctive energies, and his shy request to kiss Lucy after they have become engaged forms an ironic contrast to George's impulsive kiss at Fiesole. 'As he touched her, his gold pince-nez became dislodged and was flattened between them.' Foreign travel has done nothing to warm and humanize him. 'Italy had quickened Cecil, not to tolerance, but to irritation' (ch. 10). The scales finally fall from Lucy's eyes when Cecil pompously refuses to make up a four at tennis, saying that 'there are some chaps who are no good for anything but books'; and she breaks off the engagement. In the 'New Lucy', Cecil seeks to humiliate Lucy after the broken engagement: in the published novel he behaves generously. He refrains from recrimination; shows a new increase of self-knowledge, and undergoes a kind of salvation through renunciation: 'nothing in his love became him like the leaving it' (ch. 17).

A Room with a View explores the importance of telling the truth in a variety of ways: most obviously through the contrast between the free-speaking Emersons and the cautious English visitors at the Pension Bertolini: '"It is so difficult"', says Mr Beebe of the Emersons, '"at least I find it difficult – to understand people who speak the truth"' (ch. 1); more subtly through Lucy's predicament once she has fallen under Miss Bartlett's influence and embarked on a course of subterfuge and secrecy, suppressing her strong feelings for George to preserve middle-class conventions. The part that lies play in the developing action of Forster's first four novels indicates the importance he attributes to complete honesty in personal relations. More complex than John Stuart Mill's strenuous call to truth, Forster's idea of honesty implies an antithesis between the self and society, and that involves due regard for the prompting of the subconscious: '"the lie we acted has ruined our lives"' Rickie tells Agnes in The Longest Journey, '"down in what they call the subconscious self he [Stephen] has been hurting me"' (ch. 23). In A Room with a View the chapter headings draw attention to the series of lies that Lucy becomes involved in as the result of her failure to be frank and honest about what happened at Fiesole and about her true feelings for George.

Throughout the novel Forster succeeds in suggesting the conflict between the unconscious and the conscious in Lucy, as she struggles to maintain propriety in all her actions: in this respect and in her simple passion for truth, she resembles Adela of *A Passage to India*, although she is a much younger woman and possesses greater warmth and imagination. She is also an accomplished pianist. Music, which Forster believes is the 'deepest of the arts' and which he frequently employs to fine effect, releases her spirit, and acts as an index to her changing moods and unconscious feelings, as she moves from one composer to another. She learns to live as she plays – heroically. In the first version of the novel, Lucy had been an inconspicuous accompanist at the concert that was to form the central episode, whereas in the published novel she is a skilled soloist; the difference is important. Lucy's dreams also reveal the strength of her unconscious emotions. And a change in her voice conveys more than she cares to make known about her repressed feelings for George Emerson. But more important than music, dreams, and voice for revealing Lucy's internal conflicts are her dramatic encounters with George himself and her subsequent attempts to repress the emotions they spontaneously evoke. One of these encounters, when she and Cecil and her mother come upon the impromptu swimming-party, reveals George as near-naked, natural, uninhibited man. This is an excellent example of Forster's attempt to anglicize the Pan motif and to combine social comedy and symbolic significance. Cecil takes inept control, Mrs Honeychurch is motherly.

> 'Hush, dears,' said Mrs Honeychurch, who found it impossible
> to remain shocked. 'And do be sure you dry yourselves thoroughly
> first. All these colds come of not drying thoroughly.'
> 'Mother, do come away,' said Lucy. 'Oh, for goodness' sake,
> do come.'
> 'Hullo!' cried George, so that again the ladies stopped.
> He regarded himself as dressed. Barefoot, bare-chested, radiant
> and personable against the shadowy woods, he called:
> 'Hullo, Miss Honeychurch! Hullo!'
> 'Bow, Lucy; better bow. Whoever is it? I shall bow.'
> Miss Honeychurch bowed (ch. 12).

This high-spirited bathing episode, like other bathing scenes in Forster's fiction, acts as a baptism into brotherhood; in this case, for George, Freddy, and even temporarily for Mr Beebe, the clergyman. It also offers a potential rebirth into naturalism for the silent Lucy, who has once bathed in the pool herself, but has since been taught to feel embarrassment. For the men it was an eternal moment: 'on the morrow the pool had shrunk to its old size and lost its glory. It had been a call to the blood and to the relaxed will, a passing benediction whose influence did not pass, a holiness, a spell, a momentary chalice for youth' (ch. 12). In *Where Angels Fear to Tread*, Philip and Gino share a sacramental chalice, Rickie and Stephen are offered a similar moment in *The Longest Journey*, and Clive and Maurice swim through the waters of the dyke on the expedition from Cambridge in *Maurice* (ch. 13). But what, we may ask, is Lucy doing here? It is as if a lady had invaded the sanctity of the Cambridge swimming club, where Oscar Browning and his cronies bathed 'in a state of primitive nudity' and young men 'ran quite naked in crowds over the green grass' (GLD, p. 31). Actually the comic–serious bathing scene serves its function of establishing the value of naturalness and spontaneous joy in *A Room with a View*, but the essence of its eroticism is homosexual, as is the description of Gerald's beauty in *The Longest Journey*, 'just when he began to be beautiful the clothes started'; and Lucy can hardly be expected to be as stimulated by naked man as her creator nor as amused by the antics of the three men around the sacramental pool.

It is the central weakness of the novel that Lucy's emancipation from the spirit of muddle should have to come from Mr Emerson ('beware muddle'), when the reader feels it should come from his son. In refusing to acknowledge her love for George, Lucy was 'disordering the very instruments of life'. In the first version of the novel, George was an aesthetic prig; in the 'New Lucy' he was an ideal figure, a compound of noble peasant and Cambridge culture, killed off by his creator when he rode his bicycle into a tree in a storm; while in *A Room with a View*, he is a complex but negative figure, an imperfect product of his father's system of natural education, too passive to justify his final claim to Lucy, '"Well, I acted the truth."'

Since George is too weak to sustain his symbolic role as the embodiment of naturalism, the main weight of the novel's meaning falls elsewhere, not on character, but on visionary moments and dialogue. It falls especially on the simple-life philosophy of 'comradeship' and respect for the body somewhat tiresomely unfolded by old Mr Emerson, a compound of his famous American namesake and the Utopian Socialist, Edward Carpenter, a great champion of 'comradeship', comradeship democratic and homosexual. When Lucy turns from George, she joins the ranks of the benighted, 'who follow neither the heart nor the brain, and march to their destiny by catch-words.' When she pretended to George that she did not love him, and pretended to Cecil that she loved no one, 'the night received her, as it had received

Miss Bartlett thirty years before' (ch. 17). But, in spite of these solemn phrases, this is a comedy not a tragedy; and so it seems absolutely right that Lucy should be given a second chance. Even Miss Bartlett has one and enjoys a minor redemption, for she allows Lucy's final meeting with old Mr Emerson which she could have prevented, and thus permits the reunion with the unsuitable George.

Later when George and Lucy talk over past events on their honeymoon, Lucy is at first inclined to ascribe Miss Bartlett's action to 'muddle', but George proposes another explanation, more in keeping with the psychological subtlety of the novel as a whole.

> 'I'll put a marvel to you. That your cousin has always hoped. That from the very first moment we met, she hoped, far down in her mind, that we would be like this – of course, very far down. That she fought us on the surface, and yet she hoped' (ch. 20).

Forster was always fascinated by the connections and contradictions between the meanings on the surface and meanings deep down, between what he called the 'upper personality' and the 'lower personality', in writers and in ordinary people, fascinated too by the 'subterranean', a fact often ignored by critics who describe his characters as divided into sheep and goats, red bloods and mollycoddles. The connection the characters have to make

> is between the upper and literate reaches of the mind and the lower and unwashed, or proletarian, levels of consciousness, which can no longer be downtrodden and despised; for they are ready to strike back, and to withdraw their energies, if they are not accepted and set free (Hampshire, 1969, p. 47).

In this early novel, Forster explored the interaction of the different levels of consciousness in a manner that foreshadows both *Howards End* and *A Passage to India*, but because *A Room with a View* is a light domestic comedy, he subordinates psychological analysis to humour and to the moral education of the heroine. The result is a lively rendering of English manners at home and abroad. Yet it is clear from the ending of *A Room with a View*, as it is from the ending of *Where Angels Fear to Tread* and a passage in the 'New Lucy' which speaks of the lovers as Tithonus and Aurora, 'with the little stupid world spinning beneath them', that Forster found it easier to mythologize the ideal harmony of love than to present it in concrete human terms.

Youth enwrapped them; the song of Phaeton announced passion requited, love attained. But they were conscious of a love more mysterious than this. The song died away; they heard the river, bearing down the snows of winter into the Mediterranean.

This very English couple become one with the natural lovers on the carriage to Fiesole and with the world of myth and poetry. The mysterious, the elemental, and the unseen are thus accommodated within the rational world of Edwardian comedy, but the lovers' happiness seems precarious, not only because it is visionary, and a trifle disembodied, but because the eternal world they have glimpsed at Fiesole and at Windy Corner belongs to European pastoral and cannot easily survive in the modern industrial society to which they must return and live out their lives.

Where Angels Fear to Tread

Where Angels Fear to Tread, like many of the short stories, was inspired by the spirit of place. The little town of Monteriano, with its many towers and steep winding ascent, is based on the medieval town near Florence called San Gimignano, where Forster stayed on his visit to Italy, and the novel was still called 'Monteriano' in proof stage, not only on the title-page, but on all the running heads. It was published as Forster's first novel, under its present title, in 1905, although as we have already seen, the novelist had earlier begun work on what was later to become *A Room with a View*. Both novels evoke the atmosphere and spirit of Italy with special intensity. In *Where Angels Fear to Tread*, the contrast between Italy and England serves an even more important structural function than in *A Room with a View*. At one time the novel was to have been called 'The Rescue', and Forster drew up a simple timetable of the rescues in the manuscript, now in the British Museum. From this it is clear that Lilia Herriton leaves London for Italy in November 1902; Philip Herriton, her brother-in-law, sets out to rescue her from an unsuitable Italian marriage in February 1903, but arrives after the marriage with Gino, the son of an Italian dentist, has already taken place; Lilia dies in December of the same year, having given birth to a son, and the second rescue party to bring back the baby sets out in July 1904. The manuscript note then refers to 'The 2nd two days', and 'The return', that is, Philip's and Caroline's return after the disaster of the baby's death. Since the actual outline, consisting of barely more than twenty-odd words, appears on the verso of the last page of the manuscript, it was probably a check on chronology rather than a guide. It is an extraordinarily mature manuscript for so young a writer, and contains little evidence of fumbling or uncertainty. But the manuscript variants are sometimes illuminating, especially references to Philip's love of England and the strength of his unwillingness to return to Italy. Also interesting are his more detailed attempts to apportion responsibility for the baby's death, contained in two paragraphs subsequently omitted from the beginning of chapter 9.

In the novel that Forster was to write next, *The Longest Journey*, the opening conversation reveals that one of the Cambridge idioms of the day was to ask of anyone whether he was 'saved' or not. This had nothing to do with evangelical religion. The phrase was a convenient piece of social shorthand to indicate whether the person belonged to the group of people that one liked and intimately knew. To belong to such a group the person had to be (a) serious, (b) sensitive, (c) in love with truth and beauty, (d) prepared to place the integrity of the inner life above questions of correct behaviour. Much the same question tended to be asked by the inhabitants of Bloomsbury and to some extent determined whether one were accepted into the magic circle or not. It was an exclusiveness that had its positive and negative sides ('hardly a state of mind which a grown-up person in his senses could sustain', J. M. Keynes once remarked).

Where Angels Fear to Tread is a novel about being saved. Two ideas of being saved are played off against each other. One is the idea of spiritual salvation, of saving one's inner integrity, of achieving wholeness of being. Philip Herriton and Caroline Abbott reach out towards this in their best moments. The other is saving face, the whole business of sending out rescue parties to prevent an undesirable marriage or, subsequently, to provide a loveless but socially respectable upbringing for the child of such a marriage. Old Mrs Herriton, a devious suburban arch-plotter, who does not believe in 'romance, nor in transfiguration, nor in parallels from history, nor in anything else that may disturb domestic life', and her odious daughter Harriet, are the chief champions of this particular brand of saving. In reading the novel it will be noted that the word 'save' recurs repeatedly in thematically significant passages. Ultimately, the working out of this contrast between two different kinds of salvation ends in some confusion, a confusion that may reflect unresolved muddle in the novelist's own mind. When Caroline Abbott confesses to Philip at the end of the novel that she had been in love with Gino from the beginning – a confession that rightly comes as a surprise, but also as a confirmation of the reader's deepest intuitions – she seems to muddle the two kinds of salvation: spiritual and prudential. She tells Philip that if Gino had asked her, she would have given herself 'body and soul'.

> 'That would have been the end of my rescue party. But all through he took me for a superior being – a goddess. I who was worshipping every inch of him, and every word he spoke. And that saved me' (ch. 10).

Saved her from what? Caroline, who is granted a vision of the wholeness of life, the tower rooted in the earth, its top shining in the sun, a young woman who is not only sensitive to truth and beauty but who is also able to act, unlike the hesitant Philip, congratulates herself on being saved from Gino, the one character in the novel who serves as a touchstone of spontaneity and the truth of the instinctive life. In a context of spiritual values she congratulates herself on a prudential escape. There is something very muddled here, surely.

What is the explanation of this confusion? It is something that goes to the roots of Forster's fictional world, the idea of the 'eternal moment'. This permeates his vision and finds its simplest expression, as we have seen, in the two short stories, 'The Road from Colonus' and 'The Story of a Panic'. The eternal moment is Forster's main way of creating a bridge between the phenomenal world and spiritual reality. Something that happens in the external world is recognized as a manifestation of inner truth, it is treasured in the mind, and thus becomes the guiding light of all our moral being. But two features deserve special notice. The actual experience tends to stop short before fulfilment or fruition; or, if there is fulfilment or partial fulfilment, it is immediately followed by death, for example Gerald's death in *The Longest Journey*. In *Where Angels Fear to Tread*, there is no fulfilment for Caroline, only a vision of love. The second feature to notice about the eternal moment is that it is closely linked to the symbolic moment of choice, which, 'if a man accepts, he has accepted life, but which if he refuses he joins the ranks of the benighted'. This brand of secular Calvinism is the least satisfactory aspect of Forster's fiction. It is at variance with the facts of our moral lives and can only be defended by saying that it is the novelist's means of highlighting or dramatizing the importance and consequence of our moral actions and of showing the connection between visionary moments and practical and ethical consequences. To return to

Caroline's confession at the end of *Where Angels Fear to Tread*, 'And that saved me', it is now apparent that only by preserving her from full commitment to her love for Gino could Forster grant her an eternal moment, an eternal moment by reference to which she would judge all things thereafter. In the process she is protected, like many of Forster's characters, from discovering the reality of sexual desires and from any enduring commitment to life.

Where Angels Fear to Tread is a beautifully composed novel. It has an effortless symmetry and graceful proportion, certainly effortless compared with the more contrived structure of *Howards End* and the more consciously created patterning of *A Passage to India*. The structure is not triadic, as it is in *The Longest Journey* and *A Passage to India*, but is marked out by the two rescue operations to Monteriano and the appalling interludes of life in Sawston. The main elements in the composition are thus the two visits and their consequences. From these, Forster develops the radical contrast between the passionate, instinctive life of the Italian town Monteriano and the snobbish, convention-ridden provinciality of Sawston. But he is too subtle an artist to construct a novel on crude and obvious contrasts. Monteriano has its own snobbery and provincial limitations, as Lilia discovers as soon as she tries to escape from domesticity and share the brotherhood of man, enjoyed by her Italian husband in café society. In the conversation between Gino and Spiridione, his friend from the customs house, Forster captures the machismo and complicity of Latin male society with its total exclusion of the woman except as a topic of conversation, and the rapid alternations, 'at one moment full of childishness and tender wisdom, the next moment scandalously gross' (ch. 3). And then again Italy, far from acting as a liberating experience for Philip Herriton, at first only reinforces his moral priggishness, his complacent superiority, his innate aestheticism – his tendency to see all life 'as a spectacle'. Indeed, the novel opens with irony that Philip, who is so obviously still the conventional Englishman in spite of his 'continual visits to the Continent', should counsel Lilia to be *un*conventional and to go off the main tracks and see the little towns. And there is added irony in his advice to 'love and understand the Italians, for the people are more marvellous than the land.' Lilia certainly falls in love with one Italian, but this was not at all what Philip had meant; and the choice of Gino, the son of a dentist, doubles her folly in his eyes. Her vulgarity is established from the first moment that we see her 'sprawling out of her first-class carriage' (the manuscript shows that the word was changed from the less expressive 'peeping' to 'sprawling'). The effect is reinforced by her peals of ungovernable laughter.

Lilia has earlier married into the Herriton family, but her husband Charles died, leaving her with a daughter, Irma, to bring up. She begins to look to the obsequious but unsuitable Mr Kingcroft as a substitute for her dead husband, but Mrs Herriton nips this affair in the bud, without even the need for a rescue party, and is subsequently delighted at Philip's plan to send her to Italy. In his best Jane Austen manner, Forster invents an interchange between mother and son. Philip speaks of the purifying and ennobling effect of Italy on all who visit her:

> 'She is the school as well as the playground of the world. It is really to Lilia's credit that she wants to go there.'
> 'She would go anywhere,' said his mother, who had heard enough of the praises of Italy (ch. 1).

But Philip is not discouraged. He sees Lilia's spiritual salvation as lying in Italy and asks himself sardonically, 'Why should she not be transfigured? The same had happened to the Goths.'

If the theme of salvation is central to the meaning of *Where Angels Fear to Tread*, so too is the theme of transfiguration; and both are an expression of that widespread attempt in a secular age to invest life with meaning and significance by using religious terminology to describe heightened states of being. Salvation forms the moral centre of the novel and transfiguration is the poetic or imaginative means of achieving it. At moments of intense emotion or as the result of visionary experiences, Forster's characters are granted a view that transfigures the details of ordinary life. Even uneducated people experience such transfigurations. The experience depends as much on love and the holiness of the heart's affections, as on imaginative insight, as the author makes clear in saying of Lucy and George in *A Room with a View*, that the 'most real thing' is 'love felt and returned, love which our bodies exact and our hearts have transfigured' (RWV, ch. 16). Even the incredibly vulgar Lilia, with her talk of 'dindins' and 'go to bye bye', found her salvation in Gino as the result of an act of transfiguration: in her case, appropriately, an act of a typically sentimental and shallow kind. 'She remembered how the evening sun had struck his hair, and how he had smiled down at her, and being both sentimental and unrefined, was determined to have the man and the place together.' The transfiguring promise was genuine enough – after all

Caroline secretly shared it – but it becomes tainted by Lilia's wilful possessiveness, her desire to have both the man and the house by which she first saw him, her determination to transform Gino, the vital young Italian, into a tame English husband. Lilia's transfiguration of Gino is also coloured by novelettish expectations and values.

Lilia's experience of transfiguration is in a sense peripheral. Those that count in the working out of the theme of salvation are the transfiguring visions enjoyed by Caroline Abbott and Philip Herriton. Significantly, Philip's sister, Harriet, terrible in her self-enclosed righteousness, enjoys no such visions. Neither, of course, does Mrs Herriton, adroitly protecting Irma from any contact with reality outside Sawston conventions. Yet Mrs Herriton's impotence against natural forces is evident, and never more beautifully suggested than in the scene when she receives news of Lilia's engagement as she is planting peas. She immediately resorts to telegrams and anger and forgets the peas and the torn up letter. At night, however,

> Just as she was going upstairs she remembered that she never covered up those peas. It upset her more than anything, and again and again she struck the banisters with vexation. Late as it was, she got a lantern from the tool-shed and went down the garden to rake the earth over them. The sparrows had taken every one. But countless fragments of the letter remained, disfiguring the tidy ground (ch. 1).

Forster's removal of the unnecessary extra sentence in the manuscript 'And paper is the most indestructible of things', well illustrates his youthful powers of self-criticism.

The main point about genuine moments of transfiguration is that they reveal ultimate reality and that the memory of them endures. They are not vulnerable to cynicism or disenchantment. In *Where Angels Fear to Tread*, Forster contrasts two kinds of romance. On the one hand, there is the romance of foreign travel and refined aestheticism; on the other, there is the romance of genuine transfiguration. The distinction is made in relation to Philip. He returns from his first experience of Italy with an unreal, romantic picture of the country, of its art, and its people; and he uses this as a means of mocking at English suburban life (there is an element of Forster in Philip, as the author has confessed). Because there is something self-conscious and spurious about Philip's vision it cannot survive the disillusionment of his visit to Monteriano; because his idealistic vision of Italy cannot embrace such mundane details as the fact that Gino's father is a dentist, 'Exit spurious romance.' He returns to Sawston disenchanted, a ready prey to his mother's malign influence. Mrs Herriton has no respect for the sanctity of personal relations, only for 'personal influence' – this an utterly damning feature in the context of Forster's moral world. Caroline also returns disenchanted with Italy as the land of romance. She is dull and remorseful, since she feels responsible for the unfortunate match between Lilia and Gino. Preoccupation with the distinction between two kinds of romance and between romance and reality is a preoccupation of the age as well as something deeply felt by Forster; it is found in all the major novelists of the Edwardian period and formed the main theme of a study published by R. A. Scott-James in 1908, called *Modernism and Romance*. With the decline in religious faith and the increase in materialism, many novelists sought to endow the details of ordinary life with special meaning to find something beyond 'life's daily grey' (HE, ch. 14): self-realization, self-fulfilment, and the discovery of a personal reality become the master themes.

The working out of the major theme in *Where Angels Fear to Tread* requires that Philip and Caroline should return to Italy and experience transfiguring visions. These must restore their faith in love and beauty, they must also restore their faith in Italy as the natural home of both: the real Italy, not the Italy of the Baedeker guide. Romance now returns to Philip as the result of a trivial gesture. Gino tells Caroline that he is sorry he was rude to Philip eighteen months before when he had given him 'an aimless push, which toppled him onto the bed' ('toppled' was a second thought in the manuscript). No tall man likes to be 'toppled', remarks the author. For Caroline, romance begins to return when she pays homage to the complexity of life. The reunion of Philip and Caroline is then marked by a shared vision of the tower.

> 'It reaches up to heaven,' said Philip, 'and down to the other place.' The summit of the tower was radiant in the sun, while its base was in shadow and pasted over with advertisements. 'Is it to be a symbol of the town?' (ch. 6).

Both glimpse the truth that the prose and poetry of life are equally necessary, that the poetry does not cease to exist because there is also ugliness and vulgarity, although Caroline masks her understanding, and changes in the manuscript indicate Forster's uncertainty about their respective responses. In the manuscript, after 'Is it to be a symbol of the town?' came the passage 'She surprised him by picking up his meaning. "I think it is. And the lovely part is small and beyond our reach"' (WAFT: BM). Forster presumably saw that the omission of specific reference to Caroline's understanding of the tower would maintain her mysterious and subterranean development.

Now that Philip and Caroline's general views of life have been partially transformed, they are ready to see Gino and his son in a new light. Two set-pieces follow. In the first, which takes place in the local opera house and which is in itself splendidly operatic, as Benjamin Britten has remarked, Philip regains his radiant vision of spontaneity and human brotherhood. He is hauled up into Gino's box, and is once more enchanted by the 'kind, cheerful voices, the laughter that was never vapid, and the light caress of the arm across his back.' Wisely, Forster deleted the sentence 'It was the finest rag in the world' before publication; but it reveals the identity he sensed between the brotherhood of the Italian opera house and of undergraduate life at Cambridge. The second set-piece is Caroline's visit to Gino's house. Both she and Philip are now granted a vision. In Gino's presence, Caroline is made to feel the inadequacy of her simple code of right and wrong. 'The comfortable sense of virtue left her. She was in the presence of something greater than right or wrong.' She sees the man who had previously seemed 'cruel, vicious and vulgar' in a new light. He lifts his son to his lips. 'The man was majestic; he was part of Nature; in no ordinary love scene could he ever be so great.' She helps him to bath the child. And so the scene is set for Philip's transfiguring vision

> There she sat, with twenty miles of view behind her, and he placed the dripping baby on her knee. It shone now with health and beauty; it seemed to reflect light, like a copper vessel [radiate as she dried it: MS]. Just such a baby Bellini sets languid on his mother's lap, or Signorelli flings wriggling on pavements of marble, or Lorenzo di Credi, more reverent but less divine, lays carefully among flowers, with his head upon a wisp of golden straw. For a while Gino contemplated them standing. Then, to get a better view, he knelt by the side of the chair, with his hands clasped before him.
>
> So they were when Philip entered, and saw, to all intents and purposes, the Virgin and Child, with Donor (ch. 7).

Gino's love is sanctified in the eyes of both Caroline and Philip. There can be no question of taking the child back to Sawston with them. It's only Harriet's blind wilfulness, aided by the poor idiot – a force of nature or blind fate – that destroys Gino's son.

But the pattern of transfiguration is not yet complete. Two dramatic confrontations follow: the first is the fight between Gino and Philip and the second the scene between Philip and Caroline on the homeward-bound train. The tragedy of the baby's death challenges Philip's comprehension of life. He cannot see round it. But the dead, as so often in Forster's fiction, inspire the living.

> The passion they have aroused lives after them, easy to transmute or to transfer, but well-nigh impossible to destroy. And Philip knew that he was still voyaging on the same magnificent, perilous sea, with the sun or the clouds above him, and the tides below (ch. 9).

Accepting personal responsibility for the child's death, he is convinced that he alone should tell Gino of his son's death. In an extraordinary scene, comparable in its subterranean implications with the wrestling scene between Birkin and Gerald in Lawrence's *Women in Love*, Philip and Gino engage in a life and death struggle which serves to establish the need for personal contest, struggle, and truces within personal relations, a need later defined through Stephen Wonham in *The Longest Journey*. Caroline, who has seemed to Philip a goddess throughout the day, intervenes to save him from Gino's instinctive revenge. For Philip she becomes the embodiment of suffering humanity. 'Her eyes were open, full of infinite pity and full of majesty, as if they discerned the boundaries of sorrow, and saw unimaginable tracts beyond' – a figure strongly reminiscent of Keats's Moneta in *Hyperion*. And Philip experiences salvation. 'Quietly, without hysterical prayers or banging of drums, he underwent conversion. He was saved.' Caroline has been transfigured into a goddess, an earth-mother who heals her quarrelling sons with the milk of human kindness. She commands the two men to drink the milk that had been prepared for the baby. They drink in solemn ritual, and then Gino who is told to finish the milk 'either by accident or in some spasm of pain, broke the jug to pieces.' The sacrament is over and perfect reconciliation achieved; yet it might have been a very different scene if what the maid went for was 'the umbrella' she had forgotten as Forster wrote in an early draft, and not 'the baby's evening milk'.

The final transfiguration occurs on the return train journey to England when Philip learns of Caroline's love for Gino and realizes her self-sacrifice in going back to rescue himself from the revengeful father, whom she did not wish to see again because she was in love with him. There is a strange mixture of detachment and voyeurism in Philip's standpoint. 'And to see round it he was standing at an immense distance. He could even be glad that she had once held the beloved in her arms' – a similar voyeurism recurs in Rickie's pleasure in seeing Agnes in Gerald's arms, in *The Longest Journey*. Caroline protests that his view of her has been too refined. '"Get over supposing I'm refined. That's what puzzles you. Get over that."' The last of the many transfigurations then follows.

> As she spoke she seemed to be transfigured, and to have indeed no part with refinement or unrefinement any longer. Out of this wreck there was revealed to him something indestructible – something which she, who had given it, could never take away (ch. 10).

But Forster seems to have been very uncertain what Philip had done for Caroline. At first he wrote that he had made her life 'bearable', then he wrote 'admirable', and finally in the published text the stoical 'endurable'.

A possible sub-title to *Where Angels Fear to Tread* might be 'or the education of Philip'. His education consists in learning that life was more complex and heroic than he had thought, that it was not enough to see clearly and laugh, and that it must never be regarded as a spectacle. He is shocked out of his cynicism and aestheticism by admiration for Gino's instinctive love and for Caroline's heroic self-denial. Although he can admire both approaches to life and they appear to give him a deeper insight into reality, he can only contemplate their beauty, he cannot actively embrace them. Caroline attributes his inability to give himself up to a life of action to his mother's influence: Philip lacks passion, is curiously sexless, and even in the act of seeing Caroline as a goddess, is partly reverting to his earlier aestheticism; this inveterate custom of translating unmanageable life into manageable art, is a habit of mind Philip's creator partly shares. The indecisive end to Philip's relations with Gino and Caroline reflects the author's ultimate failure at this stage in his career to connect the ordered pursuit of culture and the disordered life of the emotions. 'The object of the book is the improvement of Philip, and I did really want the improvement to be a surprise', Forster explained in a letter in 1905 (Gowda, 1969, p. 127).

In a characteristically self-deprecating remark, Forster once said that he was not really a novelist at all, because he had only succeeded in drawing three types of people: the people he liked, the people he disliked, and the person he thought he himself was. In *Where Angels Fear to Tread*, the people he dislikes are clearly Mrs Herriton and her daughter Harriet, the people he likes are Gino and Caroline, and the person he thinks he is, is Philip, a kind of Prufock figure, 'I am not Prince Hamlet; nor was meant to be.' Yet there is an important distinction to be drawn between Philip and the voice of the novelist in this novel. Both are in quest of truth and beauty, both seek to connect the prose and poetry of life, and both remain ironically detached from much that goes on. But the quality of their irony is radically different. In Philip, irony is the cynical expression of a man who feels that he has been let down by his trust in beauty. The author's irony, on the other hand, is not cynical, but salutary and necessary. It represents the free play of the rational mind on all the materials of experience. It is the expression of a mind attached to no fixed system of values, open to many forms of experience. At every turn and corner irony corrects and keeps in check imaginative excesses or flights of fancy. It neither denies nor disavows the truths of the imagination, but it preserves the author from sentimentality, if not wholly from a secular religiosity. Most important of all it quietly calls in question the simple oppositions on which the plot rests and makes us aware that Gino is not only the embodiment of natural passion but a remarkably conceited and obtuse young man. Yet there are some passages in which the author and character are too alike. And it was only in the character of Fielding in *A Passage to India* that Forster succeeded wholly in distancing himself from his fictional *alter ego*. The weakest passages in *Where Angels Fear to Tread* are those in which Forster identifies himself too closely with Philip and seems almost to endorse his snobbish and inadequate, aesthetic response to life.

In *Where Angels Fear to Tread* the novelist appears as someone who prides himself on his good taste, on his ability to detect and expose affectation and vulgarity. But he is attracted towards a form of instinctive energy that transcends questions of good taste. While the plot of the novel asserts the supremacy of an energy that has 'no part with refinement or unrefinement', an energy that is embodied in Gino and Caroline, the commentary has a faint tinge of aesthetic snobbery. In some passages the author speaks with the tones of the cultural snob who knows what to admire and what not to admire. The Baedeker tradition has something to answer for in this early novel and so too has the youth of the author.

Any account of the serious themes of the two Italian novels is likely to make them appear more solemn than they really are. In fact, the predominant tone is light and witty. The dialogue is always entertaining, the observations amusing, the capturing of the fine nuances of social behaviour unerring in its accuracy. Both novels have a controlled Mozartian exuberance that conveys a spirit of youthful joy in creation. Many admirers of them probably remember particular scenes, comments, snatches of dialogue, or minor characters long after they have forgotten the more important details of plot or theme. Windy Corner would be incomplete without the games of tennis and bumble-puppy, and Freddy's schoolboy puns; while the Pension Bertolini would be equally incomplete without the two Miss Alans, those indomitable spinsters left over from the mid-Victorian period, whose plan to go to Greece is not a mere convenience of the plot, but proof that they can recognize the heroic when they encounter it. It is amusing to recall how serenely Mrs Honeychurch presides over her household at Windy Corner, how magisterially she dismisses Cecil Vyse's high ideals. '"If high ideals make a young man rude, the sooner he gets rid of them the better"'; and how swiftly Mr Beebe transforms himself from natural man enjoying the fun of bathing naked in the woods to his clerical self when he hears people approaching: 'his voice changed as if every pine tree was a Rural Dean.' The portrayal of Lucy's acute embarrassment as she listens to Cecil reading Miss Lavish's novel, with its highly coloured account of George's kiss is simultaneously amusing and deeply moving. And finally how firmly the last sentence of *Where Angels Fear to Tread* returns us to mundane reality after the lofty heights of Philip's contemplation of Caroline as a goddess. 'They hurried back to the carriage to close the windows lest the smuts should get into Harriet's eyes.' In the Italian novels, we trust Forster the visionary because his visions are so firmly rooted in reality.

4

The Longest Journey

In *A Room with a View* and *Where Angels Fear to Tread* the juxtaposition of Italy and England serves as a major structural principle for contrasting two approaches to life: the instinctive and the conventional. In the three English novels, *The Longest Journey* (1907), *Howards End* (1910), and *Maurice* (written 1913–14), the structure rests on contrasts within English society; consequently communities and houses serve a more important symbolic role than in the Italian novels. Thus the tripartite division of *The Longest Journey* into Cambridge, Sawston, and Wiltshire corresponds to three different responses to life; it also marks the main stages in the development of the hero, who – we are told – was sensitive to places and 'would compare Cambridge with Sawston, and either with a third type of existence, to which for want of a better name, he gave the name "Wiltshire"'. In *Howards End* there is no similar formal division; but Mrs Wilcox's house Howards End is contrasted with London to symbolize the conflict between continuity and change in English society in the Edwardian period. The spirit of place, previously associated in the short stories and Italian novels with classical myth and Mediterranean culture, now assumes a distinctly English form; moreover, the individual's moments of truth, the symbolic moments in his spiritual development, are now presented in relation to a larger, public theme.

This theme is England, the continuity of the English tradition, the question of who shall inherit England, which all three novels specifically ask. Each attempts to convey an answer in a final pastoral coda: the scene in which Stephen Wonham, who guides 'the future of the race', takes his daughter into the woods to sleep; the scene in which Helen Schlegel and her baby assume the role of inheritors in the hay field in *Howards End*; and the escape to happiness 'in the greenwoods' for Maurice and Alec at the end of *Maurice*. The nature of the answer is not very convincing, particularly in the light of later historical development, as Forster admitted towards the end of his life, saying that the English countryside had lost its plausibility and so too had the established home as a symbol of continuity. It is not only the concern with the relationship between the individual and the spirit of England that these three novels have in common, however. They also assert the supremacy of imaginative vision; they explore the possibilities of man living in harmony with the earth; they are centrally concerned with the sanctity of personal relations, with the need 'to connect'; and they all show that ultimately 'the inner life pays', an ironic reversal of the commercial ethics of the day.

The Longest Journey is Forster's most autobiographical novel. In the Introduction which Forster wrote in 1960 for the World's Classics edition of the novel, he confesses that although it has proved the 'least popular' of his novels, it was the one he was 'most glad to have written'.

> For in it I have managed to get nearer than elsewhere towards what was on my mind – or rather towards that junction of mind with heart where the creative impulse sparks. Thoughts and emotions collided if they did not always co-operate.

As the story of a young man who struggles to retain his human and artistic integrity, *The Longest Journey* makes an illuminating comparison with James Joyce's *A Portrait of the Artist as a Young Man* (1916) and Lawrence's *Sons and Lovers* (1913); and, as the story of the painful initiation of a young man into life, with Butler's *The Way of All Flesh* (1902). In Forster's Italian novels, it will be recalled, there is a strong antithesis between two kinds of young men and consequently two responses to life, between aesthetes, such as Philip Herriton, and the embodiments of natural passion, Gino or George Emerson. *The Longest Journey*, because it is closely autobiographical, offers a direct insight into the original sources of this duality: salvation through culture and salvation through nature. And since it is longer and more complicated than either of the Italian novels and is moreover wholly set in England, it renders more fully the forces in English society that make it peculiarly difficult for anyone to be both cultured and natural at the same time.

The basic story of *The Longest Journey* is simple but there is the inevitability of Greek tragedy and of Ibsen's still-topical *Ghosts* in the complex interaction of past and present that leads to the denouement.

In the first section, Cambridge, we meet the hero, Rickie Elliot, an undergraduate with the hereditary defect of a lame foot; he is not particularly clever, but is full of high ideals and intent on learning to love and understand everyone. This part of the novel expresses a radiant vision of human fellowship. In the Sawston chapters, we watch the progressive deterioration of Rickie's character under the influence of his wife Agnes, an unimaginative and untruthful woman, and of her brother Mr Pembroke, a housemaster at Sawston school where Rickie has become a teacher. The ideals of human fellowship and the pursuit of reality are replaced by the worthless ideals of the school, by a life of compromise and deceit and the acceptance of the second best. In this novel Rickie is faced with a symbolic moment of choice. He learns that the coarse, virile young man, Stephen Wonham, who lives on his aunt's farm, is his own illegitimate brother. Although he longs to grasp the moment and greet Stephen as a brother, he is prevented from doing so by Agnes, who is more concerned with saving face in society than with truth and salvation. The moment passes and Rickie becomes muddled. When he discovers that Stephen is the son not of his detested father but of the mother he had loved, he regards Stephen as a symbol of her frailty and needs to learn painfully that he is a symbol of his mother's love. Throughout these later sections, Rickie's transformation of experience into abstractions expresses the victory of Sawston over Cambridge, the triumph of life lived at second-hand over the fearless immediate grasp of reality. In the last section of the novel, Wiltshire, Rickie loses his own life in saving Stephen from being run over by a train. After Rickie's death, Stephen thinks of him lying in the earth. 'The body was dust . . . The spirit had fled, in agony and loneliness, never to know that it had bequeathed him salvation.'

Clearly another story about salvation, yet equally important is the theme of illusion and reality. Indeed, the novel opens with a group of undergraduates grappling with one of the central problems of European philosophy: is reality in the object or in the mind of the perceiver? Is the cow really there? From this point, the word reality recurs repeatedly. Stewart Ansell, with all the pedantic integrity of the undergraduate philosopher, a pedantry that nevertheless 'lay close to the vineyards of life', refuses to recognize the existence of Agnes Pembroke, whose entrance interrupts the discussion, even though she bounds in with the brash confidence of someone who has just got herself engaged to a handsome young soldier, Gerald. By Ansell's standards, she has no reality; she is a figment of Rickie's diseased imagination. Subsequently, Rickie tells Agnes that she must mind such a 'real thing' as Gerald's death and much later that Stephen must be told such a 'real thing' as his parentage. At Sawston he prays to be delivered 'from the shadow of unreality that had begun to darken his world'. When he has finally left his wife and turned back to literature he finds happiness, 'because, as we used to say at Cambridge the cow is there. The world is real again.' But the sceptical, mocking Mrs Failing tries to discredit his rediscovery of happiness and reality.

Forster has admitted that when he wrote *The Longest Journey* he had several different ideas of reality in his mind.

> There was the metaphysical idea of Reality ('the cow is there'): there was the ethical idea that reality must be faced (Rickie won't face Stephen); there was the idea, or ideal of the British Public School; there was the title exhorting us in the words of Shelley not to love one person only; there was Cambridge, there was Wiltshire (LJ, 1960, Introduction, pp. ix-x).

With so many different ideas 'whirling around' in his mind, it is hardly surprising that the novel operates on many levels and is not entirely free from confusion. Moreover, in developing these various conceptions of reality, the novelist was very conscious of forces tugging him in opposite directions. On the one hand, he felt inspired by the spirit of place, which seemed to offer him authentic insights into reality. On the other hand, he felt the 'spirit of anti-literature' making him go 'deliberately wrong'. By the spirit of anti-literature he means the tug towards artificial and self-conscious writing. It has been suggested that the element of literary self-consciousness, opposed as it was to the inspirational, may have been a device for covering up 'scandal', a contrivance to divert attention from the 'authorial self-portrait' (Stone, 1966, p. 186). But it seems simpler to assume that it sprang primarily from a youthful compulsion to achieve fine effects through literary imitation, especially imitation of writers who celebrated the spirit of the earth, for example, Meredith, Richard Jefferies, and W. H. Hudson. Moreover, the evidence of a cancelled passage imitating Meredith and other changes made in the manuscript lend weight to this simpler stylistic explanation.

The first idea of *The Longest Journey*, 'that of a man who discovers that he has an illegitimate brother', came to the author as early as 18 July 1904; then, between 1904 and 1907, 'other ideas intervened to

confuse or enrich the original theme.' But it was the spirit of place
which 'fructified' his meagre conceptions of the 'half-brother', as
Forster's Introduction to the novel in 1960 and the essay 'Three
Countries' make clear. In them, he explains that the dry bones of the
story were 'vivified by the sudden irruption of the Wiltshire countryside' at Figsbury Rings, an ancient encampment five miles outside
Salisbury consisting of an 'outer circle of embankment and an inner
circle, and in the centre . . . one tree'. The site became Cadbury Rings
in the novel. Speaking of their influence, in the essay 'Three Countries',
he writes:

> There's no case here of the direct inspiration which Italy gave me.
> But sitting upon the Rings several times and talking to the
> shepherds who frequented them, I had an emotion appropriate
> to the work in hand and particularly to the creation of one of
> the characters in it. Stephen Wonham. This rustic hero is not to
> everyone's taste. He can be boorish and a bore and when he gets
> drunk it is not upon wine. But he belongs to the countryside,
> he faces reality and he is the inheritor (KCL).

Forster's imagination caught fire on the Rings, just as it had caught
fire in response to the spirit of Cambridge, 'the fearless, uninfluential
Cambridge that sought reality and cared for truth'. From this compound *The Longest Journey* is created.

In this novel about the quest for truth each of the main characters
represents a different approach to reality. For Rickie it is the way of
imagination, reflected most obviously in his short stories, the visionary
qualities of which satisfy neither his wife nor his potential publisher.
For Stephen Wonham, it is the way of instinct; for Stewart Ansell it is
the way of the intellect. The novel as a whole suggests that no one
approach is sufficient but that all are necessary. Plot, characterization
and imagery establish a series of confrontations and contrasts between
the three different approaches which are defined and illustrated in a
variety of ways: through the young men's families, the houses they
inhabit, their response to money, friendship, love, and nature. The
rather awkward flashback in the Madingley Dell when Rickie tells his
friends the story of his life establishes him not only as the product of a
loveless marriage but as a lonely city-dwelling child. 'He had opened
his eyes to filmy heavens, and taken his first walk on asphalt. He had
seen civilization as a row of semi-detached villas, and society as a state
in which men do not know the men who live next door'. In his

loneliness he would sob and ask 'Shall I ever have a friend?' (compare Maurice's quest for the elusive friend). The flashback also establishes that Rickie hated his mocking father, adored his mother, who 'was afraid of intimacy, in case it led to confessions', and felt remorsefully responsible for her death because he wilfully disobeyed her order to put on his overcoat on the day she died.

Rickie has no permanent home. He is dependent for hospitality on relations and friends: his cousins, the money-conscious Silts, 'who combine to a peculiar degree the restrictions of hospitality with the discomforts of a boarding house'; and the Pembrokes, Herbert who teaches at Sawston and his sister Agnes who keeps house for him, a house in which 'neither the cry of money nor the cry for money shall ever be heard.' This is an index of their gentility and that unreal attitude to money common in their class, which Forster had encountered in his great-aunt Marianne Thornton. In fact to exclude the topic from polite conversation was a convenient device for ignoring economic privilege in the late Victorian and Edwardian period. And Agnes's silent but single-minded legacy-hunting illustrates how hypocritical the convention was.

Stewart Ansell's harmonious background is a complete contrast to Rickie's rootlessness and the Pembrokes' dissociation of culture from money. Ansell, who is a composite picture of Forster's Cambridge friends H. O. Meredith and the brilliant scholar Alfred Ainsworth, is the son of a successful suburban draper. Although his father knows nothing about philosophy, he loves his son and believes that he should be free to do what he wishes. The family, consisting of the father and two sisters, live over the shop. When Rickie visits Ansell, he contrasts the 'live' money that rattles through their tills with the 'dead' money that comes silently to him through the death of others. The Ansell family background, while acting as an obvious symbol for the wholeness of life that is attained through frankness and love and the union of money and culture, serves as an effective counterweight to Stewart Ansell's own somewhat pedantic separation of philosophy from life. In contrasted but related fashion, Stephen Wonham's coarse animal nature, his simple instinctive response to the earth and the local peasantry is set against the gentler and more civilized background of ideas provided in an unpublished book by his uncle, Mr Failing. These ideas, a combination of abstract nature worship and Utopian Socialism are strongly reminiscent of the thought of Edward Carpenter, author of *Civilisation: its Cause and Cure* (1889), a once popular critique of the coming machine age. By placing the representatives of the three approaches to reality in such fully and appropriately realized settings, Forster increases the social and symbolic resonance of the novel and prevents it from becoming either thinly allegorical or overtly didactic.

Poets and novelists sometimes see their 'intentions' more clearly in retrospect than at the time of writing, especially when provoked or given a nudge by subsequent criticism, as Forster was nudged by Lionel Trilling's book to see *Howards End* in Trilling's terms. Caution is therefore required in interpreting their remarks. Yet Forster's Introduction, written more than fifty years after the novel, offers a suggestive and succinct account of the quest for truth and the struggle between opposed characters and forces for possession of Rickie. Having spoken of Cambridge as the place where truth and reality are worshipped, he writes:

> Ansell is the undergraduate high-priest of that local shrine, Agnes Pembroke is its deadly debunker. Captured by her and by Sawston, Rickie goes to pieces, and cannot even be rescued when Ansell joins up with Stephen and strikes (Introduction, p. xi).

The account is especially interesting since it defines the conflict in the simplest possible terms and assigns to Ansell a role that he does not quite fulfil in the novel. At one time Forster gave him a more active part in bringing Stephen and Rickie together, but omitted it from the published novel. In reading the author's simple outline we need to remember that the conflict is a sex battle as well as a battle for truth. The Cambridge ideal of male friendship – and by implication the ideal of personal relations – excludes heterosexual love; the woman becomes an object of suspicion and is regarded either as an intruder or as something unreal. When Lytton Strachey went through the records of the Cambridge Apostles it became clear that most were homosexuals though not practising ones.

Agnes, on entering the magic Cambridge circle, instinctively recognizes Stewart Ansell as the enemy who must be won over or defeated. The ensuing conflict springs from sexual jealousy as much as from different standards of truth. One scene establishes clearly the intimate bond that exists between Stewart Ansell and Rickie (ch. 7). Rickie gives Ansell a garland of flowers, he speaks of 'a kind of friendship office, where the marriage of true minds could be registered', and Ansell pulls him down affectionately by the ankles. Returning to this chapter after reading *Maurice* and the homosexual short stories, one sees immediately that the relationship is essentially homosexual. The two places that Rickie comes to associate with happiness are his rooms in Cambridge and the Dell at Madingley. He would like to extend this happiness to all, but both places are in fact places of seclusion (though not necessarily symbolic 'wombs'), open only to the elect, with Stewart Ansell occupying a central place. Agnes breaks into both magic circles. Her first victory is complete when she calls Rickie into the Dell at Madingley and enfolds him as her lover: her second at Cadbury Rings. When Mrs Failing informs Rickie that Stephen Wonham is his stepbrother, and Rickie, in a moment of understanding not horror, calls out 'Stephen', it is Agnes, not Stephen who answers and who 'caught him to her breast'. Agnes, like Miss Bartlett in *A Room with a View*, blots out the distant view, and therefore reality.

A further example of the way the struggle for truth is supported and qualified by overtones of sexual possession lies in the tentative hint that Agnes's opposition to Stephen Wonham arises partly from his similarity to her dead fiancé, Gerald. In chapter 31 of the published text, the fact that Agnes identifies Stephen with Gerald is only hinted at. Stephen tells Rickie that 'She looked at me as if she knew me, and then gasped "Gerald", and started crying.' But, in an earlier manuscript version the identification is made dramatic. Agnes throws herself into Stephen's arms when she calls him Gerald. This unconscious dimension in Agnes's character, stronger in the manuscript than in the published version, casts a sympathetic light on her inner conflict and hidden motives. Yet the chill analysis of her as someone who was not 'conscious of her tragedy' in the printed text, someone from whom 'the inner life had been withdrawn', firmly relegates her to the ranks of 'the benighted'.

When Agnes and Rickie announce their engagement, before Stephen Wonham enters the action, the philosopher Stewart Ansell sums up the situation.

> She is happy because she has conquered; he is happy because he has at last hung all the world's beauty on to a single peg. He was always trying to do it. He used to call the peg humanity. Will either of these happinesses last? His can't. Hers only for a time. I fight this woman not only because she fights me, but because I foresee the most appalling catastrophe. She wants Rickie, partly to replace another man whom she lost two years ago, partly to

make something out of him. He is to write. In time she will get
sick of this. He won't get famous. She will only see how thin
he is and how lame. She will long for a jollier husband, and I
don't blame her. And, having made him thoroughly miserable
and degraded, she will bolt – if she can do it like a lady (ch. 8).

The prediction of this born misogynist proves accurate – except that
it is Rickie who bolts. Stewart Ansell's objections to Agnes are simple
and fundamental, as he explains in a letter to Rickie. They are '(1) She
is not serious (2) She is not truthful.' The action of the novel endorses
this analysis.

The change of scene from Cambridge to Cadover – 'the perilous
house' – is important in a variety of ways. It introduces two new
characters who are to play vital parts in the novel: Mrs Failing, a
spiteful sardonic old woman, who is Rickie's aunt; and Stephen
Wonham. The change marks a crucial stage in the development of the
theme of brotherhood. It also introduces the first of the many references
to the railway-crossing, thus prefiguring Rickie's death there. And it
brings a new spirit into the novel, the spirit of Wessex: pagan, natural
and instinctive, a manifestation of the continuity of rural England, a
spirit embodied to some extent in Stephen. Mrs Failing, who invites
the newly engaged couple to Cadover, suggests another kind of continuity. In her is continued the heartlessness of Rickie's dead father: his
sterile aestheticism, his delight in playing cruel tricks on people. Mrs
Failing begins by playing a trick on Agnes by pretending that the
unshaven Stephen is a peasant. In the older woman, Agnes meets her
match: the two women, adept in the art of compromise, form a truce
in deceit. Agnes connives in Mrs Failing's scheme to send Stephen
away after the aunt's revelation that he is Rickie's brother; they thus
prevent Rickie from greeting him and acknowledging the relationship.
When Agnes discovers that Mrs Failing has not told Stephen, she
announces triumphantly to Rickie, 'Dear, we're saved!' Her complicity
in this scheme of false salvation is complete. And Rickie is pained and
shocked.

The description of Rickie's and Stephen's ride to Salisbury brings
together the theme of brotherhood and the theme of the continuity of
England in a deeply moving fashion; it conveys a sense of some ultimate reality lying behind favoured spots of English countryside; and
it offers authentic intimations of infinity. The occasional lapses into
religiosity of phrase – they 'were approaching the Throne of God' –

are counterbalanced by the comedy of Rickie's failure to manage his mount and by the coarse humour of the soldier they meet who sings rhymes about Aunt Emily, until Stephen topples him in the mud. In this whole section much is made of settling one's differences by physical contest, but without the sadistic overtones that accompany Gerald's bullying, or Mrs Failing's delight in cruelty, or Agnes's repeated talk of horsewhipping. Rather this part establishes the value of personal conflict, the reality of which is finally confirmed by Stephen's frank contest with Mr Pembroke over the division of the profits from Rickie's short stories and by the contrast made by Stephen between the sham values represented by Mr Pembroke and the earthy reality of riding on Salisbury Plain by night (ch. 35). Stephen, who serves to link the ideals of fraternity and the English spirit, is not merely a healthy animal, 'with just enough soul to contemplate its own bliss', in touch with nature, completely at home with the morals and manners of the local peasants. In his simple fashion, he is, like Stewart Ansell, a philosopher in search of truth, absurd as his sixpenny rational tracts may be. He is also imaginative, like Rickie; a child of poetry and rebellion, although his imagination expresses itself more naturally and in a less literary form: 'he lived too near the things he loved to seem poetical.' Since the novel is to end with Stephen as the 'inheritor' of England, it is important that he should not appear as a crude embodiment of the primitive, but should contain within him the potentialities, at least, for intellectual and imaginative development. There is a world of difference too between his vital, good-natured, shambling confusion as he ignores social restraints and the spiritual muddle that overwhelms Rickie, a muddle that arises from social compromise and self-delusion.

Forster was wise to omit a long fantasy about the naked Stephen's encounter with the earth in the Salisbury ride episode, since it was a bad instance of the tug of 'anti-literature' and disastrously lowered Stephen's potential as an inheritor instead of raising it. In his Introduction to the novel, he has given a not completely accurate summary of the deleted part. Near the beginning of the cancelled section, there is an invocation to the woodland deities to guard Stephen (at this stage called Harold Wonham). '"O nymphs and woodland Fauns! O dryads and satyrs! O all ye hosts of earth whose deity I am compelled to greet! . . . Guard, O guard, this inefficient and most bumptious youth who advances without a talisman against your suspected powers."' The young man feels that he is pursued by an unseen presence; and bumps into a huge grey shape (a tree): 'his brain had been wiped clean, and he was a little child. Liking the smooth bark, he laid his cheek to it and kissed the living wood, again and again. Then he stood up smiling, but full of reverence' (MS, KCL). Meredith's account of Richard Feverel's night ride in the Rhineland forest was Forster's main model here, although the celebration of man's kinship with the earth could be found in a multitude of post-Darwinian writers. In the published novel, Stephen experiences a moment of panic fear when pursued by a flock of sheep, but the other elements connected with Pan disappear. Forster makes the point about his genuine contact with the earth more neatly and economically by picturing Stephen's contempt for one of Rickie's fanciful stories about getting in touch with nature when he reads it on the roof at Cadover. He exclaims, 'In touch with Nature! What cant would the books think of next. His eyes closed. He was sleepy. Good, oh good! Sighing into his pipe, he fell asleep' (ch. 12). Stephen's faults are obvious, but they do not spring from the undeveloped heart. He is a genuine Pagan 'who lives for the Now', the very opposite of Henry Wilcox in *Howards End*, who 'lived for the five minutes that have passed, and the five minutes to come' and who 'had the business mind' (HE, ch. 29).

The central part of *The Longest Journey*, 'Sawston', provides a convincing indictment of the system of education that produces the undeveloped heart in the English middle classes. Forster here draws on his own public school, Tonbridge, probably exaggerating little, as fellow sufferers at other schools testify. Recalling Goldsworthy Lowes Dickinson's miseries at Charterhouse, he once remarked '. . . as generation after generation of sensitive boys record their experience in them, one marvels why the boarding house system continues at all, and why the middle classes still insist on so much discomfort for their children at such expense to themselves' (GLD, ch. 5). Of course, the answer was that, in Forster's day, a public school education was both an assertion of economic status and an almost essential passport to administrative power in England and the British Empire. The end justified the means, even though the recognizable public school figure who was produced was damaged for life as a private individual. In the Sawston chapters, Forster connects the public and the private theme. His public theme is the education of an Englishman and the future of England: his private theme is the individual's quest for truth, love, comradeship, wholeness of being. It is appropriate that Rickie's moral deterioration should be set against a background of the shoddy second-hand values taught at Sawston. Although Rickie himself has suffered as a boy at a public school and is determined to spare others similar suffering, he is power-less to do so. He becomes enmeshed in a network of petty intrigue and deceit that culminates in a painful case of bullying. Sawston is the exact antithesis of Cambridge. It worships success, not truth; it believes in 'personal influence', not 'personal relations'; it seeks to develop *esprit de corps*, not brotherhood; it claims to be the 'world in miniature', to speak for the world and not just for itself. '"The good societies [Stewart Ansell tells his listeners] say, 'I tell you to do this because I am Cambridge'. The bad ones say, 'I tell you to do that because I am the great world'. . . . They lie"' (ch. 7). Sawston is an enclosed, self-sufficient world in which spiritual muddle and unreality flourish. The fogs blot out the light. Rickie's marriage brings not the looked-for vision but phantoms and spectres as grey and ghastly as those that haunt the paintings of Eduard Munch or the plays of Ibsen and Strindberg. After the death of Agnes's child, the departure of the bullied Varden, and Rickie's total disenchantment with Agnes, those two very different apostles of truth, Stewart Ansell and Stephen Wonham, invade this unreal world and restore some sense of reality.

The dramatic climax of the Sawston chapters comes with Ansell's arraignment of Rickie and Agnes before the boys at Sunday dinner. Benjamin Britten has compared these recurrent big, rather melo-dramatic scenes in Forster's fiction to operatic set-pieces. This scene at Sawston comes nearer to the trial scene in *A Passage to India* than to the fight between Philip and Gino in *Where Angels Fear to Tread*, but the analogy with opera is appropriate to all three and comes as a useful reminder not to judge such set-pieces by purely realistic standards. The contrast between the isolated, accusing figure of Stewart Ansell, and the petty formality of the dining-room, with its 'imperial port-raits', Union Jack, and figures at high table is a fine piece of theatre that dramatizes the actual clash of values. The success of the whole scene depends on multiple ironies. Ansell believes that Rickie knows nothing about having a brother; Rickie believes that he knows all. It is only when Rickie refers specifically to his 'father's disgrace' that the secret is given to the world.

'Please listen again,' resumed Ansell. 'Please correct two slight mistakes: firstly, Stephen is one of the greatest people I have ever met; secondly, he's not your father's son. He's the son of your mother.'

It was Rickie, not Ansell, who was carried from the hall, and
it was Herbert who pronounced the blessing –
'*Benedicto benedicatur.*'
A profound stillness succeeded the storm, and the boys,
slipping away from their meal, told the news to the rest of the
school, or put it in the letters they were writing home (ch. 27).

In the final section of the novel, 'Wiltshire', the development of the
different ideas of reality and of the relationships between the characters
is complicated and confused. The question of ethical reality (will
Rickie accept Stephen as a fellow man, a brother?) becomes inextric-
ably mixed up with another notion of reality, psychological and spiritual in origin. The working out of the ethical theme requires that
Rickie should cease to see Stephen as a symbol, either of his father's or
his mother's frailty and see him as a man. But the working out of the
psychological theme and the theme of continuity requires that Rickie
should see his mother in Stephen and see him transfigured by the
mother's love. When Pembroke tells Rickie that he should mind all
the more on finding that it was his mother who was at fault, Rickie
replies gently, '"I have been too far back"', an evocative phrase, first
used of the effect of Stephen's conversation with Ansell in a cancelled
version of chapter 31, a phrase that foreshadows Forster's definition of
prophecy in *Aspects of the Novel*. Rickie continues: '"Ansell took me a
journey that was even new to him. We got behind right and wrong, to
a place where only one thing matters – that the Beloved should arise
from the Dead"' (ch. 31). It is clear that Stephen becomes transfigured
and sanctified as a reincarnation of his mother's love. But the author
cannot logically endorse both the ethical and the spiritual ideas of
reality. Is it possible to ascribe the idea of the Beloved rising from the
grave as just one more of Rickie's illusions? Hardly, with the abundant
evidence of the author's own belief in the influence of the dead in the
other novels, and his stout defence of 'ancestor worship' when challenged about this element: '"The present is so heavy and crude and so
vulgar that something has to be thrown into the opposite scale . . .
This is not a private fancy of mine: all races who have practised ancestor
worship know about it."'
In the published version of *The Longest Journey*, the very Shelleyan
incident when Rickie watches Stephen's 'transfigured face' as he lights
a paper boat that becomes a rose of flame and passes under one of the
arches of the bridge, is the most striking visionary moment of the

novel. It clearly carries the full weight of the author's imaginative approval; yet what it endorses is Rickie's acceptance of Stephen as a symbol, not a man. Moreover, a later passage that speaks of the 'mystic rose and the face it illuminates' further clarifies Stephen's symbolic transfiguration into an image of the dead mother. In the cancelled sections that exist only in the manuscript, the theme of the mother's spirit living through Stephen is even more strongly stressed. An early version of chapter 32 includes two examples of the dead surviving in the living. One is Agnes's momentary identification of Stephen with her dead lover Gerald: he recalls 'all the radiant possibilities that perished on a suburban football field'. Stephen understands intuitively and is 'transfixed with pity'.

> 'Poor girl – has it been like that – don't think I shall ever tell
> him – Ah poor girl!' Then the moment passed, the spirit returned
> to the grave, the lips were those of a stranger, and the memory of
> them an eternal shame.

Agnes's identification is clearly an illusory vision, the product of psychological guilt. The second survival from the dead is not illusory, however, although it, too, is connected with repressed guilt, Rickie's confused feeling that his failure to obey his mother's injunction to wear his overcoat was responsible for her death. In this version, the school is on fire. Stephen and Ansell urge Rickie to leave the burning house at Sawston,

> 'No one's stopping!' they cried. 'Come our way. Come back to
> the things you've forgotten.'
> For a moment he murmured about duty.
> 'But he must have a great coat!' said Stephen. 'He can't go
> without a great coat.'
> To Rickie also a mortal spirit was incarnate in immortal flesh.
> Last time, when that voice had said those words, he had silenced
> it fretfully [cf. end of ch. 2]. He obeyed it today, and the three
> of them followed the course of the storm (MS, KCL).

In the later published version, Forster still suggests that Rickie goes with Stephen because he hears his mother's voice speaking through him and not because he accepts Stephen's ethical argument, '"Come with me as a man . . . Not as a brother; who cares what people did years back."' But he no longer makes the point dramatically but through commentary and he omits the link with the overcoat.

Habit and sex may change with the new generation, features may alter with the play of a private passion, but a voice is apart from these. It lies nearer to the racial essence and perhaps to the divine; it can, at all events, overleap one grave (ch. 31).

Ultimately the two approaches to brotherhood interweave and overlap but are never satisfactorily reconciled. Rickie and the author appear to endorse ideals of transfiguration, while Stephen appeals to a rough and ready ethical ideal based on common humanity. As a further paradox the novel ends with the triumph of Stephen's elemental qualities, but only because the dead Rickie had 'bequeathed him salvation'.

Much of the awkwardness in the final section of *The Longest Journey* also comes from the novelist's attempt to establish Stephen as someone fit to be an 'inheritor', first, in the sense of inheriting the qualities possessed by his farmer father and his gentle mother, the qualities of 'poetry and rebellion' that brought them together; and second, in the sense of inheriting the spirit of England's past, a past seen as essentially rural, associated with ancient Wessex, pagan rather than Christian. At this late stage in the plot, Forster suddenly switches to the past and relates the story of how the young farmer Robert fell in love with Rickie's mother, waited patiently, and finally ran away with her to Stockholm where Stephen was conceived. For the reader, Robert achieves a symbolic rather than a real existence. He is clearly intended to embody the spirit of the earth. 'As he talked, the earth became a living being – or rather a being with a living skin – and manure no longer dirty stuff, but a symbol of regeneration and of the birth of life from life' (ch. 29). Certainly his practicality shows up old Mr Failing's shadowy ideals of love and brotherhood, his firm grasp of the actual forms a healthy contrast to Rickie's father's abstractions and cynicism. Even for Mrs Failing the two lovers are no 'ordinary people', but 'forces of nature'. And yet in the midst of this overt celebration of love, nature, and the spirit of the earth, there comes a chill qualifying passage. It is put in the mouth of the prosy Mr Failing certainly, but on the evidence of Forster's own eulogies elsewhere of 'Love the Beloved Republic', it expresses the author's view that the republic 'will not be brought about by love alone. It will approach with no flourish of trumpets, and have no declaration of independence. Self-sacrifice and – worse still – self-mutilation are the things that sometimes help it most.' Mr Failing uses these sentiments to recommend an immediate rescue party to Stockholm; but they reverberate with a wider significance in the novel as a whole. After Rickie's brief vision of happiness and brotherhood at Cambridge, the emphasis falls on suffering, self-sacrifice, self-mutilation. Is Rickie's death at the railway-crossing to be seen as a necessary act of self-mutilation in the service of 'Love the Beloved Republic'? And, autobiographically, a mutilation of one part of the self that another part may survive?

While Forster constantly emphasizes that Stephen inherits his parents' loving spirit, he places a quite extraordinary stress on his drunkenness and animality, especially in the final chapter. This may be partly to justify Rickie's sense of desertion and spiritual bankruptcy and partly to prevent the 'inheritor' figure who represents the continuity of England from being refined away into a sentimental symbol. But the various sides of Stephen's character never come together as a whole. He is required to represent too many of the qualities Forster admired and to represent them in too simple and elemental a form. A good example of this oversimplification relates to the working out of the theme of personal relations. When Rickie reviews the watchwords that had ruled his life at Sawston, watchwords such as 'Organize', 'Systematize', 'Fill up every moment', 'Induce *esprit de corps*', he sees that 'they ignored personal contest, personal truces, personal love.' Stephen, in his relations with the local peasants, exemplifies the importance of 'personal contest', like Gino and Philip in *Where Angels Fear to Tread*. But he represents in a very rudimentary fashion the middle way between the preciosity of Cambridge's ideal of personal relations and the neglect of all personal relations at Sawston. Thematically, then, he contributes something to the ideal of wholeness, but there is little to suggest that Stephen was capable of wholeness of being himself, of uniting the monk and beast in man. There is altogether too much beast.

Why does Rickie save Stephen's life twice? First, he saves him from toppling over the banisters at Dunwood House; then, later, he saves him from being run over at the level-crossing. Why should the saving occur twice? And why should Rickie survive the first and die in the course of the second? The questions are not easily answered, but the attempt to answer them takes us to the heart of the novel. The first incident when Stephen throws a brick through the study window, wrecks the hall, lurches up the stairs, and nearly falls over the banisters, establishes Rickie's release from remorse and his consequent capacity for instinctive action. While Herbert Pembroke is calling for the police, Rickie has already saved Stephen. The simplicity of his greeting, '"Hello, Stephen!"' stresses his intuitive acceptance of his brother.

Hither had Rickie moved in ten days – from disgust to penitence, from penitence to longing, from a life of horror to a new life, in which he still surprised himself by unexpected words. Hello, Stephen! For the son of his mother had come back, to forgive him, as she would have done, to live with him, as she had planned (ch. 31).

To Agnes, Stephen seems 'a man of scandal'; to Rickie, he is 'a symbol of redemption'. Neither acknowledges him as a man 'who would answer them back after a few hours' rest.'

Forster's early attempts to imagine the confrontation and Rickie's decision to go with Stephen were sentimental and melodramatic. In the first of these Stewart Ansell accepts Rickie's invitation to Dunwood House, sleeps the night beside the drunken Stephen, and later prepares Stephen to accept a life shared with Rickie. A highly emotional scene between Stephen and Rickie follows in which Rickie constantly returns to the theme of his mother's resurrection in Stephen. In a later version Forster reduces the Ansell/Stephen explanation by condensing the essentials into dialogue at the beginning. The sentimental confrontation between the half-brothers follows. Rickie pleads for forgiveness. '"Son of my mother, kiss me; forgive me."' He then speaks in prophetic vein of the dream he had after his child's death and of his newly gained vision of human continuity (Forster's master theme) as the result of seeing his mother resurrected in Stephen. 'Rickie gazed at the pure stream to which he would never contribute and watched it broadening to the sea.' Mawkish as this scene is, it does clarify Rickie's later action in the published novel in sacrificing his life for Stephen at the railway-crossing. At the end of this version storms gather; Agnes, who is terrified, throws herself into Stephen's arms; part of the school is struck by lightning; and Rickie follows the fleeing Stephen, obedient this time to the voice of his mother, as it speaks through Stephen and tells him to bring his great-coat. Forster was wise to omit most of the details in these two early versions and to retain only brief references to Ansell's intervention and the exact details of Rickie's dream. He showed a true craftsman's skill in combining both in a short semi-dramatized résumé of Rickie's moral and spiritual progress. This then leads up to his decision to leave Agnes and follow Stephen.

However, the confrontation at Sawston cannot mark the climax of the relations between Stephen and Rickie. Between this incident and the later one at the level-crossing, Rickie passes through stages of intense spiritual struggle. At Sawston he confesses to Stephen that ever since he failed to give himself up to the spirit of the ride to Salisbury, he has 'taken the world at second-hand'. He fights against Mrs Failing's cynicism, against her denial that the earth may 'confirm' men's love, her denial that it will, in the words of her husband, '"suffer some rallying-point, spire, mound, for the new generation to cherish"' (ch. 34). The memory of Stephen sailing the paper boat, the 'mystic rose', and the tunnel 'dropping diamonds', comes back to Rickie as he drives away from Cadover. 'He stood behind things at last, and knew that conventions are not majestic, and that they will not claim us in the end.' Indeed, his liberation seems complete, more complete than Philip's at the end of *Where Angels Fear to Tread*. And yet he moves forward, not to freedom and self-reliance, but to 'self-sacrifice' and 'self-mutilation'. When he recognizes Stephen as 'a hero' fighting against social injustice, fighting, too, against the 'Wilbrahams and Pembrokes who try to rule our world', he feels that it is 'worth while to sacrifice everything for such a man'. But when he discovers that Stephen has broken his promise not to drink, his whole moral world collapses. His trust in the earth becomes implicated in his broken faith in Stephen.

> 'May God receive me and pardon me for trusting the earth.'
> 'But, Mr Elliot, what have you done that's wrong?'
> 'Gone bankrupt, Leighton, for the second time. Pretended again that people were real. May God have mercy on me!' (ch. 34).

And it is in the spirit of defeat that 'wearily' he does 'a man's duty' and pushes Stephen to safety off the railway-line, saving his brother at the cost of his own life.

How extraordinary all this is. What it seems to suggest is that Forster was unable to imagine any future for a liberated Rickie in an Edwardian novel, or indeed in Edwardian society. He therefore huddles together a series of spiritual crises to make his death appear convincing and necessary. The ending also suggests the victory of self-disgust over self-renewal, or at least the author's disgust with the refined squeamish side of his nature that lacked the courage to accept the coarse animality of Stephen. Rickie has been drawn towards two men, the intellectual Stewart Ansell and the physical Stephen Wonham. He cannot accept either, or reconcile such contrasting responses to life within himself, and so must die. In *Maurice*, written a few years later, but not published in his lifetime, Forster was able to deal more frankly with the theme of brotherhood and love between men: the ideal of 'comradeship and ecstasy'. In *The Longest Journey*, he is driven into using a number of artistic subterfuges to mask his real theme. This enables him to explore areas of experience that interested him but not to carry out the exploration to its logical conclusion. Rickie, in the novel, at first vows never to marry because of his inherited deformity. But he does marry, and not only fathers a child, who is even lamer than himself, but feels guilt-stricken for his offence against the child, his wife, and himself. It requires little ingenuity to substitute homosexuality for inherited deformity. And the question whether a man will accept his illegitimate brother, given the strong taboos against frank acceptance of illegitimacy in the Edwardian middle class, may be another subterfuge for asking the question, will a man accept a form of sexuality that is forbidden by society. Moreover Agnes feels 'menaced by the abnormal', overtly by Rickie's deformity and Stephen's illegitimacy, but subconsciously by male comradeship (chs 1, 14 and 15). Since the publication of *Maurice* in 1971 and the posthumous homosexual short stories in 1972, the meaning behind these artistic subterfuges becomes more apparent. But this new way of reading the novel, although it may illuminate much that has always seemed obscure, still does little to clarify the confusion of themes and symbols within the novel.

Two rather different views have been taken of this confusion. Lionel Trilling, one of Forster's most perceptive critics, sees it as a failure to master technique, the kind of failure that one expects to find in an early but ambitious novel. John Harvey, on the other hand, sees it as an expression of a confused and inadequate vision of life.

> *The Longest Journey*, then, despite – or perhaps because of – its local successes is a failure as a whole. The disparate elements of which it is composed are never brought together into any kind of unity; at best they lie uneasily side by side; more often they actively quarrel with each other (Bradbury, 1966, p. 127).

There is undoubtedly confusion, not simply rich ambiguity. And it is confusion of vision as well as of technique. But the final impression of the novel is more unified than patient analysis would lead one to expect. Although we cannot say what Forster said of Ibsen, 'Everything rings true and echoes far because it is in the exact place which its surroundings require', we can say that the great imaginative scenes in the novel cohere in the memory more firmly than Harvey suggests.

The vision of Agnes's and Gerald's kiss, the parallel scenes in the Cambridge Dell and in the Cadbury Rings, the ride across Salisbury Plain after which Rickie takes 'the world at second hand', Ansell's dramatic irruption at Sawston school, the paper boat 'burning as if it would burn for ever', Rickie's death and finally the pastoral coda: all these come together in the memory as an affirmation of the rightness of a life lived close to the rhythms of nature, a life passionate and instinctive. And Demeter, the earth goddess, who transcends sex, says Forster in 'Cnidus' (AH), binds together the two generations: she presides over Mrs Elliot's experience of instinctive love for Robert, her farmer lover, and over Rickie's and Stephen's experience of the earth and their mother. *The Longest Journey* is something more interesting than a splendid failure or a flawed masterpiece. It is a novel that challenges most of our settled critical categories and is a landmark in Forster's fictional development.

5

Howards End

When *Howards End* appeared in 1910, it was widely praised; and many reviewers took the opportunity it offered to survey the novelist's development. The anonymous reviewer in the *Times Literary Supplement*, for example, remarked that Mr E. M. Forster had 'now done what critical admirers of his foregoing novels' had 'confidently looked for'; he had now 'put right' the faults of his 'clever, imperfect slightly baffling' earlier novels (Gardner, 1973, p. 125). Like the earlier works, *Howards End* is built on a major antithesis, the contrast between the Schlegel and Wilcox ways of life, but it is one that has deeper social implications than the contrasts in the earlier novels. The contrast is no longer between spontaneity and convention but between culture and materialism, both in the lives of individuals and in the life of society. Indeed, the growing materialism of the Edwardian age and the challenge of the machine to traditional culture were topics no responsible novelist could ignore. The mood is still that of social comedy, but the comedy bites deeper and embraces a broader spectrum of English society, so that the novel becomes a 'Condition of England' novel, as well as a brilliant Edwardian comedy of manners. It illustrates very well what has been called Forster's 'Coleridgean urge to include everything, to see every side of every question, to allow every viewpoint' (Beer, 1962, p. 198).

The initial action, as in *Where Angels Fear to Tread*, concerns a rescue party; but, whereas in that novel the two rescue parties provide a main structural principle, in *Howards End* Mrs Munt's expedition to rescue Helen Schlegel from Paul Wilcox is mainly a means of launching the reader into the major contrast between the Schlegels and Wilcoxes. In addition it provides, through Helen, the first insight into the 'panic and emptiness' that lie behind the confident Wilcox fortress. Since the novel has a wider theme than either personal salvation or the difference between true and false salvation, Forster's favourite comic device has to undergo subtle transformation if it is still to function as an integral part of his fiction. Thus, after the first three chapters, the idea of the rescue party as a means of saving someone from a misguided marriage or from unconventional behaviour is replaced by operations to rescue a house from ownership by a stranger or to rescue a clerk from descent into the abyss of poverty and social degradation. The Wilcoxes' concerted attempt to retain Howards End after Mrs Wilcox's dying wish that it should go to Margaret Schlegel (in early working notes she 'refuses the legacy') may be seen as a form of rescue party. The advice to change his job given to the young clerk, Leonard Bast, whom the Schlegels meet at a concert, may also be seen as a rescue operation, so too may Helen's ill-fated expedition to Oniton to obtain social justice for the Basts, and Margaret's visit to Howards End to rescue Helen from her supposed madness. The two Schlegel sisters rescue their old relationship from misunderstanding and disaster through love, tenderness and imaginative sympathy 'the past sanctifying the present; the present, with wild heart-throb, declaring that there would after all be a future'; they thus prove that 'the inner life had paid'. Margaret also stages a rescue operation to save the broken Henry Wilcox, whose previously impregnable fortress has collapsed after his son, Charles, has been sentenced to three years' imprisonment for manslaughter. Surprisingly the manuscripts show that Forster had written six chapters without knowing whether Charles would kill Leonard or Leonard Charles. Bast's death, brought about by a 'weak heart', by Charles's blow with the Schlegel sword, and by the weight of books falling on him, makes a fitting symbolic end, though Strachey's friend Carrington, for one, could not see why Leonard must 'fall down dead with the books on top of him'. Like James's young hero Hyacinth Robinson, in *The Princess Casamassima*, he is finally destroyed by the culture he so ardently pursues.

Howards End takes up and expands the theme touched on at the end of *The Longest Journey*: who shall inherit England? In the earlier novel, the inheritor is Stephen Wonham, the young English pagan, in touch with the earth, alive to the wisdom of the body, who is the illegitimate son of a farmer and a gentlewoman. Alone at night with his sleeping daughter on the Wiltshire downs he meditates on his fate. 'Though he could not phrase it, he believed that he guided the future of our race ...' The word 'our' reveals too obviously the authorial approval and the whole passage is over-assertive rather than imaginatively convincing.

This pastoral coda, however, together with the poetic evocations of the spirit of Wessex, reflects Forster's preoccupation with the future of England in a novel that is primarily concerned with the fate of its passive and ineffective hero, Rickie. By contrast, *Howards End* is not the story of a young man's imaginative and emotional development, but the story of two strongly contrasted groups of people; consequently it distributes its imaginative sympathies over a much wider range of characters than *The Longest Journey*. In addition it offers a deeper insight into the interaction between character and society, and recognizes frankly the importance of money and work.

The changes are no doubt partly due to a general maturing of the novelist's vision (it was surprisingly mature from the start); but they were also prompted by the growing national concern with the 'Condition of England', a concern reflected in a large number of works, fictional and non-fictional, published in the early years of the century. Beginning in the last decades of the nineteenth century, a series of reports had drawn attention to the problem of the poor in the big cities. Charles Booth's *Life and Labour of the People of London* (1889), the first systematic and comprehensive study, was followed by Seebohm Rowntree's study of the slums of York, *Poverty: A Study of Town Life* (1901), L. C. C. Money's *Riches and Poverty* (1905), Will Reason's *Poverty* (1909), and Philip Snowden's *The Living Wage* (1912). But most influential of all was Sidney and Beatrice Webb's *Minority Report of the Poor Law Commission* (1909), which prepared the way for subsequent legislative action. The popular success of *The Condition of England* (1909), by C. F. G. Masterman, a member of the Liberal Government from 1908 until 1915, establishes clearly the wide interest taken at the time in urgent social issues.

It was not only the problem of the poor that troubled the conscience of the nation, but the emergence of the great cities. In an essay written in 1904, Masterman wrote:

> In England the cities are most monstrous, and black, and
> disorganized; and the aggregations which sprawl at the mouths
> of the rivers or amid the wastes of the manufacturing districts
> most effectually challenge the advocate of any life that is secure,
> and passionate, and serene. These aggregations are something new
> in the history of things, to which no former time can furnish
> any precedent or parallel (Masterman, 1904, p. 47).

87

It was this sense of the newness of the problem and the bewildering feeling of ceaseless flux that acted as a challenge and an inspiration to such novelists as H. G. Wells, Galsworthy, and Forster. A similar vision of the monstrous city and the destruction of feudal rhythms of life appears in another of Masterman's works, significantly entitled *From the Abyss* (1903). Although purported to be written by an inhabitant of the abyss, few could have been deceived, as the approach is so obviously that of a middle-class evangelical liberal.

In much of the imaginative literature of the Edwardian period, including Forster's *Howards End*, certain themes assume a new importance: the city; the division of the nation into the rich and the poor (a division first noted by Disraeli in *Sybil*, 1845); the threat of the abyss to those perched perilously on the lower verges of gentility, like Forster's Leonard Bast; the destruction of the older agricultural rhythms of life and the violent emergence of a new urban order (recorded and lamented by Richard Jefferies, W. H. Hudson, George Sturt and, most memorably, in D. H. Lawrence's early novels); the mixed blessing of Empire and Imperialism; the immediate threat posed by the other great Imperial power, Germany, explored most dramatically in Erskine Childers's *The Riddle of the Sands* (1903) and H. H. Munro's *When William Came* (1914). The Edwardian period, far from being a period of settled calm, was one of continuous unrest and troubled analysis; this is reflected not only in the literature of the Edwardian propagandists, H. G. Wells and George Bernard Shaw, in *Tono Bungay* (1909) and *Heartbreak House* (1917), but in the work of the less politically committed writers, Henry James, Galsworthy, and Ford Madox Ford. Galsworthy's *Fraternity*, almost exactly contemporary with Forster's *Howards End*, reflects similar social preoccupations. Ford Madox Ford's novels render the major tensions of the age, and mirror the breaking down of old codes of behaviour, especially the code of gentlemanly honour in *The Good Soldier* (1915), while his little known impressionistic pageants, *The Soul of London* (1905), *The Heart of the Country* (1906), and *The Spirit of the People* (1907), provide further evidence of the concern with the changing ethos of England and the challenge of London. It is against this background of social and political upheaval and the writing it produced that Forster's *Howards End* needs to be seen if it is to be judged aright.

The novel opens informally on a quiet domestic note. Nothing could be more casual than its opening sentence: 'One may as well begin with Helen's letters to her sister.' But the letter that follows, naturally and unobtrusively, sounds the opening notes of two of the major themes of the novel. The first is the antithesis between the Wilcoxes (commercialism and power) and the Schlegels (culture, or 'sweetness and light'). The second is the importance of continuity, symbolized in the house Howards End, which, as we have already seen in chapter 1 was based on Rooksnest, in which Forster lived until he was fourteen. Helen's impulsive excitable nature emerges clearly from the first letter; so, too, does her susceptibility to atmosphere and to people totally unlike herself. Her subsequent seduction of the lowly clerk, Leonard Bast, at Oniton may seem improbable. (Was she 'got with child by Leonard Bast or by his fatal forgotten umbrella. All things considered', Katherine Mansfield mocks, 'I think it must have been the umbrella.') But, in fact, Helen's susceptibility to opposites – an aspect of the 'only connect' theme – provides the necessary psychological link between her brief love for Paul Wilcox and her even briefer affair with Leonard, and nearly makes both credible.

The letter with which *Howards End* opens is a brilliant piece of impressionistic writing. It not only introduces major themes, images, and major characters by name; it also evokes the mysterious spirit of Mrs Wilcox: 'Trail, trail, went her long dress over the sopping grass, and she came back with her hands full of the hay that was cut yesterday.' It is vital to the success of the book that the novelist should create the sense of a benevolent 'presence', in complete harmony with the house, not just a character. And it is important, too, that the reader should remember the details of the grass and hay, since they are taken up later in the novel and act as a recurrent motif, first associated with Mrs Wilcox, but subsequently with Margaret Schlegel, as she gradually develops her intuitive powers and thus assumes something of the indefinable wisdom of Mrs Wilcox. Helen's next letter fills out details. 'Mrs Wilcox, if quieter than in Germany, is sweeter than ever, and I never saw anything like her steady unselfishness . . .' The third letter announces that Helen and Paul, the younger son, are in love. The rapidity and compression of the writing is astounding in the opening chapters of the novel. But it was not always so. At first, as the manuscripts now published reveal, Forster overloaded the writing with unnecessary detail, especially in describing the Schlegels' house, at Wickham Place (Abinger: HE MSS, p. 3). The published text contains a perfect balance between circumstantial and representative detail.

The well-intentioned aunt, Mrs Munt, rushes off to intervene. By

the time she arrives at Howards End, the crisis is over and there is no
need for a rescue party. Helen has realized her mistake. However, her
telegram to her sister, Margaret, 'All over. Wish I had never written.
Tell no one – Helen', arrives too late to stop Aunt Juley. The aunt – a
wonderful comic creation, who nearly became an example of 'a
character running away' from the author, as the manuscript shows –
has something of the concentrated singleness of purpose that the
Wilcox family exemplifies. 'To history, to tragedy, to the past, to the
future, Mrs Munt remained equally indifferent; hers but to concentrate
on the end of her journey, and to rescue poor Helen from this dreadful
mess.' She mistakes the elder son Charles for the younger Paul, and
the whole episode of the car ride from the station is created in the best
spirit of English domestic comedy. But the comic misunderstanding of
identity, here as elsewhere in the novel, never disguises the deeper
significance of the incident. Falling in love, an aspect that should remain
essentially personal, as Margaret reminds her aunt, has become involved
in the public life of 'telegrams and anger' that always surrounds the
Wilcoxes. Mrs Munt, by talking about Helen to Charles, has offended
against Margaret's principle that personal relations are private, '"would
you please only talk the thing over with Helen."' Charles, furious at
being taken by surprise and indignant at his younger brother's folly,
immediately challenges him to own up, when he and Mrs Munt arrive
at Howards End. '"Yes or no, man; plain question, plain answer."'
At this juncture Mrs Wilcox gently and affectionately intercedes. It is a
memorable moment in the novel. All feel her presence and are silent.
For the reader she seems to embody the spirit of peaceful reconciliation
without ceasing to be a tactful mother of a headstrong and difficult
family.

> 'Charles dear,' said a voice from the garden. 'Charles, dear
> Charles, one doesn't ask plain questions. There aren't such things.'
>   They were all silent. It was Mrs Wilcox.
>   She approached just as Helen's letter had described her, trailing
> noiselessly over the lawn, and there was actually a wisp of hay
> in her hands. She seemed to belong not to the young people and
> their motor, but to the house, and to the tree that overshadowed
> it. One knew that she worshipped the past, and that the
> instinctive wisdom the past can alone bestow had descended upon
> her – that wisdom to which we give the clumsy name of
> aristocracy.

The aristocracy to which she belongs is Forster's spiritual aristocracy that he was later to define in his essay 'What I Believe' (TCD), but which he celebrates in all his novels.

Some obscurity surrounds the inner crisis that Helen experiences as the result of her love for Paul. In Forster's novels, as in those of Henry James, the gap between the external event and the crisis of consciousness it prompts is often extremely great, what E. K. Brown calls 'the chasm between the world of actions and the world of being' (Gardner, 1973, p. 371). With both authors it is important therefore to be sensitive to submerged connections. In *Howards End* we receive little aid from the author. This may be because he himself is uncertain whether Helen's experience constitutes an 'eternal moment' or not. For the reader, certainly, it is doubtful whether her brief love for Paul is a glimpse into the reality of instinctive passion that is to act as a guiding light for the rest of her life (compare, for example, Agnes and Gerald in *The Longest Journey*); or whether, on the other hand, it is an illusory experience, brought about by her temporary infatuation with the unfamiliar Wilcox world of masculine power and dominance. Although almost everything points to the second interpretation, there are enough residual echoes of earlier Forsterian modes of thought to suggest that it is not completely illusory. Moreover, later in the novel, Leonard Bast, like the heroes and heroines of the earlier novels, treasures up his eternal moment of conversation with the Schlegels, anxious not to tarnish it by later 'trivial or awkward contacts'. Forster certainly sees the absurdity of Leonard's overvaluation of the moment, his timidity, his genteel withdrawal from a society in which he feels ill at ease. But he seems less critical of Helen's moment at Howards End. The conversation between the two sisters after Helen's visit helps to clarify Helen's experience and to define the two women's respective attitudes to it. The exchange also relates the specific incident to the wider themes of the novel. Margaret, with her natural genius for generalization – a genius not incompatible with a respect for what Blake called 'minute particulars' – reflects on the significance of this whole encounter between the life of culture and the life of 'telegrams and anger'.

> I've often thought about it, Helen. It's one of the most interesting things in the world. The truth is that there is a great outer life that you and I have never touched – a life in which telegrams and anger count. Personal relations, that we think supreme, are not supreme there. There love means marriage settlements;

death, death duties. So far I'm clear. But here's my difficulty. This outer life, though obviously horrid, often seems the real one – there's grit in it. It does breed character. Do personal relations lead to sloppiness in the end? (ch. 4).

In the action that follows, both sisters are thrown into the world of 'marriage settlements', and 'death'. We then witness their attempts to harmonize the 'inner world' of personal relations and the life of the spirit with the 'outer world' of telegrams and anger. This they do through love and imagination and the discovery of their roots in the earth. Their success in reconciliation is far greater than Rickie's in *The Longest Journey*, but it is not achieved without some sense of loss.

The epigraph 'only connect', which unaccountably dropped out of the 1924 reprint and many subsequent editions, tells the reader immediately that the master theme of *Howards End* is harmony. This sets it in the English Romantic tradition, that tradition that had as its central ideal the imaginative reconciliation of opposites. Typical expressions of this ideal are Blake's 'without contraries there is no progression', Coleridge's 'balance and reconciliation of opposite or discordant qualities', Keats's constant striving to unite thought and feeling, and Wordsworth's vision of the harmony between man and nature. Forster's recognition that the principle of polarity operates in society as well as in the life of the individual forms a further link with this tradition, although he attempts nothing so positive and all-embracing as Coleridge's philosophic distinction in *Church and State* between the forces of permanence and the forces of progression in society. Forster's approach to society is intuitive, tentative, unsystematic. It is not philosophic. But it shares with the great Romantics a visionary and prophetic quality which springs primarily from his Burkean sense of the continuity of past, present, and future in the life of the nation and the life of the individual. His vision of the continuity within personal relations appears most obviously in the reunion between the two sisters, 'the past sanctifying the present', while the continuity in national life appears clearly in the description of the Dorset coast at the end of chapter 19, the vision of England as 'a ship of souls, with all the brave world's fleet accompanying her towards eternity', an overwritten passage certainly, but visionary and prophetic in tone and embodying the ideals of harmony and continuity untarnished by provinciality or jingoism.

The ideal of a realizable harmony at the levels of both private and public life is implicit throughout the novel. *Howards End* seeks to transmute the muddle of existence into the mystery of life, to transform the horrors of industrialism into a plausible pastoral vision. In relation to the private life, the most explicit expression of the theme of 'only connect' occurs at the beginning of chapter 22.

> Margaret greeted her lord with peculiar tenderness on the morrow. Mature as he was, she might yet be able to help him to the building of the rainbow bridge that should connect the prose in us with the passion [MSS and span our life with beauty]. Without it we are meaningless fragments, half monks, half beasts, unconnected arches that have never joined into a man.

This romantic Wagnerian image of the 'rainbow bridge', with the contrasted 'unconnected arches', lacks the remote austerity of the image of the overarching sky in *A Passage to India*, but it symbolizes the ideal reconciliation of opposites more adequately than the image in *The Longest Journey*: '"There wants a bridge,"' Stephen exploded.

In *Howards End*, Margaret's task in helping Mr Wilcox to achieve internal harmony is defined:

> Only connect! That was the whole of her sermon. Only connect the prose and the passion, and both will be exalted, and human love will be seen at its highest. Live in fragments no longer. Only connect, and the beast and the monk, robbed of the isolation that is life to either, will die (ch. 22).

The ultimate challenge comes when Henry Wilcox, who has himself been guilty of seducing Jacky Bast when she was a girl, refuses to allow Helen, now eight months pregnant with Leonard Bast's child, to sleep a night at Howards End. Up to this moment, Margaret has remained passive, seeking to remake her husband's personality through sympathy, insight and kindness. But now this all changes.

> 'You have not been yourself all day,' said Henry, and rose from his seat with face unmoved. Margaret rushed at him and seized both his hands. She was transfigured.
>   'Not any more of this!' she cried. 'You shall see the connection if it kills you, Henry! [MS has the stronger 'Connect! You shall connect if I kill you'] You have had a mistress – I forgave you. My sister has a lover – you drive her from the house. Do you see the connexion? Stupid, hypocritical, cruel – oh, contemptible! –

a man who insults his wife when she's alive and cants with her memory when she's dead. A man who ruins a woman for his pleasure, and casts her off to ruin other men. And gives bad financial advice, and then says he is not responsible. These men are you. You can't recognize them, because you cannot connect (ch. 38).

Here, then, the central theme of 'only connect' has deep personal and social implications: it is as if we had strayed temporarily into an Edwardian theatre and were listening to one of the many stage attacks on the dual morality of the day.

The all-embracing theme of harmony appears in a variety of ways, not all of them equally successful. It is explored through the private lives of individuals, through the conflict of classes, through the conflict of national traditions, English and German, reflected in the Schlegel family background, with the 'good' German father uniting the best of both traditions; and, symbolically, through the descriptions of nature, so that the wych elm that shelters Howards End comes to represent the protective masculine principle guarding the feminine principle. The two together form an ideal of perfect companionship, or as Forster frequently calls the ideal relationship for which Margaret strives, 'comradeship': '"In dealing with a Wilcox, how tempting it was to lapse from comradeship"', she realizes. Since comradeship is the word used for male friendship in several novels, it provides an interesting verbal link between Forster's homosexual and heterosexual ideal, just as in Edward Carpenter's writing and Forster's *Maurice* it links the idea of male love and socialist brotherhood.

Within the framework of the major contrast between the Wilcoxes and the Schlegels, Forster creates a lively sense of human diversity, and the novel ends with a passionate vindication of diversity as the principle that alone gives meaning to life, a principle with special appeal to someone who felt himself to be in some sense an outsider. '"All over the world men and women are worrying because they cannot develop as they are supposed to develop"', Margaret observes, and advises Helen, '"Develop what you have"', appealing finally to the principle of 'Differences – eternal differences', as adding colour to life's 'daily grey'. Paul, Charles and Mr Wilcox are all sufficiently differentiated (with Charles a crude parody of his father). The women, too, are neatly differentiated, for example, Evie, Henry Wilcox's companionable daughter, and Dolly, Charles's silly wife. And Mrs Wilcox seems to have little in common with the rest of her over-confident practical family although she does in fact share their lack of interest in ideas. She also shares their practical grasp of material reality, but it is the earth and not its man-made products that she grasps so tenaciously. She, too, has her special kind of confidence, based on instinctive goodness. Paradoxically it is lack of confidence that leads to her son Paul's failure of nerve with Helen.

Within the Schlegel circle there are similar paradoxes and evidences of human diversity. The two sisters, Margaret and Helen, based partly on Goldsworthy Lowes Dickinson's sisters and also on Virginia Woolf and Vanessa Bell, are sharply differentiated. Margaret is intellectual, imaginative, contemplative, has a 'profound vivacity' but is completely lacking in physical charm. Helen is impulsive, potentially 'heroic', as her response to Beethoven's Fifth Symphony and subsequent actions demonstrate, definitely pretty, 'rather apt to entice people, and in enticing them to be herself enticed'. The latter remark throws a world of light on her affairs with Paul and Leonard. The brother Tibby, like Margaret, disdains 'the heroic equipment'. Created with great subtlety and ironic humour, a fact often ignored by many readers much to the author's regret, Tibby illustrates that it is possible to be intelligent, cultured and well bred and yet be incapable of personal warmth. Music, books, and pictures have developed Tibby's mind and taste; they have not developed his heart. He is a less important but more shrewdly observed case of the 'undeveloped heart' than Ronny Heaslop in *A Passage to India*. With perhaps touches of Lytton Strachey in his sprawling languor and exhausted aestheticism, he exhibits the limits of culture when not infused with human passion. At moments of crisis, as when Helen asks him to send the £5,000 to Leonard Bast, he acts formally and correctly, but from no deep inner spring of action. He 'had never been interested in human beings', and his 'attention wandered when "personal relations" came under discussion' (ch. 30).

Sameness and human difference cross class as well as family boundaries. Leonard Bast, an inspired guess at an unknown class and way of life, resembles the Wilcoxes in his desire for quick returns, though what he wishes to acquire is culture not cash. He thus exemplifies how difficult it is in a materialistic age for the newly educated to avoid the values of an acquisitive society. But Leonard also resembles the Schlegels. This appears most clearly in his hunger for the infinite and his potential heroism (the promise and withdrawal of the heroic is a continuous preoccupation in the novel). Critics have dismissed Forster's creation of Jacky Bast as a piece of unfeeling class-consciousness, 'a failure of charity and imagination', according to one writer. There is some truth in this. But it is worth noticing that she and the upper middle-class Dolly are drawn into close parallel by similar incidents relating to broken photographs (ch. 7 and ch. 8). We are thus made to see that both are silly coarse women; class is largely irrelevant. Jacky provides the connection between the 'abyss' and the 'goblin footfall', between the social and metaphysical nightmare; after her call at Wickham Place, Margaret feels that she 'had risen out of the abyss, like a faint smell, a goblin footfall, telling of a life where love and hatred had both decayed' (ch. 13). Throughout the novel such interminglings of character, class and behaviour remind the reader of life's complexity and prevent him from oversimplifying the dramatic interplay of opposites, from seeing them in simple black and white. Moreover, the novelist's ironic tone and characteristic detachment reinforce the sense of complexity; so, too, do the recurrent phrases and images, phrases such as 'telegrams and anger', hands 'on the ropes of life', 'only connect', and images such as the wisps of hay. All of these symbolize systems of value, but in such a way that each implies its opposite, with which it occasionally interchanges, a system of 'contraries' ultimately Blakean in its dynamic complexity.

There is a world of difference between the simplicity of the original idea and the complexity of the finished novel. In a diary entry for 26 June 1908, Forster wrote:

> Idea for another novel shaping, and may do well to write it down. In a prelude Helen [*substituted for* the sister] goes to stop with the Wilcoxes, gets engaged to the son & breaks it off immediately, for her instinct sees the spiritual cleavage between the families. Mrs Wilcox dies, and some 2 years later Margaret gets engaged to the widower, a man impeccable publicly. They are accosted by a prostitute. M., because she understands & is great, marries him. The wrong thing to do. He, because he is little, cannot bear to be understood, & goes to the bad. He is frank, kind & attractive. But he dreads ideas (Abinger: HE, p. vii).

Another early jotting speaks of Margaret having a child and her husband Henry being angry because it does not 'nail her down' (Abinger: HE MSS, p. 355). It is clear that from the start Forster imagined a double encounter with the Wilcoxes, first by Helen and then by Margaret; both encounters were intended to prove unsatisfactory, though in different ways. In the finished novel, we are not made to feel that for Margaret to marry Henry was 'the wrong thing to do', though there are difficulties in understanding just why she did so; neither does Mr Wilcox go 'to the bad' after the marriage; yet undoubtedly these phrases from the diary do throw light on some of the ambiguities and implausibilities in the published novel. Margaret's salvation of Wilcox in the penultimate chapter is a brief, perfunctory, patched-up job, although the sympathetic reader has little difficulty in imagining the extent of his conversion by filling out the details given in the last pages. But the earlier images of marriage as a 'net' and a distorting 'glass shade' are not conducive to a reconciling harmony and the phrase 'someday she would use her love to make him a better man' suggests a curiously calculating and utilitarian approach towards the task of redemption. The reference in the manuscript note to Margaret's having a child seems to suggest that at one time Forster envisaged the new social harmony in England as springing from a union of Bloomsbury and big business rather than Bloomsbury (Helen) and the Board School (Leonard). However, it is dangerous to infer too much from these early jottings, since the characters' relations are primarily conceived in psychological terms. It seems likely that as the idea of the novel took hold of Forster and the characters and actions developed, he became more and more conscious of the sociological significance of the clash between the Schlegels and Wilcoxes. The social analysis grows organically with the characters and the story; it is not superimposed. Here, surely, we see the radical difference between the novelist and the political theorist as a critic of society.

In creating the mental and physical furniture of the Wilcoxes and Schlegels, Forster exhibits a confident grasp of socially significant detail. Houses, especially Howards End, play a vital part in the imaginative organization of the novel. All the characters are, in some sense, modern nomads, in search of a spiritual home. London, with its 'sense of flux', is but a foretaste, for Margaret Schlegel, of this 'nomadic civilization'. Homes are made by people, but only by those capable of love and affection and inspired with a vision of continuity. It is clear that for the Wilcoxes houses must always remain houses, to be bought and sold for profit, part of the general machinery of living, to be dispensed with when no longer of practical value. Mrs Wilcox makes Howards End a home. When she meets Margaret she sees someone capable of doing the same. She recognizes her as her 'spiritual heir', in fact. For Margaret, Oniton Grange might have become her home, but Mr Wilcox rides rough-shod over her tender imaginative feelings and sells it on the grounds that it is damp. All the dense circumstantial details relating to houses and blocks of London flats build up a powerful contrast between the forces of permanence and the forces of change. As a symbol for meaningless movement, distorted perception, and widespread pollution, Forster uses the motor car to intensify the impression of an age of rapid and bewildering change. How brilliantly he creates the sense of unreality and blurred focus in the car ride to Oniton as the scenery merges and congeals like porridge, and how subtly he suggests the desperate measures necessary for Margaret to reassert contact with the earth.

Because Forster invests the ordinary objects of modern civilization with spiritual or sociological significance there is little need for the kind of overt comments that are common for instance in Wells's *Tono Bungay*. True to his own admonition, only connect, he penetrates to the underlying connections between things. A particularly good example is his description of the furniture in Mr Wilcox's flat in Ducie Street. There the phrase, 'it was if a motor-car had spawned', establishes a connection, which undercuts Margaret's romantic attempt to 'derive the modern capitalist from the warriors and hunters of the past', her attempt to see the dining-room 'as an ancient guest hall'. Equally incisive in its sociological penetration is the account of Wilcox's office at the Imperial and West African Rubber Company, some details of which emphasize the soulless uniformity that lies at the heart of capitalist endeavour and others its far-reaching imperial power. Henry Wilcox is illuminated by a light that flickers on the map of Africa not by the sun that transfigures Forster's youthful heroes. It is worth noting, too, that the 'Waste Land' details of Leonard's and Jacky's stale uncommunicative exchanges and sterile love actually antedate T. S. Eliot's famous poem and may have contributed something to its tone and idiom. Forster had considerable difficulty with this scene, as the different manuscript versions reveal (Abinger: HE MSS, pp. 46–50), but the final result is strikingly authentic in atmosphere and idiom.

A characteristic weakness of the liberal humanist is his tendency to underestimate the importance of money and work. Forster is certainly not guilty of this in *Howards End*. The novel frequently draws attention to the paradox that it is the representatives of culture, the Schlegels, who talk frankly about money, while the captains and crew of industry, the Wilcoxes and Leonard Bast, find such talk embarrassing. The Schlegels

> held that reticence about money matters is absurd, and that life would be truer if each would state the exact size of the golden island upon which he stands, that exact stretch of warp over which he throws the woof that is not money. How can we do justice to the pattern otherwise?

Margaret calls it 'going through life with one's hand spread open on the table' (ch. 7). Wilcox, who is nearly a millionaire, shuns discussion of his exact wealth before marriage, so Margaret, with a comically exaggerated sense of her own income, tactfully conducts the necessary domestic arithmetic in abstract tenths. And this is the man who arranges marriage contracts for others and rules over a vast financial empire! He cannot talk about money in relation to himself, because, as Forster suggests, like other men of power, he has never learned to say 'I', that is to accept personal responsibility for his wealth. Here there are interesting parallels with Nietzschean and Shavian ideas of the 'Superman', glanced at lightly in the text (ch. 27). Where Shaw in his plays and Wells in *Tono Bungay* tend to concentrate on the mechanics and outward show of Edwardian plutocracy, Forster penetrates more deeply to its psychological origins. In the case of Margaret Schlegel, however, he seems hardly aware that her obsessive talk about inherited wealth may spring as much from neurotic guilt as from frank honesty, as may her extreme sensitivity to the 'odours from the abyss – odours the more disturbing because they were involuntary' (ch. 26). Can we really doubt that the creation of Margaret Schlegel in part assuaged the author's conscience as an inheritor of unearned income and as a member of a financially privileged circle? 'Money plays a much larger part than it should in your conversation', said one of Forster's friends. 'It is true', wrote Forster in his private Commonplace Book, 'but how to cure myself at 53. The ugly habit has crept on me.'

It is the sudden irruption of Leonard Bast rather than the problem of who is to inherit Howards End that raises the sharpest issues about money and work. After Leonard has visited Wickham Place to recover his umbrella and after the Schlegels have seen the Wilcoxes in the flat opposite – a potential threat to Helen's peace of mind – Margaret boasts that she has no fears of the Wilcoxes, '"there's never any risk as long as you have money. Money pads the edges of things".' For the reader, her subsequent argument obviously embraces the unknown visitor on the edge of the abyss, Leonard Bast, as well as Paul Wilcox. '"You and I and the Wilcoxes,"' she remarks to her sister, Helen, and their aunt Mrs Munt,

'stand upon money as upon islands. It is so firm beneath our feet that we forget its very existence. It's only when we see someone near us tottering that we realize all that an independent income means. Last night, when we were talking up here round the fire, I began to think that the soul of the world is economic, and that the lowest abyss is not the absence of love, but the absence of coin' (ch. 7).

After this confession she imagines 'the tragedy last June if Helen and Paul Wilcox had been poor people, and couldn't invoke railways and motor-cars to part them.' This is specially apposite coming as it does immediately after the account of the loveless, poverty-stricken Bast *ménage*. The subsequent narrative does not confirm Margaret's neurotic fear that the 'soul of the world is economic', but it does explore very fully the various attitudes to money and the inevitable consequences of loss of money and work. *Howards End* does this more sensitively and imaginatively than most Edwardian novels.

That the Wilcoxes and the Schlegels inadvertently combine to bring about Leonard's financial ruin (a detail which came late in the planning of the novel) expresses the equal responsibility of the capitalist and liberal idealist for the state of society. Neither family, however, can be held directly responsible for Leonard's fate. Wilcox honestly believes that the Porphyrion Fire Insurance Company is in a bad state and that Margaret's friend should 'leave the ship before it sinks' – a typical piece of commercial morality. Margaret, with every good intention, passes on the information. In fact, it turns out to be ill-founded advice and Leonard comes to face the abyss. This is mainly through leaving a safe job; but it is also through Helen's impetuosity in rushing the Basts up to Oniton and then forgetting to give them their return tickets. Love and money, in a characteristic Forsterian fashion, become intermixed and exchangeable. Helen gives herself to Leonard, not in the spirit of instinctive joy, but 'heroically', as a sacrificial victim from the class responsible for his ruin. And, subsequently, since their sexual union does nothing to alleviate her guilt, she offers the £5,000 that Leonard proudly refuses.

Similar substitutions of money for love occur frequently in Forster's fiction, in Philip's offer of money to Gino, in Rickie's offer to Gerald, and in Maurice's and the other homosexual heroes' attempts to reward their lovers. There is obviously rich material here for psychological speculation, as Wilfred Stone has shown in his analysis of the themes of love and money in Forster (Stallybrass, 1969, pp. 107–21). Certainly one cannot fail to see the wide gap that separates the surface meaning and the deep social grammar of the patterns of love and money. Forster makes conscious play of material and spiritual currency, 'these are moments when the inner life actually "pays"', but he exposes more of himself than he perhaps realized. He also exposes the tensions and ambiguities of the Edwardian age as it groped its way towards creating a new ethic of love and money. He renders what eludes easy explanation. By doing so he achieves a special kind of truth, a truth similar to that revealed in James's novels on love and money, *The Princess Casamassima* (1886), *The Awkward Age* (1899), and *The Golden Bowl* (1904). By contrast Galsworthy offers a sentimental and simplistic picture, seeming in *Fraternity* (1909) to endorse the class hypocrisies and financial evasions of the middle class in the denouement, where Hilary Dallison saves caste by leaving money for the little nameless artist he has been in love with, and escapes abroad. *Howards End* is free from such clichés and evasions. It is the work of an artist with a deep intuitive understanding of society and a fine critical intelligence.

The Schlegels are attracted towards the Wilcoxes because they admire their positive qualities and because they are conscious of the characteristic weaknesses of their own circle. They admire the Wilcoxes' energy, their power to command, to organize and control, their talents for honest hard work. At first both Helen and Margaret are led to overestimate these qualities, taking them for the only reality that matters, simply because they themselves do not possess them. But Helen's sight of the frightened Paul at the breakfast table after they have become engaged reveals the 'panic and emptiness' that lies behind the façade of power, and Margaret's further contact with Mr Wilcox forces her to modify her notion of him as the embodiment of reality. His confident hold 'on the ropes of life' proves illusory; he is sharp-sighted about work but obtuse about personal relations; and his fortress crumbles when the past catches up with him. 'He lived for the five minutes that have passed, and the five minutes to come; he had the business mind' (ch. 29). This is a continuous motif. But for the novel to succeed Wilcox must be positively attractive both as an individual and as a socially representative figure. Otherwise Margaret's marriage becomes psychologically improbable and their symbolic

union meaningless. In the original plan for the novel, recorded in
Forster's diary, Wilcox is to be 'frank, kind & attractive'. This he is,
but what he lacks for all his energy, his preservation of the 'self-
confidence and optimism of youth', and his overgrown schoolboy
charm, is personal magnetism and positive sexuality. In the latter
respect he is not sufficiently Margaret's opposite. As a representative
social figure he works well enough. Forster does not, as Lawrence
thought, 'make a nearly deadly mistake glorifying those *business* people
in *Howards End.*' What he does do is to give them sufficient positive
qualities to make the dynamic tension between the Wilcoxes and
Schlegels illustrative of the major conflicts in Edwardian society.

One explanation for Wilcox's attraction for Margaret has not always
been recognized. He embodies the importance of work, not normally a
sufficient reason for deciding to marry a man, certainly, but for Margaret a vital one. She comes to recognize that the world of culture
would not exist without the Wilcoxes' hard work, that life on an
inherited income, however gracious and conducive to personal relations, lacks an essential ingredient: work. Whereas Carlyle, Ruskin and
William Morris had preached the gospel of work to invest the new
forces of industrialism with value and to abate social discontent, Margaret applies this gospel to the leisured middle class. She uses it to
justify the commercial activities of the Wilcoxes. However, neither
she nor her creator seems able to imagine work except in terms of the
counting house: of the labour of farm-workers or factory-workers the
novel has nothing to say. Margaret also uses the gospel of work to
rebuke Tibby for his empty life. 'I believe that in the last century men
have developed the desire to work,' she tells him, 'and they must not
starve it.' As one who sympathizes with some of the ideals of 'The New
Woman', many of which were reflected in the suffragette movement
and such novels as Gissing's *The Odd Women* and Wells's *Ann Veronica*,
Margaret extends her gospel of work to women although she herself
does not work and resorts to the 'methods of the harem' in order to
influence Mr Wilcox. The time will soon come, she hopes, when 'not
to work' will be as shocking as '"not to be married" a hundred years
ago'. Yet, in her private debating society, she develops a philosophy of
money, not work. For her the salvation of the Basts lies in money.
'"Give them money. Don't dole them out poetry-books and railway-
tickets like babies. Give them the wherewithal to buy these things."'
Until Socialism comes, she insists, '"give people cash, for it is the warp
of civilization, whatever the woof may be. The imagination ought to

play upon money and realize it vividly, for it's the – the second most important thing in the world"' (ch. 15).

Helen, on the other hand, before she is afflicted with guilt and remorse, sees that it is work not money that Leonard Bast needs. It is to persuade Margaret to speak to Henry about work for Leonard that she brings the Basts to Oniton. '"It's work he wants," interrupted Helen. "Can't you see?"' But Leonard denies this. He 'was near the abyss', remarks Forster, 'and at such moments men see clearly.' Leonard fears that once out of his little groove he will stand no chance of a similar job. He also fears that gifts of money will destroy rather than save. 'Their friends give them money for a little', he explains, anticipating his own fate, 'but in the end they fall over the edge.' Here Forster exaggerates the immobility of labour in the Edwardian period but not the damaging effects of driblets of charity. Masterman's *From the Abyss* vindicates Leonard's fears of the abyss, with its accounts of the disastrous effects of 'gusty benevolence' and its vision of life as a 'continual struggle, a balance on an edge perpetually crumbling', where the 'hunger of the infinite' such as Leonard's must remain unsatisfied or be socially disruptive. The manuscripts of *Howards End* reveal that Forster added details to stress this theme, for example, Margaret's distress in chapter 13 at 'the odours from the abyss' (Abinger: HE MSS, p. 115).

Helen, always more absolute than Margaret but no less intuitive, holds Wilcox directly responsible for Leonard's ruin and argues on the basis of abstract justice and duty that he should find him a job. She does not, of course, know at this stage that Wilcox had earlier ruined Jacky Bast (one notices again the erotic/economic parallels). Margaret will have nothing to do with Helen's abstractions and speaks with the cool sceptical voice of Cambridge and the Fabian Society when she finally agrees to ask Wilcox's help. '"Nor am I concerned with duty. I'm concerned with the characters of various people whom we know, and how, things being as they are, things may be made a little better"' (ch. 26). The reader finds it hard to forgive her for deciding not to accept Henry's help once she has discovered about his past with Jacky. Reasons are given and the awkwardness hurried over; but on reflection it is clear that Henry has been saved from remorse and the possibility of social embarrassment at the expense of the Basts, who thereafter sink into the abyss. The plot and the author's sensibility pull in opposite directions here, for there is no mistaking his acute insight into the lives of those perched on the edge of the abyss, his deep compassion for them, and his extraordinary skill in evoking their predicament. He may have read Masterman's *From the Abyss*, for Masterman had been on the board of the *Independent Review* and had reviewed Forster's novels at great length. The author certainly took something from a man who ran a mining paper and who, Forster records in his diary on 10 February 1909, 'made me see how wide an abyss opens under our upper class merriment & culture' (Abinger: HE, p. xi).

Almost a year later, Forster made another comment in his diary that throws light on a major theme of the novel. 'Am grinding out my novel into a contrast between money & death – the latter is truly an ally of the personal against the mechanical' (Abinger: HE, p. xi). Preoccupation with death in *Howards End* leads neither to morbidity nor to the high proportion of deaths that critics of Forster's earlier novels so frequently laughed at. Helen speaks for her creator in the coffee-room scene in Shropshire. In reply to Leonard's desperate outcry, '"the real thing's money, and all the rest is a dream",' Helen answers:

> 'You're still wrong. You've forgotten Death.'
> Leonard could not understand.
> 'If we lived for ever, what you say would be true. But we have to die, we have to leave life presently. Injustice and greed would be the real things if we lived for ever. As it is, we must hold to other things, because Death is coming. I love Death – not morbidly, but because He explains. He shows me the emptiness of Money. Death and Money are the eternal foes. Not Death and Life. Never mind what lies behind Death, Mr Bast, but be sure that the poet and the musician and the tramp will be happier in it than the man who has never learned to say: "I am I"' (ch. 27).

The Wilcoxes, she sees, are 'deeper in the mist than any', and for all their building of empire, don't see that Death alone is 'imperial'. Leonard is puzzled by all this, but to Helen the mystery becomes clearer. '"Death destroys a man; the idea of Death saves him."' This paradox, which was enunciated by Michelangelo and which Forster probably came across in Arthur Symons, Helen then expands by declaring that Love and Death are the eternal adversaries and that in this contest 'the thews of love have been strengthened.' It is a vision similar to Keats's idea of the world as a 'vale of soul-making'. '"So never give in," continued the girl, and restated again and again the vague yet convincing plea that the Invisible lodges against the Visible.'

The qualifying word 'vague' sounds the necessary note of scepticism; it reinforces the reader's confidence in the novelist's integrity.

How does Forster accommodate the Infinite and the Unseen in a 'Condition of England Novel'? Mainly through two modes of writing, later labelled 'Rhythm' and 'Prophecy' in *Aspects of the Novel*. By 'Rhythm' he means a pattern that grows organically from within and is not mechanically superimposed. A novel that is 'stitched internally' develops through 'repetition plus variation', so that the meaning expands in the reader's mind creating a special kind of wholeness. Obviously Rhythm is of special value in a novel that develops a vision of harmony and offers a critique of individual and social fragmentation. Repeated images such as the wych elm, flowers, and wisps of hay, and repeated antitheses such as those between Death and the Idea of Death, the Seen and the Unseen, are some of the most obvious examples of this process. In addition to creating an impression of wholeness, artistic and social, Rhythm also creates a special kind of resonance suitable for communicating the impalpable and the numinous, for suggesting the Infinite and the Unseen.

'Prophecy' like Rhythm conveys the sense of the Infinite. In a prophetic writer like Dostoevsky, Forster remarks,

> the characters and situations always stand for more than themselves;
> infinity attends them, though they remain individuals they
> expand to embrace it and summon it to embrace them; one can
> apply to them the saying of St Catherine of Siena that God is in
> the soul and the soul is in God as the sea is in the fish and the
> fish is in the sea (AN).

The world of the prophetic novelist 'reaches back' and it reaches out. But in Forster the prophetic element is always muted. The tone is in a minor not a major key. There are always ironic qualifications.

One simple and effective way in which Forster achieves a sense of mystery and prophetic resonance is by withholding information and then releasing it so that we experience a sudden flash of illumination. For example, when Mrs Wilcox, describing the details of Howards End, refers to Charles Wilcox's delight in motoring, Margaret says:

> 'I suppose you have a garage there?'
> 'Yes. My husband built a little one only last month, to the
> west of the house, not far from the wych elm, in what used to
> be the paddock for the pony.'
> The last words had an indescribable ring about them (ch. 8).

For the attentive reader, particularly one familiar with Forster's technique, the passage creates a minor sense of mystery. A few chapters later, when Mrs Wilcox is dead, the vital information that the old lady loved the paddock more than the garden itself is released. It is we, not the characters, who 'connect'. We suddenly see the whole thing in a new perspective. The trivial details relating to paddock, garage, and motor-car, have assumed a prophetic dimension. The mind reaches back and sees the old agricultural rhythms destroyed by the civilization of mechanical appliances, one spot loved by an old woman, full of intimate associations, thoughtlessly destroyed.

A further way in which Forster achieves a prophetic dimension is through his adaptation of the Gothic mode. In the Romantic period, Gothic novelists contracted the whole world into an eerie castle. They then chilled the blood by exploiting suspense and introducing ghosts, spirits, and strange happenings. *Howards End* might be considered Gothic in two senses: it contracts the spirit of England within a single house; it also exploits the Gothic mode to cause a frisson, a shudder of horror and delight. The most striking example occurs when Miss Avery suddenly appears in what Margaret had believed was an empty house.

'Is that you, Henry?' she called.
There was no answer, but the house reverberated again.
'Henry, have you got in?'
But it was the heart of the house beating, faintly at first, then loudly, martially. It dominated the rain.
It is the starved imagination, not the well-nourished, that is afraid. Margaret flung open the door to the stairs. A noise of drums seemed to deafen her. A woman, an old woman, was descending, with figure erect, with face impassive, with lips that parted and said dryly:
'Oh! Well, I took you for Ruth Wilcox.'
Margaret stammered: 'I – Mrs Wilcox – I?'
'In fancy, of course – in fancy. You had her way of walking. Good day.' And the old woman passed out into the rain. (ch. 23).

Some readers may dismiss this as meretricious spookiness. On the other hand, I think it truer to say that Forster successfully manipulates a well-known novelistic tradition, the Gothic, to produce supernatural vision through physical shock. He wants to suggest that the house has a life of its own, that it is attended by a maternal spirit. It would have been crude to introduce the ghost of Mrs Wilcox. Instead, he ties the scene down to reality by introducing Miss Avery, the woman who would have been the mistress of Howards End if Tom Howard had not been killed in the war. And Miss Avery, the rightful spiritual owner, as it were, addresses Margaret as 'Mrs Wilcox', thus raising her to the status of new spiritual heir. Later in the novel, Forster exploits Miss Avery's eccentricity by having her unpack all Margaret's furniture in Howards End, thus suggesting her full physical possession of the house. The withholding and sudden release of information and use of the Gothic are but two devices Forster uses to create the prophetic, thus accommodating the Infinite to social criticism. Elsewhere a particular tone of voice creates the prophetic dimension.

From its first publication, *Howards End* has been widely praised: for its deft social comedy, for its conscious artistry and beauty of design, for its symbolic power, for its ripe wisdom, and for what the anonymous reviewer in the *Nation* in November 1910 called 'its far sighted criticism of middle class ideas', a form of praise that implicitly links it with Matthew Arnold's *Culture and Anarchy*. It is certainly a novel about culture and society and is so recognized by Raymond Williams in his book with that title. The Wilcoxes ignore culture; Leonard Bast seeks to acquire culture; the Schlegels accept culture. For them it is an integral part of life. They had not, Forster remarks, 'mistaken culture as an end.' *Howards End* is pre-eminently the representative Edwardian novel. What prevents it from becoming one of the world's great novels is a distinct sense of strain and a lack of human warmth. Late in life, Forster analysed his own dissatisfaction with it. 'Have only just discovered why I don't care for it; not a single character in it for whom I care. . . . I feel pride in the achievement, but cannot love it, and occasionally the swish of the skirts and the non-sexual embraces irritate' (CB, May 1958, KCL). Yet the evidence of the novel suggests that he once cared about Leonard Bast and the minor character Tibby; both radiate the artist's delight in the joy of creation. He obviously cared about Mrs Wilcox, and he cared about Margaret and Helen, who represent two sides of his own character. But all three women are slightly out of focus. It matters little with Mrs Wilcox of whom it is specifically said 'she and daily life were out of focus: one or the other must show blurred.' With Margaret and Helen it is different. When the two sisters talk, they charm; when Forster describes them they often repel: there is an unbridged gap between their attractive minds and their outward femininity. Even in Margaret's talk there is a note of shrill hysteria when she is in the company of other women. It is as if Forster can be just to individual women and just to the feminine principle as it counteracts and modifies the masculine principle: what repels him is women in a group. It is not surprising to find that after writing *Howards End* he made a conscious attempt to escape from the 'swish of skirts' by concentrating more of his imaginative powers on the relations that really interested him, the relations between men. This he did in the unfinished *Arctic Summer, Maurice*, and the homosexual short stories.

6

Posthumous Fiction

Arctic Summer

In *Howards End*, the ideal, only connect, is more convincingly rendered through the reconciliation of Margaret and Helen than through the union of culture and commerce, or culture and the common man. It is a vindication of personal relations, especially between those of the same sex, rather than of social harmony. The two sisters are both deeply imaginative, yet quite clearly Margaret represents the intellectual and Helen the heroic approach to life. The antithesis continued to fascinate the novelist and in his next work, *Arctic Summer*, begun soon after *Howards End*, he embodied it in the conflicting approaches to life of two men: Martin Whitby, an intellectual, and a heroic character called Clesant March or Cyril March, in different versions of the novel. The choice of two women in *Howards End* had obviously limited the thematic possibilities of the conflict. In the newly sketched work, Forster hoped to escape 'the swish of skirts', and to render the alternatives, heroic and intellectual, so that they embraced the major divisions in modern civilization. But the attempt proved abortive.

One problem that he failed to solve satisfactorily was that of creating a suitable setting in which to present the continuing strength of the heroic tradition, trying at one stage Italy and at another England. Another problem was to envisage what kind of relationship the antithetical men might enjoy as the reconciliation became more personal and less ideological. After working on the new novel during 1911, Forster laid it aside when he left for India in October 1912. When he returned he brought with him several chapters of a novel on India. This, in its turn, was shelved when a momentary physical contact with Edward Carpenter's friend and servant, George Merrill, provided the creative spark for an explicitly homosexual novel, *Maurice*, written in 1913–14. Thereafter, he returned to the homosexual theme in various short stories. None of his later fiction, except a brief extract from *Arctic Summer*, was published during Forster's life. It is with this extremely revealing, hitherto unpublished material, that this chapter is concerned. Clearly, all earlier interpretations of Forster's artistic development require to be modified in the light of this new evidence.

There are no less than four different manuscript versions of *Arctic Summer*; these have been called the Cyril Version, the Tramonta Version, the Radipole Version, and the Aldeburgh Version by Elizabeth Ellem, who has made a detailed study of this unfinished novel (Ellem, 1973, pp. 1087–9). Although the manuscript material amounts in all to about 56,000 words, there is much reduplication, and the story does not advance very far in any one of the versions. The first of these, bearing the date November 1911 on one page, is the Cyril Version, more fragmentary than the Tramonta Version, but, like it, beginning with a scene on Basle station and then moving to Italy. Cyril March, an ambitious soldier, has a brother Robin, who is at Cambridge and who plans to enter Holy Orders. Robin 'goes wrong' and Cyril holds himself responsible. The disaster brings Cyril, the chivalric soldier, close to Martin Whitby, the man of intellect and culture, whom he has first met at Basle station. Somewhat improbably Cyril is seeking redemption in fighting for the Turks against Italy, 'a clear issue . . . there aren't many'. Martin hopes that Cyril's redemption will come ultimately from the love of his sister Dorothy. However, as Miss Ellem remarks, 'Cyril has retained not only the ideal of purification through warfare, but the role of chivalry towards women', so that although he can accept Martin's love gratefully, he feels that 'Women are different; you must be worthy of them or the whole thing goes.' Martin, who has modified his own rather arid intellectualism under his sister's influence, tries to carry Cyril along with him. And this is as far as this version develops.

The Tramonta and Radipole Versions make an interesting contrast because the setting of one is Italian and the other English. In the Italian or Tramonta Version, Martin Whitby, a Treasury official, who is travelling in company with his mother-in-law Lady Borlase and his wife Venetia, is saved from being swept under a train by a young man who has 'the look and gesture of a warrior'. He turns out to be a young soldier, Clesant March (the 'Cyril' of the other version), bound for the renaissance castle, Tramonta, which contains frescoes depicting the battle of Lepanto, described as 'the last of the crusades'. Martin Whitby offers to obtain the necessary *permesso* from the owner in Milan. Clesant accepts, but is irritated by the idea that they should all go to Tramonta together; and his growing dislike of Martin increases, as the result of Martin's 'ungentlemanly' exposure of a silly joke played by the owner's daughter at Milan. When Martin arrives at Tramonta with Lady Borlase and Venetia, his wife, he ascends a tower and sees a view where 'form had wedded colour and behind their union stood Romance blessing it'. But the great moment in his life occurs when he sees an image of Clesant in the fresco of the soldiers marching off to the battle of Lepanto. As Miss Ellem remarks, 'He sees in the marching band the qualities – instinctive courage, colour, romance – that he had briefly perceived on Basle station', when Clesant's heroism rescued him from death. 'As long as he stayed in Tramonta,' Forster writes, 'the vision persisted. He saw neither the man nor the picture, but a power behind both, to which he could give no name.' In many ways, all this marks a regression into the world of the early Italian novels rather than an advance. Martin, like Philip Herriton in *Where Angels Fear to Tread*, registers the changes in his response to Italy on revisiting the country, both have 'tower visions', and both seek to connect art and life. Yet we note a difference: Martin has a mature sense of form that he shares with his thirty-year-old creator and with a later fictional creation, Fielding, in *A Passage to India*.

The Radipole Version was obviously an attempt to escape from the Italian world of the earlier novels, but it does not really break new ground. The opening action takes place in England not Italy. The setting, at Radipole, a public school that glorifies sport at the expense of scholarship, marks a return to the ethos of the Sawston chapters of *The Longest Journey*. In this version, it is at Radipole that Martin Whitby and Clesant March first meet, when Martin presents the school prizes. The masters and boys dislike his speech about the importance of books and kindness. Clesant alone listens, but when Martin says that he does not like his choice of a prize, the boy replies that he has not liked his speech. For this piece of rudeness, a master makes him apologize, and gives him lines. Martin then meets Clesant's elder brother Lance, who has come to fetch the boy home; he finds himself attracted to Lance and agrees to meet him later in London. If the opening suggests a return to the public school world of *The Longest Journey*, the description of Captain and Mrs March's house, Monkswear, suggests a return to the world of *Howards End*, in which Mrs Wilcox's house represents values that transcend the shabby conventions of suburban or metropolitan life. The presiding genius at Monkswear is Mrs March. The following passage, which differs from a similar passage in the Tramonta version through its special emphasis on the mother's heroic ambitions for her sons and the harmony suggested between the contemplative and active sides of medievalism well illustrates Forster's attempt to give a specifically English setting to the chivalric idea in the Radipole Version.

> Seen from above the place suggested a lair, and she entertained the notion willingly. She liked to think of the brood that was growing up in it, and would presently steal upon their astonished prey, for she had high if vague aspirations for her sons. Seen from below it had another aspect which pleased her equally. The monks and their weir had gone, but a flavour of pre-reformation times remained, and here she ruled like a Lady Abbess, making allowances in a calm deliberate way for the fervency of youth. . . .

But the attempt to domesticate the chivalric ideal proved a failure; and, when in 1951 Forster produced the Aldeburgh Version, from which he read extracts at the Aldeburgh Festival, it was to the Italian, Tramonta Version that he returned, which at least had the virtue of unity of mood and tone, even if it did not extend his fictional range beyond that of his earlier writing, as he had hoped it would.

In a note to the Aldeburgh Version, Forster discussed the three main problems he faced in creating the character of the heroic man, March. First there was the question of how a man who is 'first and foremost heroic' should be presented in the modern world; and he concluded that the only way would have been to present him impressionistically, and to root him as little as possible in society, and 'let him come and go unexplained'. T. E. Lawrence (Lawrence of Arabia), whom Forster did not know in 1911, offers 'a hint' of how it might be done. But, of course, to choose a socially rootless hero would be to restrict not expand the novel's vision in comparison with the panoramic vision of society presented in *Howards End*. The second problem was to involve March in the sophisticated social circles he despised. Forster's solution was to invent a brother, Robin or Lance, according to the different versions. The brother then gets into trouble and would be rescued by Martin Whitby, so that young March becomes 'devoted to Martin and thinks there is no-one like him in the world and will sacrifice anything to make him happy'. The third problem, which has already been touched on briefly, was 'What is going to happen?' Forster searched in vain for a solution.

> I had got my antithesis right. The antithesis between the civilized man, who hopes for an Arctic Summer, and the heroic man who rides into the sea. But I had not settled what was going to happen, what the major event is to be.

A novelist needs 'a solid mass ahead' or 'a mountain round, over or through which the story must somehow go.' But even the Great War did not provide an answer, because – as Forster is too reticent to admit – the answer was not to be found in the international situation, but in honesty about his own homosexuality. In 1951 he wrote:

> In a sense I see the end more clearly today, for I have lived on to an age when not only March can't get what he wants but Martin can't either. The novel could have ended with two companions in defeat. But such an ending doesn't interest me.

An end involving 'two companions in defeat' presumably lost most of its appeal once Forster had written *Maurice*, in which he granted his male lovers a triumph in exile and presented the possibility of a redeemed England through their classless love.

Maurice

There were rumours during Forster's lifetime that there was a completed novel in manuscript, but on the whole *Maurice* was a well-kept literary secret. The original inspiration, as we have already seen, came on a visit to Edward Carpenter in September 1913, and by July 1914 Forster had completed the first version of the novel. He revised the awkward last part in 1919 and again in 1932. Then, in 1959–60, he subjected the text to a more thorough revision and left a note that read 'Publishable, but worth it?' The answer must surely be 'yes', partly on the basis of the novel's considerable merits and partly for the great light it throws on Forster's dilemma as an artist and as a man: how to come to terms with his own sexuality in a society that imprisoned homosexuals and censored homosexual literature. Among the small circle of friends to whom he showed the earliest version of the novel, H. O. Meredith, upon whom the character of Maurice was partly based, showed no interest, an unexpected response that nearly caused Forster to abandon further composition; Goldsworthy Lowes Dickinson, whose homosexual autobiography later passed into Forster's hands, was naturally encouraging; Lytton Strachey, who thought the ending highly improbable and Forster's idea of male copulation too embarrassingly self-conscious, nevertheless 'enjoyed it very much'. Yet the novel remained unpublished for many reasons. At the time of its original composition there could be no thought of publication; moreover the later banning or prosecution of such books as D. H. Lawrence's *The Rainbow*, and Radclyffe Hall's *The Well of Loneliness* must have confirmed Forster in his decision not to seek publication – he did indeed protest publicly against these and other acts of censorship. There were also strong personal reasons for not publishing: the novel contained thinly veiled portraits of living people and Forster's natural reticence and respect for the feelings of other people, especially those of his mother, who had found *Howards End* shocking, restrained him from submitting the manuscript to a publisher. Even in its final 1959–60 version, Maurice is only a sketch of a novel, written primarily for the author himself and for a small circle of friends, all of whom had a special interest in the theme of homosexuality. The absence of a bracing tension between the author and a wider public accounts for the unworked thinness of much of the narrative, its self-indulgent tone, the too intermittent play of irony. Clearly one of the worst evils of literary censorship is that it drives the writer in on himself, with a consequent impoverishment in moral vision and literary style. In *Two Cheers for Democracy*, Forster makes the revealing comment that people do not realize that censorship of a book 'may have impaired the creative machinery of the writer's mind.' For all its artistic merits, *Maurice* is an exercise in personal therapy not a finished work of art.

The plot of *Maurice* is simple, too simple, indeed; and no doubt had Forster from the beginning been writing for publication he would have developed a more intricate pattern of characters and events. The story centres on Maurice Hall's parallel and contrasted relations with two young men. First, he is loved by and loves a fellow Cambridge undergraduate, Clive Durham. But Clive's homosexuality is only a temporary stage in his development; he discovers that he is capable of normal heterosexual relations, is repelled by masculinity, including Maurice's, and gives himself up wholly to the rather trivial duties and responsibilities of a country gentleman. Maurice then meets a second man, Alec Scudder, and ultimately discovers perfect happiness in this relationship, now able to recognize frankly 'the wisdom of the body', as he had not been able to in his platonic relationship with Clive.

Ironically he meets Alec at Clive's dilapidated country estate, Penge. Even more ironically, Alec is only an under-gamekeeper there. With sly humour Forster has noted that he is senior in date to the 'prickly gamekeepers of D. H. Lawrence'. The happy ending for the two men involves retreat to the 'greenwoods', but it carries with it – however improbably – the suggestion that the future of England belongs to them. 'They must live outside class, without relations or money; they must work and stick to each other till death. But England belonged to them. That, besides companionship was their reward.' And, in the cancelled Epilogue of the 1913–14 version, Maurice's sister Kitty, many years later, comes across them living out their greenwoods idyll as woodcutters, 'they had stayed disintegration & combined daily work with love' (KCL). Thus *Maurice* reveals clearly what neither the final coda of *The Longest Journey* nor that of *Howards End* makes clear, that the fusion of classes in a redeemed England is at least in part an apologia for and a celebration of the middle-class homosexual's love for a strong man in the class below him. Private and public myths share a common structure.

Within the relatively simple framework of the plot there is considerable complexity. Maurice is neither a psychological case history nor a prose poem in praise of homosexuality, in the Dorian Gray vein. Forster's mode is still domestic comedy and there is still a fairly subtle interplay of poetic vision and comic spirit, although the comedy in the main affects only the minor characters. It hardly touches the protagonists. Forster's lack of detachment towards two of the major figures – his sympathetic involvement with Maurice and his disgust with Clive, the sexual turncoat – undoubtedly disturbs the unity and tone of the whole work. The cast is reasonably large, but only the three men are more than lightly sketched. Many of the very English scenes spring vividly to life, as when the well-intentioned Mr Ducie, in the opening scene, instructs the unheeding Maurice in the technical details of sex. He does so by drawing the male and female sexual organs on the sand. But when he sees people approaching, he rushes to blot out the traces, 'sweating with fear'.

> 'Sir, won't it be all right?' Maurice cried. 'The tide'll have covered them by now.'
> 'Good Heavens . . . Thank God . . . the tide's rising!'
> And suddenly for an instant of time, the boy despised him.
> 'Liar,' he thought. 'Liar, coward, he's told me nothing.' . . .

Then darkness rolled up again, the darkness that is primeval but
not eternal, and yields to its own painful dawn (ch. 1).

The final sentence adds a characteristic Forsterian touch, linking finite
and infinite; premonitory in tone, it holds out a qualified hope to
Maurice and to mankind. And the hero actually recalls the incident
later as he lies in Alec Scudder's arms (ch. 38).

In sketching Maurice's early development, Forster draws on some
of his own experiences, as he had done in *The Longest Journey*; for
example, Maurice's relationship with the garden-boy, George, parallels
Forster's with Ansell. But, in other respects, Forster makes his hero as
unlike himself as possible. Maurice Hall is hearty, athletic, slow and
conventional in his responses; he has no literary or artistic ambitions;
and, on being sent down from Cambridge for missing lectures, he
becomes a stockbroker. Yet despite the dissimilarities, Maurice shares
something of his creator's fineness of imaginative perception. Since we
are specifically told that at Sunnington, his public school, he had lost
the clearness of vision 'which transfigures and explains the universe',
and not enough happens to him later as the result of his relationship
with either Clive or Alec to restore it, the imaginative dimension of
Maurice's character becomes slightly improbable. It is recognized for
the device that it is, a device for communicating the author's own
superior insight into the events and a means of eliciting sympathy for
the sexual outsider, the man who has 'cut himself off from the
congregation of normal man' (ch. 42).

In the first of the novel's four unnamed divisions (chapters 1–11),
the reader follows Maurice's life from his last day at prep school to the
exalted moment of recognition when his Cambridge friend Clive calls
to him in sleep and Maurice, 'laying his hand very gently upon the
pillows', answers 'Clive'. Maurice Hall, like all Forster's heroes is
fatherless. His mother is affectionate but overprotective; his two sisters,
Ada and Kitty, likeable; his upbringing a comfortable suburban one,
with things arranged so that he may grow up like his 'dear father in
every way'. The first emotional crisis arises when he comes back from
prep school and discovers that the garden-boy George is no longer
there. His mother mistakes his tears for signs of overtiredness; but the
description of his night terrors and of the comfort he derives from the
whispered name of George, establishes this incident as an unconscious
intimation of his psychological need for a male friend and lover. It
thus foreshadows the first visionary moments with Clive and Alec, a

connection that is firmly reinforced later by recurrent allusion and image.

The theme of the ideal friend, later to be expanded in the first part of *A Passage to India*, is further developed in the account of Maurice's life 'as a mediocre member of a mediocre school' at Sunnington, where all is muddle and obscurity, except for two recurring dreams. In the first:

> He was playing football against a nondescript whose existence he resented. He made an effort and the nondescript turned into George, that garden boy. But he had to be careful or it would reappear. George headed down the field towards him, naked and jumping over the woodstacks. 'I shall go mad if he turns wrong now,' said Maurice and just as they collared this happened, and a brutal disappointment woke him up (ch. 3).

This is clearly a fictionalized use of Forster's experiences with Ansell amid the haystacks. Maurice's second dream 'was more difficult to convey', because 'nothing happened'.

> He scarcely saw a face, scarcely heard a voice say 'That is your friend', and then it was over, having filled him with beauty and taught him tenderness. He could die for such a friend, he would allow such a friend to die for him; they would make any sacrifice for each other, and count the world nothing, neither death nor distance nor crossness could part them, because 'this is my friend'.

After his Confirmation, Maurice tries to persuade himself that the 'friend' was Christ. Although he cannot find a suitable embodiment of his vision, it remains 'more real than anything he knew'. He passes through an 'obscene' stage at school and then begins 'to make a religion of some other boy'; and, through a close friendship with one, develops his capacity for the feelings of 'beauty and tenderness that he had first felt in a dream'; and then 'the growth stopped'. He begins to feel the conflict between the call of friendship and the demands of 'good form'. A joking suggestion that he was in love with a master's wife made by Dr Barry, a friend of the family, makes him long to be 'a little boy again, and to stroll half awake for ever by the colourless sea' (ch. 4).

The Cambridge of the remaining chapters of Part I is unmistakably the Cambridge of Forster's youth, with its details of luncheon with cheerful Deans, pianolas, expeditions by motorcycle and sidecar, and its thinly disguised portraits of real people, Lytton Strachey as Risley for example – actually Forster first met Strachey in G. M. Trevelyan's rooms and was scared off by his extraordinary voice and behaviour, as a paper to the Memoir Club reveals (KCL). It is equally the Cambridge of *The Longest Journey*, seen through the eyes of one of the athletic set that Rickie wished to regard as brothers. Yet it is in no sense a mere repetition of the earlier novel. The affected young undergraduate Risley, with his exaggerated gestures and curious habit of heavily accenting one word in each sentence, is the first to attract Maurice's attention. He thoroughly shocks Maurice by calling his relative, the Dean, a 'eunuch'. '"You could call your cousin a shit if you liked, but not a eunuch. Rotten style!"' But, all the same, this forms Maurice's initiation into the irreverent frankness of Cambridge; and the unknown beckons.

It is in the course of paying a visit to the 'queer fish', Risley, that Maurice meets Clive Durham, who has come to borrow pianola sheets of – inevitably – the Pathétique. Maurice soon finds himself out of his depths in the clever conversation and rushes out into the night. But he waits around until after midnight, hoping to intercept Clive Durham, who eventually appears and invites him, 'out of civility', to have a drink. Clive is tired, and Maurice drinks up and leaves.

> It was absolutely quiet now, and absolutely dark. Maurice walked to and fro on the hallowed grass, himself noiseless, his heart glowing. The rest of him fell asleep, bit by bit, and first of all his brain, his weakest organ. His body followed, then his feet carried him upstairs to escape the dawn. But his heart had lit never to be quenched again, and one thing in him at last was real (ch. 6).

Maurice has discovered the illusive 'friend'. But progress towards greater intimacy is chequered. At first, Maurice is shocked at Clive's declaration of love, and a coldness develops. He tries to love women unsuccessfully; and then, when he comes to accept the naturalness of homosexual love, he finds to his dismay that Clive insists that it should remain platonic. His agony works inward and he discovers the 'I' that he, like the Wilcoxes, had been 'trained to obscure' (ch. 10). At last he learns to connect the 'idealism and brutality that ran through boyhood'; they are 'joined at last, and twined into love'; it was 'neither body or soul, nor body and soul, but "he" working through them both' (ch. 11). The way is now prepared for the slightly unrealized midnight revelation when Maurice answers Clive's sleeping call. This brings to a close the first part of the novel.

The second part explores the developing relations between Maurice and Clive, the two years' happiness they enjoy after Maurice has been sent down from Cambridge, Clive's psychic illness, his search for health in Greece, his discovery that he is 'normal', and his return home. The peak of the relationship is the whole day's outing by motor-cycle from Cambridge. They leap forward into 'the fens and the receding dome of the sky. . . . They cared for no one, they were outside human-ity, and death had it come would only have continued their pursuit of a retreating horizon' (ch. 13). The imagery here, as in *A Passage to India* so many years later, places human relations within a perspective of a receding infinite. The whole day, it is stressed, was ordinary, 'yet it had never come before to either of them, nor was it to be repeated'. Maurice's later visit to Penge confirms them in their new-found happi-ness. Like a lover from one of the earlier novels, Clive appears with 'the sunlight behind him'. They develop a new language for their love. Concerned as they are 'with a passion that few English minds have admitted', they establish 'perfection in their lives, at all events for a time' (ch. 16).

In *Maurice*, Forster's young men are as prone to swooning and faint-ing fits as the heroines of Victorian fiction, but these sudden collapses are clearly intended to represent intense raptures and, more import-antly, psychic break-downs. Clive's sudden fainting at dinner two years later, during one of Maurice's visits to Penge, is at first un-explained or rather passed off as a relapse after 'flu. What has happened, as an ingenious but clumsy retrospective account makes clear, is that during Clive's first bout of 'flu, he has begun to discover his normality through attraction to the nurse. His breakdown thus arises from his inability to connect his old knowledge and his new understanding of his nature. It has another cause in his instinctive revulsion from Maurice's masculinity. Forster arranges the narrative so that Clive's letter from Greece announcing his self-discovery comes almost as much as a surprise to the reader as it does to Maurice: '"Against my will I have become normal. I cannot help it."' Yet the farewell scene before the departure for Greece, when Maurice stays at Clive's flat, in spite of Clive's polite discouragement, reveals essential features of the disintegrating relationship; it therefore prepares the reader for Clive's telegram. The coming together of the two men in bed (bodies not touching) suggests the lonely frustration of each. Clive, who lacks the self-knowledge to understand the sources of his unhappiness and discontent, plunges into morbid speculations about death and an eternity made up of triviality. '"Would that we had never been lovers. For then, Maurice, you and I would have lain still and quiet."' By contrast, Maurice throbs with passion that he refrains from expressing through tender regard for Clive. The text stresses the ideal of 'tenderness', as Lawrence's text does in *Lady Chatterley's Lover*; later with Alec the ideal becomes the peculiar combination of 'toughness and tenderness', that Forster looked for in life. Maurice hopes that he can cure Clive's strange breakdown where the doctor has failed, and, even after he receives the telegram from Greece, he is confident he can restore the former relationship. He writes cheerfully to summon Clive to return from Greece, but his reference to Mrs Durham's dreadful mistake in closing a right-of-way is one of those details that Forster delights to include in his fiction, a recognition of the deep structure underlying public and private morality; the same motif of the right-of-way recurs in the short story 'Arthur Snatchfold' (LTC, p. 107).

The account of Clive's return from Greece is one of the most expressive episodes in the novel. Clive, at this stage, we must be made to see, is about to enter a world of convention, of stifling emotion, with his psychic energies bound in the loose but smothering ties of a respectable marriage with Anne. He does not immediately answer Maurice's summons, but returns from Greece at his own leisure; and, on not being met, goes straight to the Halls' house in the suburbs, only to find that Maurice is not there. He feels himself strongly drawn towards Ada, because her voice reminds him of Maurice. She represents a midpoint between his old and new desires, a 'compromise between memory and desire'. In her simple unargumentative way, she represents the 'tenderness' that 'reconciles present with past'. Earlier in this scene, Clive has associated the Hall women with the 'evening primroses that starred a deserted alley at Penge'; and, since the evening primrose has been the symbol of his happiness with Maurice, this detail unobtrusively signals the transposition of Clive's values. So, too, does the dramatically conceived entry of Maurice. The two sisters, who are taking First Aid classes, ask if they may use Clive as a patient, and he is 'happy to be bandaged'. Thus, when Maurice arrives, looking 'like an immense animal in his fur coat', he finds Clive swathed and imprisoned in bandages. '"So you don't love me?"' he challenges, still confident in his powers to win Clive back to reality, but no challenge can now rescue Clive from his chosen social cocoon. Appeals to the past, Maurice's dismissal of middle-class comfort and respectability, his insistence to Clive that '"You and I are outlaws",' have no effect, because they are based on the assumption that Clive is simply muddled, not irrevocably changed. Maurice cannot believe in the reality of Clive's changed sexuality, because it proved an illusion in his own case when he willed himself to make love to Miss Olcott. The mention of this incident exasperates Clive. '"Oh for God's sake, Maurice, hold your tongue. If I love anyone it's Ada."' He gives her simply as an example. But Maurice cannot accept her exemplary function and is stung to jealousy and rage at what he considers disloyalty. Although the novel presents the reversibility of homosexuality through Clive, Forster is unable to present the process fairly and dispassionately.

Things go badly out of focus at the beginning of the third part of the novel. There is the sentimental emphasis on Maurice's loneliness 'One cannot write these words too often: Maurice's loneliness: it increased.' There is the improbable and unrealized interview with his dying grandfather, who has rejected 'orthodox' views of the Unseen for an absurd but more sincerely felt parallel between God and the sun; and there is the moving but unconvincing elevation of Maurice to the status of a hero of humanism:

> he hadn't a God, he hadn't a lover – the two usual incentives to virtue. But on he struggled with his back to ease, because dignity demanded it. There was no one to watch him, nor did he watch himself, but struggles like his are the supreme achievements of humanity, and surpass any legends about Heaven (ch. 28).

Fielding, in *A Passage to India*, can just about sustain this role; Maurice cannot; and the attempt to make him do so represents a fatal confusion of identities between creator and created.

A succession of incidents, presumably invented to exhibit something of the possible range of homosexual relations, convinces Maurice of the necessity of seeking medical aid. The first is when he is strongly tempted to seduce a personable young Woolwich cadet, nephew of the local doctor; the next concerns a client, a handsome young Frenchman,

> While they chaffed, a familiar feeling arose, but this time he smelt attendant odours from the abyss. 'No, people like me must keep our noses to the grindstone, I'm afraid,' he replied, in answer to

the Frenchman's prayer to lunch with him, and his voice was so
British that it produced shouts of laughter and a pantomime
(ch. 30).

The next concerns a boy at the East End Mission from whom Maurice
is saved because 'the feeling that can impel a gentleman towards a
person of the lower class stands self-condemned' (did Forster enjoy
writing that?). But it is an incident with a stout, greasy-faced man in a
railway carriage that makes Maurice decide to consult a doctor. The
main point is that lust has replaced love and Maurice is appalled. But
there is a good deal of muddled thinking here about sexual and social
issues. Lytton Strachey queried some of it in a letter to the author,
asking why he should regard the Dickie incident with such grave
disapproval, and remarking facetiously that what was wanted as a
solution to all Maurice's problems, was 'a brief honeymoon with that
charming young Frenchman' who would have shown Maurice that
'it was possible to take the divagations of a prick too seriously'
(12 March 1915, in Gardner, 1973, p. 431).

Neither Dr Barry nor the Harley Street hypnotist whom Maurice
consults is able to cure him. Dr Barry is too old-fashioned to do much
more than increase Maurice's sense of guilt; and, by the time he pays
his second visit to the fashionable hypnotist (a nice period touch this –
seen also in Gerald Hamilton's *Desert Dreamers*, 1914), his union with
Alec Scudder has confirmed him in full knowledge of his homosexuality. In the 'terminal note' to Maurice, Forster glances at his
difficulties in leading up to Alec. He there notes how necessary it was
that Alec should 'loom upon the reader gradually'. In fact, the novelist
succeeds remarkably well in his declared aim of developing Alec from
'the masculine blur past which Maurice drives into Penge, through the
croucher beside the piano and the rejecter of a tip . . . into the sharer
who gives and takes love'. Alec's emergence from the greenwoods
imparts an appropriate mythic dimension to his character and pre-
figures the lovers' happy, greenwoods exile. Alec comes as an answer
to Maurice's feeling that 'he himself was an outlaw. Perhaps among
those who took to the greenwood in old time there had been two men
like himself – two. At times he entertained the dream. Two men can
defy the world' (ch. 26). In his Commonplace Book Forster wrote
'two people putting each other into salvation is the only theme I find
worthwhile. No rescuer and rescued, not the alternating performance
of good turns, but it takes two to make a Hero' (CB, KCL).

There are just enough details about Alec's parents, education, and plans to emigrate to ground him in social reality. Moreover, the process by which Maurice connects the isolated details relating to Alec and then relegates them to the darkness is completely convincing. After his walk in the shrubbery he feels back

> to the incidents of his arrival, such as the piano-moving: then forwards to the incidents of to-day, beginning with the five shillings' tip and ending with now. And when he reached 'now', it was as if an electric current passed through the chain of insignificant events so that he dropped it and let it smash back into darkness (ch. 37).

It is in the darkness that Alec comes. 'Ah for darkness . . . the darkness where we can be free.' Maurice, unable to sleep, has the illusion 'of a portrait that changed, now at his will, now against it, from male to female, and came leaping down the football-field where he bathed' – an obvious variation of his early dreams of the garden-boy George. He yearns for love and infinity of space – 'big spaces where passion clasped peace, spaces no science could reach . . . and arched with majestic sky and friend'. Later he springs up, asleep, flings open the window with the cry '"Come."' Alec, who has been waiting below, answers the call. '"Sir, was you calling out for me? . . . Sir, I know . . . I know" and touched him.' What is so revealing about this scene, apart from the element of wish-fulfilment, is the particular configuration of images. Here, in a diminished form, are all the images that were made so meaningful in *A Passage to India*. In *Maurice*, the call 'Come' is an appeal that receives a human answer: in *A Passage to India*, the call is to Krishna and remains unanswered, yet must continue to be made, as Professor Godbole insists. The contrast reflects the difference between writing privately – indulging in a sentimental dream – and dealing publicly with the real world; it also reflects the advance in wisdom and maturity Forster made between 1914 and 1924.

Throughout the novel, but especially in the fourth and final part, homosexual and social themes reinforce one another. In sleeping together at Penge, the upper-class Maurice and the under-gamekeeper Alec offend against the social and sexual taboos of Edwardian society, yet neither can at first abandon inherited attitudes and manners of speech. The precise rendering of the conflict between love and social conditioning gives the last chapters a complexity that is largely absent in previous sections. Maurice's dream of an ideal friend, embarrassingly sentimental when it first appears, is now placed in a more realistic and ironic context.

> 'Did you ever dream you'd a friend, Alec? Nothing else but just "my friend", he trying to help you and you him. A friend,' he repeated, sentimental suddenly. 'Someone to last your whole life and you his. I suppose such a thing can't really happen outside sleep.'
>
> But the moment for speech had passed. Class was calling, the crack in the floor must reopen at sunrise. When he reached the window Maurice called 'Scudder', and he turned like a well-trained dog.

The image of the 'crack in the floor', which appears in Maurice's interviews with the fashionable medical hypnotist as a symbol of the uncrossable gulf that separates him from normal heterosexual love, serves here to establish the link between class and sexual taboos.

Personal and public themes fuse in the cricket match at Penge between the house and the village, an ingenious inversion of public school values and the clichés of Edwardian fiction. When Maurice joins Alec at the wicket, 'the game took on some semblance of reality'. In the context of the whole novel, their partnership at the wicket comes to represent the strength of their love and the promise of a redeemed, classless England. 'Maurice's mind had cleared and he felt they were against the whole world . . . and all England were closing round the wickets.' Forster continues:

> They played for the sake of each other and of their fragile relationship – if one fell the other would follow. They intended no harm to the world, but so long as it attacked they must punish, they must stand wary, then hit with full strength, they must show that when two are gathered together majorities shall not triumph (ch. 39).

When Clive, who has been absent on trivial affairs relating to the estate, replaces Alec at the wicket, Maurice immediately collapses and is bowled first ball. The whole scene reinforces and is reinforced by a complicated pattern of contrasts, the most obvious of them being the contrast between the adventurous spirit of an older England, the England of the greenwoods, and the formalized rituals of the Edwardian country gentry, represented by Clive's pointless activities and the dilapidated house, Penge, with its leaking roof:

> these people had the air of settling something, they either just had arranged or soon would arrange England. Yet the gate posts, the road – he had noticed them on the way up – were in bad repair, and the timber wasn't kept properly, the windows stuck, the boards creaked (ch. 16).

After Maurice's night of joy with Alec at Penge, it is not surprising that his return visit to be cured is a failure. 'By pleasuring the body Maurice had confirmed – that very word was used in the final verdict – he had confirmed his spirit in its perversion, and cut himself off from the congregation of normal men' (ch. 42). The two sides of Maurice's nature struggle for mastery, the side attracted to the 'life of the earth' and the side that says 'Anyhow, I must stick to my class.' Some dramatic event is necessary to bring about a resolution. Forster places this event ironically in the British Museum, 'the great building suggested a tomb, miraculously illuminated by the spirits of the dead.' A great Assyrian bull looks down on Alec's half-hearted attempts to blackmail Maurice. His threats represent the temporary victory of stereotyped behaviour over genuine feeling. But Maurice finds himself 'trying to get beneath the words' to the love and panic that lie beneath. He comes to recognize that 'their unison', as they move from object to object in the Museum 'at a single impulse', 'was the stranger because on the surface they were at war.' The falsity of blackmailing gesture is exposed and the real identity of the two men in shared feelings of love and fear emerges through the finely conceived encounter in the museum between Maurice and his former prep school master. Mr Ducie presents the necessary challenge from outside and a reminder of the false values of the past. He mistakes Maurice for another former pupil, Wimbleby. Maurice's lying reply, '"No, my name's Scudder",' prompts Alec to a last futile gesture: '"It isn't",' he says to Mr Ducie, '"and I've a serious charge to bring against this gentleman."' But, Maurice's lie is also a spontaneous recognition of shared identity and foreshadows his more conscious realization, after the night spent together in London, that 'they were one person.'

The conversation that takes place before Alec leaves the London hotel and Maurice returns to his former desolating loneliness is richly expressive of the tensions, uncertainties, and petty snobberies on both sides that reawaken after a night made perfect by 'the toughness and tenderness, the sweet temper, the safety in darkness'. Alec's snarling resentment at any interference with his plans to emigrate, his contemptuous dismissal of Maurice's offer of a job, his 'shrewd working class' sense of where his present interests lie, all give this scene its extraordinary psychological conviction. But they also throw doubt on the credibility of a permanent relationship between the two men. And the comment, 'Maurice saw through the brassiness to the misery behind it', does not entirely allay the reader's doubts. Yet, undoubtedly, much of the strength of this last part of the novel springs from Forster's technique of contrasting the misunderstandings and jangling disharmonies of outward appearance with the deep inner harmony that unites Alec and Maurice and which brings them together finally at the boat-house at Penge, after Maurice has entered the estate 'through a gap in the hedge', struck with 'how derelict it was, how unfit to set standards or control the future'. The love that unites them transcends class and conventional morality and constitutes a judgment on that morality.

However, there are difficulties in accepting the resolutions of both the social and the personal theme. What is the political meaning of the union in exile? Does Alec's decision not to emigrate signify that there is still scope for youthful vitality in England, even if it must hide and await its historic moment? Or do the details about emigration belong to a fictional convention familiar from early Victorian days, when the 'Colonies' were either a convenient dumping ground for scamps or a rich area for unlikely people to make good (Mr Micawber in Australia, for example). What does the union signify positively in political terms. The answer would seem to be: the coming into being of a classless society in which the bonds that bind men will be personal relations, not economic or social power. The sole justification of the cruel last chapter, so uncharitable and vindictive in its tone, is that it completes the contrast between Maurice's fulfilled love for Alec and his inhibited passion for Clive. With Alec he enjoys the triumph of personal relations based on trust, 'To be strong, to keep calm and trust, they were still the one hope'; with Clive convention and triviality supervene. Yet the defeat is more credible than the triumph, as Lytton Strachey recognized when he prophesied 'a rupture' between Maurice and Alec 'after 6 months'. What do your two young men do in bed? asked the modern American writer Gore Vidal. 'They . . . talk', replied Forster smiling. Since the life-blood of personal relations is talk, we need to believe in its reality. The novel suffers because it is so difficult to believe that Maurice and Alec could enjoy a lifetime of happiness in having their talk out and so much easier to accept the breakdown of communication between Maurice and Clive, since it is expressed through the changed quality of their talk. '"Maurice, Maurice, I care a little bit for you you know",' Clive asserts feebly at the end.

'Maurice opened his hand. Luminous petals appeared in it.
'You care for me a little bit, I think,' he admitted, 'but I can't hang all my life on a little bit. You don't. You hang yours on Anne. You don't worry whether your relation with her is platonic or not, you only know it's big enough to hang a life on. I can't hang mine on the five minutes you spare me from her and politics' (ch. 46).

Clive's final words to Maurice epitomize the victory of the formal over the personal: '"Next Wednesday, say at 7.45. Dinner-jacket's enough, as you know."' But Maurice has disappeared, leaving no trace, except a memory that comes back to Clive with the approach of old age.

The Blue Room would glimmer, ferns undulate. Out of some external Cambridge his friend began beckoning to him, clothed in the sun, and shaking out the scents and sounds of the May Term (ch. 46).

With all its obvious blemishes *Maurice* is a beautiful and poignant work: through the character of its scrupulously decent hero who liberates himself from the shackles of society it offers a vision of hope to all who feel alienated from the laws of the tribe. The alternations in mood from the ecstasy of shared happiness to the desolation of suspected desertion are deeply moving. Ultimately gratitude outweighs the bitterness of recrimination and even late in the story Clive Durham acknowledges that 'Maurice had once lifted him out of aestheticism into the sun and wind of love.' Though there are touches of the Pan motif when Alec stamps his foot and Maurice wonders whether he is a devil or an angel, the vision of rural England springs from a direct and loving observation of the beauty of the English landscape. Like Lawrence, Forster raises the contrast between agricultural and industrial England to the status of a myth, but the myth in *Maurice* belongs more obviously to the whole European pastoral tradition, with its incipient escapism and its nobles retreating to the greenwoods in the guise of shepherds. For most modern readers therefore *Maurice* is likely to appear a charming pastoral eclogue in Edwardian fancy dress.

The Life to Come and Other Stories

The fourteen stories published posthumously in 1972 cover the whole span of Forster's career and help to complete our picture of the hidden or buried Forster. Except for 'Albergo Empedocle', part of 'The Other Boat', and a relatively slight narrative contribution to the magazine *Wine and Food*, none of the material had been published before. The stories fall into two distinct groups. Those in the first group are 'Ansell', 'Albergo Empedocle', 'The Purple Envelope', 'The Helping Hand', and 'The Rock'; all are early, and have already been discussed briefly in chapter 2. The second group, belonging to a much later period, consists of the following stories: 'The Life to Come' (1922), 'Dr Woolacott' (1927), 'Arthur Snatchfold' (1928), 'The Classical Annex' (1930–1), 'What Does It Matter' (the 1930s), 'The Obelisk' (1939), 'The Torque' (1958), 'The Other Boat' (1913; 1957–8), 'The Second Course' (1944). Of these, 'The Life to Come' and the beginning of 'The Other Boat', were written before Forster's last novel *A Passage to India* (1924), the remainder were all written after his supposed fictional 'silence'. They provide conclusive evidence that his failure to write another novel after his last great masterpiece was not caused entirely by his feeling that he was out of touch with the world that had come into being since the 1914 war and could not put it into fiction (interview in *Listener*, 1 January 1959). His apparent silence was also caused by the knowledge that it was impossible to publish a novel on the theme that most interested him: homosexual relations. The editor of *The Life to Come* volume quotes a series of extracts from private papers to substantiate the point. The most interesting of these is Forster's simple statement: 'I should have been a more famous writer if I had written or rather published more, but sex prevented that' (1964). From all the evidence adduced, Oliver Stallybrass draws the following conclusion:

> Given Forster's deep inner honesty and artistic integrity, his gradual acceptance of himself as a homosexual made the decision to abandon the writing of fiction for publication heroic but almost inevitable. Perhaps we should even regard *A Passage to India* gratefully, as a magnificent rearguard action, initiated before the turning-point came with *Maurice*, and completed with the aid of a theme that relegated sex to a minor role (Abinger: LTC, p. xiv).

This is both just and shrewd, but it does ignore the evidence in Forster's Commonplace Book that he had further plans for writing novels; a novel on middle age, for example, details of which are given at the beginning of chapter 9.

The later stories in *The Life to Come*, like *Maurice*, deal overtly with homosexuality. The title story, an ironic tale of a Christian missionary whose homosexual union with a native chief, leads to the death of both men, is a simultaneous attack on religious and sexual orthodoxy. It is not surprising that Lytton Strachey, a master of ironic irreverence, should have liked this story. In fact, the attempt to combine the homosexual theme with an attack on Christian missions and imperialism only partially succeeds. 'Dr Woolacott', which T. E. Lawrence described as 'the most powerful thing I ever read', also suffers to some extent from the author's divided aims, although it is an altogether more psychologically complex story than 'The Life to Come'. Yet there is an unresolved conflict between the claims of fantasy and reality, between the private and the public theme. The country house setting, the details of the young trainee farmer's life, and the authentic dialogue locate the action too firmly in the social world for the reader to be able to accept the developing vein of fantasy and illusion. Moreover, there is the further tug between the wish to present the tragedy of a failed individual in Clesant and the tragedy of the 1914 generation in the young man who visits him. Clesant, a name already used for the heroic man in *Arctic Summer*, is a chronic invalid. He is encouraged by Dr Woolacott to give up everything that once gave meaning to life, music, intense feeling and personal relations, in order to protract his empty existence. His trouble, as he tells the young 'farm labourer' he meets and to whom he is attracted, is functional, not organic. Through the relations of Clesant and the young man, Forster develops the theme that an ecstasy in death is preferable to a life of timid joylessness. But, at the same time, he also develops a public theme about the generation who chose to die in the First World War rather than be patched up (by the Dr Woolacotts of the world) in order to live a half-life in the Waste Land years that followed. The two do not quite fuse, yet it is a haunting and strangely disturbing story.

'The Obelisk', a piece of superior bar-room bawdy, reveals Forster's ability to be funny about sex. Addressing an International Congress of Writers in Paris in 1935 on 'Liberty in England', he said that English writers were hampered because they could not 'write freely about sex', and went on to say that he wanted it 'recognized that sex is a subject for serious treatment and also for comic treatment; this later aspect of it is usually ignored' (AH). 'The Obelisk' is the story of a mild elementary schoolmaster and his wife who are separately and unexpectedly initiated into new forms of sexual experience by two sailors. The experience takes place on an expedition to a seaside obelisk. Both husband and wife attempt to cover up the fact that they had been pleasantly diverted from reaching the obelisk. The wife covers up by buying a picture postcard to find what it looks like, and the husband by talking knowingly about it. But, in fact, as the wife discovers from the woman in the kiosk, the obelisk had fallen down a week before. The sailors extract the maximum amount of bawdy innuendo from the visit. ""'Ope you showed it 'er properly while you was about it, Stan. Don't do to keep a thing like that all to yourself, you know."'' On the return coach journey the wife meditates on recent events.

> if she couldn't have seen the Obelisk he couldn't have seen it
> either, if she had dawdled on the way up he must have dawdled
> too, if she was lying he must be lying, if she and a sailor – she
> stopped her thoughts, for they were becoming meaningless. She
> peeped at her husband, who was on the other side of the coach,
> studying the postcard. He looked handsomer than usual, and
> happier, and his lips were parted in a natural smile (Abinger:
> LTC, p. 129).

The comic treatment of sex also enters the Utopian political fantasy, 'What Does It Matter? A Morality'. A story of the Ruritanian state of Pottibakia, it recounts the events that led to the country's exclusion from the comity of nations. These centre on the abortive attempts of the Head of Police to discredit the President, by exposing first his affair with his mistress and later his affair with a handsome gendarme. His plot misfires because the President's wife, like Mrs Wilcox in *Howards End*, cares only that people should not hurt one another. To the gay young gendarme who has been introducing her husband to the joys of sexual gymnastics, she exclaims: "'Young man, you didn't hurt my husband with rough jokes, I hope?'" To which he answers: "'Only in ways he enjoyed.'"

> She dismissed him and turned to the others. 'Well, there we are
> at last. I thought that someone had been hurt, and it's simply that
> two people – yes, one doesn't talk about these things of course,
> but really – what do they matter?' (Abinger: LTC, p. 142).

Although the central scene between the President and his vigorous and resourceful male lover is a piece of self-indulgent wish-fulfilment, the tale conveys the quite serious ironic moral, that the so-called civilized nations of Europe cannot recognize a nation that accepts the simple dictum that what one does in private does not matter, or, as the gendarme's moral tale about the message that passed down the ranks of Pottabakians at the Last Judgement puts it, 'Poking doesn't count.'

The two best stories in *The Life to Come* volume are 'Arthur Snatchfold' and 'The Other Boat'. In the first of these, Forster's characteristic irony and objectivity are displayed at their best; indeed it is the lack of these qualities, or their very intermittent appearance in most of the other homosexual stories that accounts for their limited success. The story concerns a homosexual encounter between an upper-class Englishman and a milkman. It explores the sensibilities and consciences of both men and casts a critical light on the effect of the law on different classes in society before homosexuality between consenting adults became legal in England. Sir Richard Conway, on a visit to the country house of an inferior business associate, Trevor Donaldson, awakes to a sense of boredom and monotony. The Donaldsons, commercial mediocrities playing the sham role of gentry, have done their inadequate best to make his visit pleasant, as Conway admits.

> 'But it's not so easy to make things nice for us business people,' he reflected, as he listened to the chonk of a blackbird, the clink of a milk-can, and the distant self-communings of the electric pump. 'We're not stupid or uncultivated, we can use our minds when required, we can go to concerts when we're not too tired, we've invested – even Trevor Donaldson has – in the sense of humour. But I'm afraid we don't get much pleasure out of it all. No. Pleasure's been left out of our packet.' Business occupied him increasingly since his wife's death. He brought an active mind to bear on it, and was quickly becoming rich (Abinger: LTC, p. 98).

Clearly Sir Richard Conway is a more reflective but less likeable Henry Wilcox.

What his life lacks, and what the costly garden that he looks out on lacks, is colour. This is promptly supplied by the appearance of the early morning milkman, with his bright canary coloured shirt and his cheerful man-to-man greeting. The next morning, Sir Richard steals out into the wood in quest of pleasure, dressed only in his pyjamas and a mackintosh. There he meets the milkman, has a jolly conversation, they understand each other's needs perfectly and satisfy them; then, Sir Richard insists that the milkman accept a present (he has carefully brought a note with him just in case); and they part.

> The affair had been trivial and crude, and yet they both had
> behaved perfectly. They would never meet again, and they did
> not exchange names. After a hearty handshake, the young man
> swung away down the path, the sunlight and shadow rushing
> over his back. He did not turn round, but his arm, jerking
> sideways to balance him, waved an acceptable farewell. The
> green flowed over his brightness, the path bent, he disappeared.
> Back he went to his own life, and through the quiet of the
> morning his laugh could be heard as he whooped at the maids
> (Abinger: LTC, pp. 104–5).

The last detail suggests that the obliging milkman is a kind of composite of Eustace ('there still resounded the shouts and laughter of the escaping boy') and Alec Scudder ('he saw a gamekeeper dallying with two of the maids'). Conway's visit to the dull Donaldsons has turned out a success after all; and he departs with his vanity flattered and with an increased sense of power.

The ironic denouement takes place in Conway's London club. The business luncheon with Donaldson, whose aluminium interests have now become opposed to Conway's, is a scene worthy of de Maupassant, as Oliver Stallybrass has observed. Conway is exhilarated when he discovers that Donaldson is on the way down and can no longer keep up his little estate; he has found out what he wanted to know: the luncheon has served its purpose. But Donaldson's chance remark about the deplorable hotel in the village and an 'extraordinary case before us on the Bench recently' arouses Conway's interest. He fears that his nice milkman may have got into a scrape. With a beautiful sense of timing, Forster uses the loquacious Donaldson to release the details of the milkman's arrest and trial so that they play on Conway's uneasy conscience. When Donaldson reports that the Bench was sorry it could not have given a heavier sentence because the man created such a bad impression and because it was all 'so revoltingly commercial', Conway is relieved – 'it couldn't be his own friend, for anyone less grasping. . . .' Relaxing, he pretends, hypocritically, to share Donaldson's righteous indignation; and it is only as the further details follow that he realizes that the man was, after all, his milkman; that he had been arrested almost immediately after leaving Donaldson's house; and that 'the old gentleman in the mackintosh' the Bench was anxious to identify was himself. His identity has remained hidden, however, through the quixotic behaviour of the milkman, who in court distracted attention from the house to the hotel. '"Th'otel. Keep to the 'otel. I tell you he come from the 'otel."' At this unconscious revelation of the man's loyalty by Donaldson, Conway is overcome with shame and remorse. His reaction is much more convincing than Henry Wilcox's when he is exposed by Jacky Bast. Wilcox collapses and releases Margaret from her engagement. By contrast, Conway's response is altogether more authentic.

> He saw that little things can turn into great ones, and he did not want greatness. He was not up to it. For a moment he considered giving himself up and standing his trial, however what possible good would that do? He would ruin himself and his daughters, he would delight his enemies, and he would not save his saviour. He recalled his clever manoeuvres for a little fun, and the good-humoured response, the mischievous face, the obliging body. It had all seemed so trivial. Taking a notebook from his pocket, he wrote down the name of his lover, yes, his lover who was going to prison to save him, in order that he might not forget it. Arthur Snatchfold. He had only heard the name once, and he would never hear it again (Abinger: LTC, p. 112).

Every circumstantial detail in this story rings true: the fake country weekend, with its pampered dogs, aching boredom, and compulsory golf; the well-upholstered hypocrisy and unreal calm of the London club; the subtle nuances in the conversation between Conway and the milkman and the tensions in the dialogue between Conway and his inferior business associate. When the theme of salvation enters the story in the last few lines it is within an ironic framework. In some ways Conway is a complex personality but he is too coarse-grained to seize the opportunities for greatness and heroic self-sacrifice matching those of his saviour. Relief at being safe from the law proves stronger than the impulse to give himself up or the feeling of shame and remorse. But he has been genuinely moved by the self-sacrifice of 'his lover, yes, his lover who was going to prison to save him'; and, with the businessman's instinct, he writes down his name lest he should forget it, as he has forgotten so many other passing events and appointments. Hovering over the whole passage is the faint suggestion that the fleeting encounter and its consequences offered a potential eternal moment, but Forster has so distanced himself from his main character and his business milieu that the amused ironic unfolding of the incident rules out the possibility of true salvation for such a worldly opportunist as Sir Richard Conway.

'The Other Boat', a much longer story that was once conceived as the beginning of a novel in 1913, is an altogether more violent presentation of the shame and remorse that may attend a homosexual affair. Lionel March (the same surname as the heroic man in *Arctic Summer*), a young soldier who has been wounded and won quick promotion in a brief engagement against the fuzzywuzzies in Africa, finds himself sharing a cabin with a wealthy young half-caste as the result of the latter's manoeuvres. By coincidence March had once played with him as a child on board ship coming back from India, when the half-caste was known as 'Cocoanut'. After taking too much champagne provided by his cabin-mate, Lionel's inhibitions are broken down and he enters into a lively give-and-take homosexual relationship. Finally, in a fit of frenzy and remorse, he murders the half-caste and jumps overboard.

In outline the story may appear improbable and melodramatic. But, in fact, the writing has much of the maturity and complexity of the writing in *A Passage to India*. The presentation of the misunderstandings and friendship between the two young men from different backgrounds is often as subtle as that of the relations between Fielding and Aziz in *A Passage to India*, and much franker. What gives the story its special distinction is its dramatization of the contrast between individual morality and the morality of the tribe. As an individual, Lionel March has no instinctive prejudice against colour or homosexuality. But his character has been conditioned by tribal morality. To illustrate its early influences, Forster begins the story with a Prelude showing how Mrs March disapproved of her children playing with little 'Cocoanut' on the voyage home and how subsequently she held him responsible for the death of one of her children. Later, Lionel's training as a soldier teaches him to accept the morality of the tribe, to do his duty, to act 'heroically', and to kill the enemies of his tribe, especially the uncivilized natives, the fuzzywuzzies. A trivial incident over the unlocked cabin door reawakens Lionel's fear of discovery and punishment by the tribe for his sexual misdemeanours. His return to the company of the 'Big Eight' on deck, all 'pukka sahibs', a conversation with his colonel, spiritual communion with his absent mother, all these arouse intense feelings of guilt and remorse. On returning to his cabin, he tries to break off the relation, but Cocoanut playfully bites the young soldier's arm.

> 'Bloody bitch, wait till I . . .' Blood oozed between the gold-bright hairs. 'You wait . . .' And the scar in his groin reopened. The cabin vanished. He was back in a desert fighting savages. One of them asked for mercy, stumbled, and found none (Abinger: LTC, p. 195).

This is one of the cases in Forster's fiction in which brutality and violence – so disturbing an element in so gentle a liberal – is given an adequate psychological and sociological origin. 'The Other Boat' is a very fine short story. The cabin scenes reveal how superbly Forster could render the crosscurrents of thought and emotion in a homosexual relationship, when he was not concerned with justifying or sentimentalizing the experience. And the early childhood section captures the inconsequences of children at play more certainly than the opening of Virginia Woolf's *The Waves*. Of all the short stories, 'The Other Boat' points towards the novels Forster might have written after *A Passage to India*, had the private censor, his reticence, and the public censor permitted.

Most of the recently published material considered in this chapter reveals the strength of Forster's underground struggle to remain a writer of fiction once he had tired of the conventions of domestic comedy and once he had come to accept homosexuality as his true theme – there were to be 'no more rescue parties' and no more 'swish of the skirts'. Interesting as a very mixed body of fiction of varying merit, this new material alerts us to the nuances of meaning in the previously published novels and short stories. In particular, it throws new light on the patterns of remorse and shame that accompany the eternal moments for the youthful lovers in the early fiction. It is now clear that the same structure of experience underlies the kisses of young men and women as the chance encounters of homosexual lovers in a non-permissive society. The experience is momentary, it offers a vision of perfect happiness, it ends suddenly, and is frequently accompanied by remorse. A challenge to society, it represents the victory of instinct over prudential considerations. When this structure of experience is applied to the conventions of domestic comedy it works through already established literary codes that we have little difficulty in interpreting, though not without occasional sense of strain when the subterranean runs counter to the surface meaning. When the structure is explored in isolation we see it for what it is. The openness proves self-defeating, however. The almost total absence of any literary tradition through which to express the reality of homosexual love leaves the writer impotent and exposed. For Maurice and Clive 'no convention settled what was poetic' and 'no tradition overawed the boys', but without a literary tradition the homosexual writer himself wears his heart upon his sleeve and runs the constant danger of writing sentimentally and with half his critical intelligence turned off. Almost equally important is the inclusion of homosexuals within a developed social morality. This did not exist when Forster wrote and hardly exists in England even today. In its absence, it is fatally easy for the minority to see themselves as the sexually elect standing above and outside the ordinary moral code or to erect a minority vision into a normative ethic. Although the homosexual writer may wish to reveal that the same moral law underlies homosexual and heterosexual relations, that love, tenderness, generosity, and sympathy are necessary virtues and that cruelty and violence are inhuman, he may find that an illiberal society drives him into claiming special privilege for a persecuted sect or accepting the stereotypes imposed by society, as Forster's character Alec Scudder, for example, assumes temporarily the stereotyped role of homosexual blackmailer – a brilliant insight this. Forster himself oscillates between these two positions. With all the new evidence to hand, it is important to resist the temptation to reinterpret the whole body of Forster's fiction along simplistic lines, discovering homosexual significance in every male friendship and asserting that all Forster's women are men in disguise; but there can be no doubt that the posthumously published writings do illuminate aspects of Forster's other fiction, especially his ingenuity in adapting established literary conventions to communicate what was most personal in his vision.

7

India, Alexandria, and India Again

As we have seen it was foreign travel that inspired Forster to be a writer. His two visits to Europe soon after leaving Cambridge marked the first stage in his development, introducing him to other scales of values to set against the conventions of the English middle class. But his early travels were restricted to 'the human norm', represented by Mediterranean culture (PI, ch. 32). His first trip to India in 1912 marked the second great stage in his maturity as a man and as an artist, introducing him to a totally alien culture. It offered him new dimensions of history, religion, and philosophy, and gave fresh insight into personal relations. The latter came largely from intimate friendships with Indians but also from observation of the strain placed on personal relations by the clash between rulers and ruled, Moslem and Hindu. Alexandria, where he lived for three years from 1915, stood midway between the alien culture of India and the familiar Mediterranean norm. It provided a resting place, a point of balance, a breathing space in which to reflect in various essays on his Indian experience, a vantage point from which to develop a new vision of life. *Alexandria: A History and a Guide* (1922) and *Pharos and Pharillon* (1923), both written when he was in Alexandria, explore the curious ways in which the great European classical tradition had been enriched, reinterpreted and much muddled by the oriental mind in Alexandria. The Alexandrian experience was thus an excellent preparation for his second visit to India in 1921 and ultimately for the composition of his masterpiece, *A Passage to India* (1924). 'As he moved further and further from home geographically', remarks Wilfred Stone, 'he came closer to home spiritually.'

India

On several occasions Forster remarked that his connections with India were 'peculiar and personal'. He went neither to rule nor to make money – the two commonest motives for Englishmen for two hundred years – but because he had made friends with an Indian, a Moslem called Syed Ross Masood, who had come over to Oxford and with whom Forster had travelled in Europe in 1907. 'When he returned to India it was agreed that I should go to stay with him.' Moreover, his friend Malcolm Darling, tutor to the young prince at Dewas, had aroused his interest in that part of India (GLD, p. 37). A further incentive to make the long voyage was Goldsworthy Lowes Dickinson's interest in the country. On 7 October 1912, Forster, together with Dickinson and R. C. Trevelyan, embarked at Naples for Bombay. By good fortune, the novelist kept a journal at the time; and, in 1962 he published extracts from it, the 'Indian Entries', in *Encounter* (January 1962). These consist of three main entry-groups covering: (1) The Voyage – Naples to Bombay (October 1912); (2) the visit to the small Indian State of Chhatarpur (November-December 1912); and (3) the visit to Aurangabad, Deccan (March-April 1913), where his host was a friend of Masood's, a young Moslem lawyer called Saeed, who clearly provided some of the inspiration for the character of Aziz in *A Passage to India*. The 'Indian Entries', and the Indian Diary from which they are taken, now in King's College Library, Cambridge, have a double interest. They exhibit Forster's sensitive reaction to a completely new world of experience. They also throw light on the genesis of *A Passage to India*.

Had Forster never written *A Passage to India*, the entries in the Indian Diary would still be worth publishing, since they record with great sensitivity and precision the impressions of an imaginative mind as it voyages into the unknown. A similarity with Coleridge immediately suggests itself; and an early entry in the Indian Diary records the sight of what Forster thought were 'water-snakes'; these naturally evoked the memory of Coleridge's *Ancient Mariner*. A comparison of Forster's journal with the journal Coleridge kept on his voyage to Malta in 1804 brings out essential differences between the socially observant novelist and the introspective poet; but it also brings out their acute sensitivity to the beauty of sea and sky, a common concern with the unity of human life, and the similarity of prose styles, flexible enough to register the widest possible range of experience.

On the first day at sea, Forster wrote a very Coleridgean account of the exact effect of the ship's prow on the water.

The water it has struck impinges on the water unstruck, so that a

mountain [MS: moustache] of white precedes it: only a rowing
boat cleaves the blue. Then – on either side of the prow – is
imprisoned a huge globe of azure which struggles to rise to the
surface and is veiled by foam. Between it and the unflecked are
frills and sprays, mostly white, but some are of the green of
glacier-streams. These are always changing in detail and arrangement, yet have fixity. The pattern of drops they make on the
outer blue is not fixed. So that there is a slow transition from our
[MS: constant] prow to the variety of the sea (IE, p. 20).

Thereafter, many of the descriptions become shorter and more impressionistic. The entry for 17 October, for example, is typical: 'Moon-set
a crescent on its back. Sunset has been like a mosque-dome. Orion lies
on his side with Sirius between him and the sea.' He is describing what
he sees, but one detail, Orion harks back to one of the dominant images
in *The Longest Journey* and the other a mosque-dome, looks forward to
A Passage to India. Another entry has the evocative sentence: 'The sea
at night hissed and sparkled but did not flame.' The statue of de Lesseps,
architect of the Suez Canal, prompts the characteristic irreverence for
the great; Forster describes it as 'pointing with one hand to the Canal
and holding a string [MS: strings] of sausages in the other.' A similar
irreverence marks his observations on his fellow passengers. A 'lady
neighbour's' comment anticipates the malicious double-think of the
female characters in *A Passage to India*:

> They tell me that young Indian's lonely. I say well he ought to
> be. They won't let us know their wives, why should we know
> them? If we're pleasant to them, they only despise us (IE, p. 21).

Clearly the society on board served as an excellent preparation for the
intolerance and inanities of Anglo-Indian life. The last entry for the
actual voyage foreshadows Forster's later preoccupation with the 'true'
and 'false' India; it also contains a retrospective glance at his Italian
experience and sums up his feelings about this voyage in which his
travelling companions had been treated as harmless eccentrics – 'the
Profs' – by his fellow passengers.

> Oct. 22. False India – a cloud bank – turned into true, a queer
> red series of hills, a little disquieting, as though Italy had been
> touched into the sinister. I had seen little yellow butterflies the
> day before, and now other kinds fluttered among the baggage.
> The Taj hotel was the most prominent building – our destination,

> but a rumour of cholera came. The last horrid meal on the horrid
> ship ended as we reached Bombay, and we went on shore in
> style in a native boat, an ugly crew but beautiful skins (IE, p. 22).

The journey over, the novelist – like Adela Quested – was eager to see
'the real India'.

Arriving in Bombay, Forster remarked that the English had 'built it
and filled it with modern toys' and had 'gone away leaving the Indians
to play there.' But, if he was disappointed with the city, he was immediately struck by the naked beauty and individuality of the Indians'
movements. Small incidents occurred during the first few days that
found their way, appropriately transformed, in *A Passage to India*. At
Peshawer, for example, Forster notes in his journal, 'Evening, so
pleasant, began disastrously for me, I lost my stud, was 10 minutes late
for dinner and it was guest night.' In the novel, it is Fielding who has
trouble with his stud and Aziz who comes to the rescue. Observing the
behaviour of the military, he noted that there were no 'gradations
between hauteur & intimacy'. Suggestions for the 'bridge party' in
A Passage to India probably came from a garden party in Simla, where
'at one end of the garden burst a gramophone – I'd rather be busy with
my little Lizzy – and at the other, on the terrace before the house,
about 20 orthodox Muslims had gathered for evening prayer.' And
comments like the one recorded of Miss Masterman played their part
in the creation of the club females in the novel. 'I came out here with
no feeling against Indians, and now I can't bear them. The change
came slowly, though I don't mind servants.' Forster does not include
this early material in the 'Indian Entries' in *Encounter*, but begins his
first main Indian entry with his arrival at the central Indian state of
Chhatarpur.

Chhatarpur contributed much to the novel. The Krishna play that
Forster witnessed at the court contained the same combination of
mystery and childish simplicity that the novelist later included in the
religious ceremonies at Mau, in the final section of the novel. The
enigmatic personality of the Maharajah contributed something to
the character of Professor Godbole, as did Forster's own Maharajah
at Dewas in 1922. In the words of the first we catch something of
the tenor and tone of Forster's fictional character.

> I try to meditate on Krishna. I do not know that he is a God,
> but I love Love and Beauty and Wisdom, and I find them in his
> history. I worship and adore him as a man. If he is divine he will

notice me for it and reward me, if he is not, I shall become grass and dust like the others (IE, p. 24).

A fuller portrait may be found in J. R. Ackerley's *Hindu Holiday*. One further contribution that the stay at Chhatarpur made to the novel was the peaceful lakeside setting at Mau – 'the only idyllic place I have seen yet.' In describing the black and gold dressed dancers in the Krishna play, Forster records his uncertainty of purpose as a novelist keeping a journal. 'What to describe – their motions or my emotions?' Aware that 'the motions are vulgarized by words – little steps, revolutions, bounds, knee-dancing', he feels his own inadequacy and begins to doubt his creative powers: ('how clumsy it gets and will my memory always breathe life into it?'). He had small cause to fear. What was needed, as he later came to realize, was the wider perspective brought by time and distance and the creative powers of memory.

The second major entry in the 'Indian Entries' relates to Forster's stay at Aurangabad, but before this, in the actual Indian Diary from which the entries were taken, are many comments that have a bearing on *A Passage to India*. At Allahabad, Forster was asked to dinner at the Collector's and spent 'not a very pleasant evening' there; he met the Spencers: he was a cultivated man with a good sense of unimaginative humour who said that he 'despised the native' at the bottom of his heart, while his wife 'hated anything Indian – Purdah parties no good. She didn't like anything. I believe this is good form.' In the novel, the English characters regulate their lives according to club rule, to rigid unthinking notions of 'good form'. Leaving Benares, Forster noted the words in block letters on marble at a railway station, 'Right is might. Might is right. Time is money. God *si* love'; the last phrase finds its appropriate place in the religious festival at the end of the novel. At Hyderabad he was quizzed about his novels by the foolish but tragic Mrs G: 'Problem novels, I suppose – Well, for my own part I think there are no problems left – all have been written about.' Hers, Forster noted was a tragic household, one that provided an insight into the lives of the Turtons and Burtons in the novel. 'She left him alone too long and he fell in love with another woman; then out she rushes from England hysterically. Now he dare see no-one and is wrapped in his work.'

The chief interest of the Aurangabad entries, printed in *Encounter*, lies in the light they throw on the relations between Fielding and Aziz. It has often been said by Forster, as well as by his critics, that Aziz was suggested by his great friend Masood; but the pages of the diary prove that Forster's relations with his host at Aurangabad, the young lawyer Saeed, were also important. The details of Saeed's house, with 'two rows of triple arches' and the square tank of green water, become incorporated into the description of Fielding's house at the government college. During a visit to court with Saeed, when a murder trial was being heard, Forster noted that the 'Punkah boy, seated at end of table, had the impassivity of Atropos', an observation expanded in the trial scene in the novel to achieve great symbolic power.

> Then life returned to its complexities, person after person struggled out of the room to their various purposes, and before long no one remained on the scene of the fantasy but the beautiful naked god. Unaware that anything unusual had occurred, he continued to pull the cord of his punkah, to gaze at the empty dais and the overturned special chairs, and rhythmically to agitate the clouds of descending dust.

Such parallels, however, are relatively insignificant compared with the record of Saeed's outburst when they were riding together. 'It may be 50 or 500 years but we shall turn you out': obviously the origin of the last scene in the novel. Equally revealing is the description of the tender farewell with which the visit ended. Having failed to buy Saeed anything to commemorate their intimate friendship, Forster writes: 'It's as if I am to do nothing for him, however slight. "The accounts of friends are written in the heart" is his explanation.' These two entries enshrine in little the essential pattern of Fielding's and Aziz's relationship.

Alexandria

When Forster returned to England from his first visit to India, he brought with him the beginnings of a novel on India, but he abandoned it to write *Maurice* in 1913–14, as we have already seen. The outbreak of war in 1914 coincided with a particularly sterile period in the author's life, and he welcomed the opportunity that service with the Red Cross in Alexandria gave to escape from the constrictions of middle-class English life and to seek new inspiration abroad. Inevitably the war intensified the jingoism in England that Forster so despised. Many of his friends and contemporaries were pacifists: Bertrand Russell went to prison for his beliefs, others became agricultural labourers as an alternative to military service, while D. H. Lawrence angrily denounced conscription from his cottage near Zennor, as he recorded in *Kangaroo*. The Bloomsbury gospel of beauty and personal relations was severely tested by the war. Forster himself saw no objection to accepting service in a humanitarian cause and so joined the Red Cross, collecting information from the wounded in the Alexandrian hospitals. In a letter to Bertrand Russell, he described how he lived in the wards, 'questioning survivors'. Although he wrote no fiction, he made 'notes on human nature under war conditions'. 'I love people and want to understand them and help them more than I did', he explained to Russell, 'but this is oddly accompanied by a growth of contempt. *Be* like them? God, no.'

The intrepid orientalist, Gertrude Bell, interviewed him in England before he left, and warned him that it was no use thinking he would get to know the people. Afterwards, he felt that he had been 'too deferential' to her, and so at his next interview with a senior Red Cross official, he became 'uppish and impertinent at the wrong moment (it's called initiative when it's at the right moment)'; and nearly missed being sent to Alexandria at all ('Lost Guide', KCL). Contrary to Gertrude Bell's magisterial prediction, he did in fact establish a wide circle of friends. These included the Swiss Director of Tramways, the French Director of Posts, an Italian composer, a Syrian Police Officer, and an Egyptian tram-conductor – in Alexandria, to his joy and relief, men were not kept apart by nationality, class barriers or stuffy conventions. He also got to know the then little-known Greek poet Cavafy, whose works he helped to popularize in England through an essay in *Pharos and Pharillon* and a later essay in *Two Cheers for Democracy*. At first he stayed in a hotel. Then he met an American widow who invited him to eat his lunch in her large garden. In a rocky creek there Forster, the creator of so many naked baptismal swimming scenes, first learnt to swim. He soon left the hotel and took a room in the house of the widow's retired Italian-speaking Greek maid, and thereafter moved wherever she moved. 'Under her relaxing sway,' he remarks, 'I gave up wearing my uniform except for my duties, and slid into a life that suited me and into a variety of acquaintances who never coalesced into a set.' In the heart of each man, Forster writes in an essay called 'Happiness' (AH), 'there is contrived, by desperate devices a magical island . . . we place it in the past or the future for safety, for we dare not locate it in the present.' He had found his 'magical island' in Alexandria.

It was a thoroughly happy period in which 'the mild and cheerful Egyptians' seemed (especially to one who had known Indians) an easy people to live with. 'But evil influences were at work.' One of these evils was the British censorship of the local press. Forster knew its effects from observation and personal experience as a journalist. Day by day he had seen the absurd spaces in the papers caused by last-minute censorship; he had also contributed numerous articles under the pseudonym 'Pharos' to the *Egyptian Mail*, a newspaper that catered for the English-speaking part of the population. Some of the articles were later published in *Pharos and Pharillon* and *Abinger Harvest*, but there are many others that deserve republication, for example 'Gippo English' (16 December 1917), with its examples of curious English culled from local advertisements, such as that of a barber who prom-ised his customers 'Antiseptic Red Cross civility and cleanliness' or the bar described as 'Alexandre's garden where Australian heroes eat and shoot'. But the title and tone of 'Gippo English' indicates that Forster, for all his genuine sympathy for the people and strong anti-imperialist views, sometimes assumes the jocular condescension of the average middle-class Englishman. And the same tone enters parts of *The Hill of Devi*, the letters he wrote home from India. In both cases he is probably consciously trying to suit his remarks to his readers. Later all this was to disappear in *A Passage to India*, where linguistic solecisms cease to be quaintly amusing and are subsumed under the twin themes of personal relations and the difficulty of communication.

In Alexandria Forster not only recaptured the easy intimacy of male friendship that he had first enjoyed in India; he also had leisure to make new literary discoveries. It was in Egypt that he first read T. S. Eliot's *Prufrock and Other Poems* and Huysmans's *A Rebours*. Eliot's poems made him aware that in a world of gigantic horror, brought into being by the war, it was the 'slighter gestures of dissent' that were alone tolerable, a lesson that bore fruit in his own political essays, especially those written just before and during the Second World War. Huysmans returned him to the world of the senses, so that 'the waves of edifying bilge' produced by the war 'rolled off', and the 'newspapers ebbed' ('T. S. Eliot', AH). In Egypt, he also had time to apply his historical training to practical purposes; from his stay there came three publications: *The Government of Egypt* (1920), *Alexandria: A History and a Guide* (1922), and *Pharos and Pharillon* (1923).

The Government of Egypt

It is a curious coincidence of literary history that chance residence abroad should have led both a nineteenth-century Romantic poet and a twentieth-century novelist to write on the political future of Egypt – Coleridge in an unpublished memorandum called 'Observations on Egypt', written when he was unofficial Secretary to the Governor of Malta in 1805-6, and Forster in a pamphlet issued by the Labour Research Department, formerly the Research Department of the Fabian Society. The pamphlet, *The Government of Egypt*, consists of two main parts: a set of recommendations made by the Committee of the International Section of the Labour Research Department, and an essay on Egypt by Forster. The most important recommendations are the recognition by Great Britain of the independent status of Egypt, the withdrawal of British troops and advisers, and the lease of the Canal Zone to Egypt for a term of years. In the brief essay on Egypt that follows, Forster makes it clear that he was in no way responsible for these recommendations, though he almost certainly sympathized with their left-wing, liberal, anti-imperialist bias. (Shortly after the publication of the pamphlet he became for a brief spell literary editor of the Labour *Daily Herald*.) The essay, based paradoxically on such 'textbooks of imperialism' as Cromer's *Modern Egypt* and Milner's *England in Egypt*, gives a highly condensed account of Egypt from the rule of Mohammed Ali to the occupation of Egypt by British troops during the First World War. It notes briefly the rise of the nationalist movement under Saad Zastaloul Pasha, his internment, the subsequent rising, the murder of British officers and the savage reprisals that followed the 'March Rebellion' of 1919, by which time Forster had actually left Egypt. At the time of writing, in June 1920, the Milner Mission to enquire into the causes of the rebellion and to recommend a constitution, was about to make its report, and Zaghoul had come to London in preparation for negotiations. To Forster, Milner seemed the worst possible choice as head of the Mission, because of his strong imperialist bias. The essay as a whole contains a judicious blend of factual statement and personal observation; it is warmly sympathetic towards the Egyptian people; but it can offer no simple solution to the country's future problems. For the reader of Forster's novels, the most interesting passages are those that reflect the writer's anti-imperialism and his comments on the 'racial arrogance' of the officials and their wives who had come to Egypt after service in India.

Pharos and Pharillon

Pharos and Pharillon is a collection of fourteen pieces, five of which were originally published in the *Nation and Athenaeum*, six of them in the *Egyptian Mail* and the remainder appeared for the first time in 1923. The volume is divided into two sections. The first, called 'Pharos', after the famous lighthouse at Alexandria, contains essays recreating the life of the city in antiquity; the second, called 'Pharillon', the name the Arabs gave to the square base of the building remaining after the collapse of the lighthouse, contains essays about the city in later times. There is some overlapping between the first section on antiquity and the historical section of *Alexandria: A History and a Guide*, but the treatment of the material is more relaxed, more general and more informal in the collection of essays. Thus, for example, both works refer to the story about the translation of the Septuagint, but it is only in *Pharos and Pharillon* that the details are expanded and the incident set in a perspective of mocking irony. Forster relates how Ptolemy chose the island of Pharos for the labour of translation.

> Here he shut up seventy rabbis in seventy huts, whence in an incredibly short time they emerged with seventy identical translations of the Bible. Everything corresponded. Even when they slipped they made seventy slips, and Greek literature was at last enriched by the possession of an inspired book. It was left to later generations to pry into Jehovah's scholarship and to deduce that the Septuagint translation must have extended over a long period and not have reached completion till 100 B.C. The Jews of Alexandria knew no such doubts (PP).

If we ask ourselves where else we have heard such a mocking irreverent tone, the answer is in Lytton Strachey, whose *Queen Victoria* (1921) and whose innovations in the art of biography Forster later praised in his W. P. Ker lecture on 'English Prose between 1918 and 1939'. But there is no question of direct influence; the two writers shared a common Cambridge ethos, sceptical and irreverent; and, on closer inspection, the similarity of style in this and in other essays does not extend very far. Forster's prose lacks the sharp cutting edge and bright metallic surface of Strachey's prose; his irony is more genial; he is more tolerant of human folly; moreover, his sensitivity to mystery, the unseen, the infinite lies outside Strachey's range. This sensitivity appears clearly in his account of Alexander's strange encounter with the Priest at Siva who addressed him as the Son of God. The description of this foreshadows comparable encounters with the unknown in *A Passage to India*. The meeting takes place beneath 'the pale blue dome of heaven', in a solitary place; no one is certain what actually happened (compare the religious ceremony at Mau in *A Passage to India*); the strangeness is consciously balanced by the matter-of-fact tone, 'a scare he did get – a fright, a psychic experience, a vision, a "turn".' And the essay, 'The Return from Siva', ends with a sentence that might have come straight out of *The Longest Journey* or *Howards End*: 'Was it explicable this side of the grave?'

In all the essays in the first part of the book, 'Pharos', Forster succeeds, as he says Theocritus succeeds, in 'wielding the double spell of realism and poetry' to evoke 'an entire city from the dead'. His poetic sense of landscape and of geological change brings the city's atmosphere alive as later it evoked the atmosphere of India in the opening chapter of 'Caves' in *A Passage to India*. He makes the great figures of the Alexandrian past realistically human without debunking them. Occasionally the attempt to humanize an old theological dispute leads to triviality and whimsy, as in the cautionary tale 'Timothy the Cat and Timothy Whitebonnet'; but in most of the essays Forster succeeds in pouring new life into old controversies and in revealing their continued relevance. All the time he is concerned with ideas that were obliged to transform themselves or perish as they passed from Greece or Palestine to Alexandria. It is with living not dead ideas that he deals. Indeed, the urgency of his need to transform his own inherited liberal humanism gives creative force to his study of cultural changes in Alexandria. This sense of involvement is clearly apparent in his personal rapport with his subject at the end of the essay on Clement of Alexandria.

> He lived in a period of transition, and in Alexandria. And in that curious city, which had never been young and hoped never to grow old, conciliation must have seemed more possible than elsewhere, and the graciousness of Greece not quite incompatible with the Grace of God (PP).

In Alexandria the ideal of 'only connect' seemed almost a reality.

The essays in the second part of *Pharos and Pharillon* range from a lively and amusing account of Mrs Eliza Fay's stay in Alexandria in 1779, based on her letters to which Forster wrote an introduction, to an appreciative estimate of a modern Greek poet, in 'The Poetry of

C. P. Cavafy'. Sandwiched in between, are essays called 'Cotton from the Outside', 'The Den', 'The Solitary Place', and 'Between the Sun and the Moon'. In the first of these, Forster expresses his characteristic dislike of the machinery of commerce, and conveys a vivid impression of the noise and confusion of the cotton trade in Alexandria. 'The Den' shows that Forster is no Coleridge or De Quincey capable of evoking the mystery of opium, yet the essay does catch the average tourist's disappointment on visiting the centres of vice in a big city. 'But we got in and saw the company. There is really nothing to say when one comes to the point. They were just smoking.' 'The Solitary Place' reveals his capacity to respond to the spirit of an un-English alien landscape that he later exploited in *A Passage to India*. Of this solitary place near Lake Mariout, Forster writes:

> It has beat a general retreat from civilization, and the spirit of the place, without being savage, is singularly austere. Its chief episode is the great temple of Abousir, which with its attendant beacon-tower stands so magnificently upon the coastal ridge. And inland lie the marble basilicas of St Menas and his holy well. But these apart there is nothing to catch the attention.

The sense of absence, exception, deprivation is similar to that evoked in the Indian novel ('Except for the Marabar Caves – and they are twenty miles off – the city of Chandrapore presents nothing extra-ordinary.') In 'The Solitary Place', when Forster comes to define the difference between the Egyptian and English plants, he stresses the 'quiet persistence of the earth', and speaks of the 'pageant of nature' passing 'like the waving of a handkerchief'. For Forster both nature and history become a passing pageant. It is this that links his vision of the life of man with the earth he inhabits. And it is the vision of history as a moving pageant that links all his work, fiction, biography, history, and guidebook.

Alexandria: A History and a Guide

What Forster said of Napoleon might equally well be said of himself: 'The Romance of the Nile Valley had touched his imagination, and he knew that it was the road to an even greater romance – India.' Many of the pages of *Alexandria: A History and a Guide* open a route that leads straight to the great Indian novel. For example, Forster's sympathetic summary of the Alexandrian philosopher, Plotinus, reveals a mind already imaginatively prepared to enter the minds of Hindu and

Brahmin. 'We are all parts of God, even the stones, though we cannot realize it; and man's goal is to become actually, as he is potentially, divine.' But the primary purpose of writing the book was to provide a practical *Guide* to Alexandria. The suggestion came from an English friend who was half German, G. H. Ludolf, who mentioned it to a local stationer and printer. It was wartime; Alexandria was full of troops; there was need for a simple well-written guide. But there were delays and the *Guide* did not appear until 1922. One thousand copies were printed; a few were sold before Forster received the news that all the remainder had been destroyed by fire. 'This blow was softened by a substantial Cheque', as the stock had been adequately insured. Then came the news that the books had not been burnt after all. A typical Alexandrian solution, 'to burn the books artificially' was found; and so *Alexandria: A History and a Guide* 'perished in personal flames'. A second edition, revised by friends, appeared in 1938. 'It did not sell well, perhaps because the Second World War started next year. Copies of it are rare.' In a typescript describing how the work came to be written, Forster records that friends suggested that there should be a third edition. 'No – there can be, there need be, no third edition', it is the 'product of a traditional age, which is at an end' (KCL). But Forster misjudged the climate of opinion and his own fame. The work passed into a third edition, and Forster duly wrote a new Preface, giving vivid personal details about its composition and of his life in Alexandria. It survives today mainly as a literary work rather than as a practical guide, read by people interested in Forster, not its subject, Alexandria.

In the novels and short stories Forster often laughs at the conventional English travellers who need a Baedeker to tell them what to see and admire, but a character in *A Room with a View* probably expresses the author's view when he says, '"It's worth minding, the loss of a Baedeker. That's worth minding"' (RWV, ch. 2). In the Preface to *Alexandria*, Forster writes, 'I have always respected guide books, particularly the early Baedekers and Murrays.' By keeping the needs of the reader always in mind and by linking the 'History' to the 'Guide' wherever possible, so that the user sees the present in the light of the past, by writing simply and colloquially, Forster has written a first-rate 'Guide'.

The opening sentences strike the chatty informal note that prevails throughout. 'The situation of Alexandria is most curious. To understand it we must go back many thousand years.' With another writer

the second of these sentences might suggest an infinite regression back-
wards, but Forster seizes on a few essentials. He conceives the history
of the city 'after the fashion of a pageant'; this links the *Guide* with the
companion volume, *Pharos and Pharillon*; it also links it with Forster's
characteristic way of seeing England's past in 'Abinger Pageant'.
Again and again, in this brief history Forster reveals his ability to write
with great distinction when summarizing the essential facts about a
character, a culture, or a philosophy. Of Cleopatra's influence on
Antony, he writes, 'She never bored him, and since grossness means
monotony she sharpened his mind to those more delicate delights,
where sense verges into spirit. Her infinite variety lay in that.' In
summarizing Ptolemaic culture, he finds an antique correlative for his
own modern ideal 'only connect': 'The Palace provided the finances
and called the tune; the Mouseion [library] responded with imagination
and knowledge; the connection was so intimate as almost to be absurd.'
And he rounds off his summary of Plotinus and Neo-Platonic thought:
'The Christian promise is that a man shall see God, the Neo-Platonic –
like the Indian – that he shall be God.'

Forster even succeeds in writing wittily about ancient theological
controversies. Such arid disputes as those between Arius and Athanasius
are enlivened by thumb-nail sketches of the protagonists: Arius
'accused by his enemies of looking like a snake, and of seducing, in
the theological sense, 700 virgins', Athanasius, strong-willed, small and
black, 'a modern street type'. He presents their theological conflicts in a
spirit of Stracheyan irreverence, allowing his humanistic irony full play
in describing their respective ups and downs and frequent banishments
and in suggesting the disparity between their un-Christian behaviour
to each other and their singleminded devotion to Christian doctrine.
After every banishment Athanasius always returned,

> and he had the supreme joy of outliving Arius, who fell down
> dead one evening, while walking through Alexandria with a
> friend. To us, living in a secular age, such triumphs appear remote,
> and it seems better to die young, like Alexander the Great, than
> to drag out this arid theological Odyssey (AHG).

Later, in a section describing the conflict between Monophysism (belief
in the single nature of Christ) and Monothelism (belief in single
will), there is a passage that illustrates perfectly Forster's skill in lucid
exposition, his gift for relating past to the present, and his controlling
irony.

If Christ has one Nature he has of course one will. But suppose
he has two Natures? How many wills has he then? The
Monothelites said 'One'. The orthodox view – the one we hold –
is 'Two, one human the other divine, but both operating in
unison'. Obscure indeed is the problem, and we can well believe
that the Alexandrians, against whom the Arabs were then
marching, did not understand Monothelism when it was hurriedly
explained to them by a preoccupied general. But it was not
without a future. It failed as a compromise but survived as a
heresy, and long after Imperial Government had disowned it and
Egypt had fallen to Islam, it was cherished in the uplands of
Syria by the Maronite Church (AHG).

Although Forster's attitude to all these controversies is one of ironic
detachment, the *Guide* throughout reveals an underlying preoccupation
with certain themes: 'only connect'; 'mystery or muddle'; what
is it that forever divides men and prevents them from achieving
the harmony they desire? Can God – ultimate reality – ever
be known? These are the master themes of the novel he was to write
after he left Alexandria and had paid his second visit to India in
1921.

India Again: *The Hill of Devi*

On 4 March 1921 Forster set out from Tilbury for his second visit to
India to take up the post of private secretary to the Maharajah of
Dewas State Senior; on this occasion, the journal he kept petered out
after two pages, and for a record of his experiences we must turn to
The Hill of Devi and *A Passage to India*. Although *The Hill of Devi* was
not published until twenty-nine years after the first appearance of the
novel, it is based on a carefully edited version of letters he wrote home
to his mother and friends during his visits to India. It also contains an
essay called 'The State and its Ruler', placed between the letters of
1912–13 and those of 1921. There is also a poignant coda 'Catastrophe',
describing the tragic events that clouded the last days of his beloved
Maharajah. *The Hill of Devi* is thus both the story of a personal pilgrim-
age, a passage to India, or the unknown – and a portrait of a prince,
perhaps a 'saint'. It is, as an Indian writer Narayana Menon, has
remarked, 'a happy relaxed book, to the point of being mischievous,
I nearly said, irresponsible' (Natwar-Singh, 1964, p. 13).

Forster was perfectly aware that in attempting to amuse his correspondents at home he was too 'prone to turn remote and rare matters into suburban jokes'. But when due allowance has been made for occasional facetiousness and whimsicality, what is most striking about *The Hill of Devi* is the author's capacity to enter into the lives and thoughts of people utterly unlike himself and to refrain from applying inappropriate Western standards to the beauty, mystery and muddle that surrounded him. Indeed, Forster was far more tolerant of the incompetence and inefficiency of Dewas than his Indian friend Masood, who paid a brief visit to the little independent Indian state soon after Forster's arrival. 'After three days of Hinduism Masood retired with his clerks and his files to Hyderabad. Our incompetence distressed him more than it could me because he saw it as an extreme example of his country's inefficiency' (HD, p. 69). In the chaos of Dewas, which blended memories of past grandeur and of spirituality with modern muddle, tawdriness and uncertainty of purpose, Forster recognized 'the fag end of a vanished civilization'. Here, then, at the other end of the world, he had found an objective correlative to his own consciousness of belonging to the end of another great civilization, 'to the fag-end of Victorian liberalism'. From this flash of recognition, from this creative rapport between observer and observed, came *A Passage to India*, the only great novel of the twentieth century to embrace the declining civilizations of the East and West in a unified vision.

In reading *The Hill of Devi* it is impossible to forget that its author also wrote *A Passage to India*, yet it has an interest and value independent of the insight it provides into the composition of that novel. The story that it relates of the dissension between the twin states of Dewas, the court intrigues, and the inevitable bankruptcy that overwhelmed the state and its ruler is a sad and poignant one. The new constitution the ruler devised, 'one of a batch which was improvised to greet the Prince of Wales', was not a success. The marriage of the Maharajah's son, the Crown Prince, to the daughter of a Chief of the Jath, a Maratha landowner in the Deccan, turned into tragedy. The Crown Prince, his mind warped by emissaries from Kolhapur, another state, fled from the court, declaring that he was being poisoned by his father. The Government of India intervened. The Maharajah tried to make foolish terms that the Prince was not to 'go to Kolhapur where his mother was, nor to Jath where his wife was; he was regarded as a Political Offender'. Negotiations between the Maharajah and the Government of India broke down. The Maharajah threatened to resign, but it was state bankruptcy in 1933 that finally brought an end to his regime. The book concludes with a photograph of the melancholy, emaciated Maharajah, taken at Pondicherry in 1934, after a penitential fast, together with a sympathetic account of his last tangled relations with the Indian Government, his lonely exile, and his death in December 1937. Judged by his actions and their political consequences the Maharajah was a failure; judged by his capacity for personal relations and cultivating inner states of being, Forster asserts, he was a saint. The discrepancy reflects to some extent the inadequacy of Cambridge and Bloomsbury values when applied to public life. In the essay 'What I Believe', Forster sadly laments that no device has been found by which the 'private decencies can be transmitted to public life.' At Dewas, Forster could do little to bring greater order into public affairs. He felt distressed at not being able to help his friend in life, suggests Ahmed Ali, 'and immortalized him after death by way of expiation' (Natwar-Singh, 1964, p. 36).

The letters on which *The Hill of Devi* is based are rich in materials that contributed to the composition of *A Passage to India*, as Perry June Levine has shown in *Creation and Criticism: A Passage to India*, an exhaustive but incisive study of the background and process of composition. Forster skilfully fused scenes, characters and episodes from his two visits to India. For example, the atmosphere of Mau, in the final section of the novel, came from Chhatarpur during his first visit, while most of the details of palace life came from life at the old palace at Dewas on his second visit. Perhaps the greatest single contribution that the second visit made was the first-hand experience of the religious festival of Gokul Ashtami, the eight-day festival in honour of Krishna, who was born at Gokul near Muttra: this inspired the last section of the novel, 'Temple'. Here the parallels are extremely close. In *The Hill of Devi*, Forster prefaces this section with the note: 'The following letters on the Gokul Ashtami Festival are the most important of my letters home, for they describe (if too facetiously) rites in which an European can seldom have shared' (HD, p. 100). What troubled him at the time was that 'every detail' was 'fatuous and in bad taste'.

The altar is a mess of little objects, stifled with rose leaves, the walls are hung with deplorable oleographs, the chandeliers, draperies – everything bad. Only one thing is beautiful – the expression of the faces of the people as they bow to the shrine (HD, p. 106).

The Maharajah alone succeeded in not being absurd. When all the details are transposed in the novel, the absurd and the sacred unite: 'God *Si* Love', 'there is fun in heaven', mystery vanquishes muddle. The actual Maharajah of Dewas, 'dancing all the time, like David before the ark, jigging up and down with a happy expression on his face', becomes Professor Godbole, who 'once more developed the life of the spirit' and placed himself in the position of God to love Mrs Moore and placed himself in her position to say to the God 'Come, come, come, come.' In addition many of the incidents recorded in the letters are incorporated into the novel: that of the snake that turns out to be a dead tree, the car accident, believed to be connected with a ghost, the queer superstition that hangs over a boat that hit a rock, and many others. *The Hill of Devi* and *A Passage to India* has each its own special kind of truth: the first tells us exactly what Forster felt at the time and is a testament to the truth of friendship, 'a sort of Dostoev-skian text written by Turgenev', according to the Indian novelist, Raja Rao (Natwar-Singh, 1964, p. 28); the second is an imaginative recreation, a truthful vision of man's quest for harmony in the modern world, or as Forster himself expressed it in a programme note to the dramatized version of the novel, a vision of 'the human predicament in a universe which is not, so far, comprehensible to our minds'.

For the making of his masterpiece, *A Passage to India*, Forster had an intimate first-hand knowledge of the hostility aroused by English rule in India, based on two widely separate visits; he had himself exper-ienced the joys and frustrations of trying to bridge the gulf that kept the English and Indians apart and of trying to create order as a minor official in a small native state; he had studied Islamic culture in Alexan-dria and India; he had witnessed many Hindu ceremonies and lived close to deeply religious men; he had known and loved Indians; and, most important of all, he had responded at the deepest level of his being to the beauty and terror of the Indian landscape.

8

A Passage to India

In *A Passage to India*, Forster draws on his two widely separated visits to India. The novel thus presents a composite picture of India and cannot be proved right or wrong by reference to historical facts relating to 1912–13 or 1921, or by reference to subsequent events in India, although the Partition of the subcontinent into Pakistan and India would seem to confirm its vision of the irreconcilable differences between Moslem and Hindu. In a piece of reminiscence, called 'Three Countries' (KCL), Forster says that he thought that he had been exceptionally fortunate in having 'three personal introductions' to India, 'the Moslem, the British and the Hindu'. The Moslem, as we have seen, came through his friend Syed Ross Masood, who showed one side of the India he knew 'in an offhand and arresting way'; the British, through officials in the civil service; and the Hindu as the result of his being Secretary to the Maharajah of the independent Hindu state of Dewas Senior. These introductions provided the basis of the tripartite structure of the novel, Mosque, Caves, and Temple.

During the first visit there was violence and acute unrest, so that afterwards 'the sense of racial tension, of incompatibility' was never absent from Forster's mind. 'It was not a tourist's outing, and the impression it left was deep.' The second visit was invaluable because it showed 'a side of India unknown to most foreigners' ('Three Countries', KCL). Forster needed the double perspective. The first attempt to write a novel on India had 'stuck' after 'half a dozen chapters'; and, although he expected that the congenial surroundings of the second visit would inspire him to go on, 'exactly the reverse happened', because there seemed to be 'an impassable gulf' between the India he was experiencing and the India he had tried to create. 'I had to get back to England and see my material in perspective before I could proceed. Perhaps the long wait was to the good and the religious atmosphere of Dewas certainly helped to establish the spiritual sequence I was seeking.' This was of special importance.

> For the book is not really about politics, though it is the political aspect of it that caught the general public and made it sell. It's about something wider than politics, *about the search of the human race for a more lasting home, about the universe as embodied in the Indian earth and the horror lurking in the Marabar Caves and the release symbolized by the birth of Krishna.* It is – or rather desires to be – philosophic and poetic, and that is why when I had finished it I took its title, 'Passage to India', from a famous poem of Walt Whitman's ('Three Countries', KCL; italics supplied).

The poetic dimension was fully attained only after careful revision. For its attainment it was necessary to dislodge the rational humanist Fielding from his central position as chief mediator of the message of the caves. In an early manuscript version of this episode, it is Fielding not Mrs Moore who confronts the caves' indifference to human values most directly. '"Have you anything to say",' he asks the caves. '"Boum".' He then recites the opening lines of *Paradise Lost* and Meredith's 'Enter these enchanted woods/You who dare', but all to no avail.

> A shout, a whistle, a whisper, all were 'Boum', loud or soft but without distinction in quality. He felt helpless and terrified, as if someone were insulting him, and through him, humanity. Once more he spoke, and with a tenderness he never admitted in his daily voice. He pleaded for all the unhappiness and misunderstanding in the world, past, present, and to come, for the misery we must all undergo, whatever our opinions and positions, and however much we dodge or bluff.

After reciting four lines from a Persian poem Aziz 'had compelled him to learn', lines that speak of the secret understanding of the heart, he thinks '"Poetry, piety, courage – nothing has value"' and shouts, in defeat or defiance, '"Go to Hell!"' By changing the focus to the intuitive Mrs Moore and the psychologically disturbed Adela, Forster deepened the mystery and heightened the visionary element. Other revisions, directed towards intensifying the enigma of India and to reducing circumstantial details in the plot and in the background of the characters' lives (Aziz's education in Germany, Fielding's past experience in running a school 'for backward youths at fancy prices'), also contributed to making *A Passage to India* the philosophic and poetic novel Forster intended.

A Passage to India is not only a natural development from the early novels and *Howards End*, but marks the culmination of Forster's vision. In the earlier novels the major theme is the individual's search for salvation or – as in the case of *Howards End* – a family in search of its spiritual home; in *A Passage to India* the theme is the plight of 'the human race'. By writing about India, Forster moved away from the limits of English society and Western philosophy and embraced the universal. But it was enlargement rather than escape; for the basic structures of experience remained the same. India offered Forster an unconscious parody of the achievements of Western rationalism in its English rulers. It also confronted him with the triumph of natural forces that such rationalism claimed to have controlled and ordered. There are obvious contrasts between this novel and its published predecessor, *Howards End*. Whereas in *Howards End* the principle of diversity provides the final vindication of personal relations, in *A Passage to India* it is precisely human diversity, the difference of colour, race, and creed, that threatens personal relations. In the earlier novel, there is the promise of a harmony between man and the earth; in the later novel the earth is frequently hostile or indifferent; the message of the caves reduces all human endeavour to a meaningless echo. It is not surprising therefore that *A Passage to India* has often been read as marking the final collapse of Forster's liberal faith: a profoundly pessimistic novel conveying no hope to mankind. Yet close attention to its structure, tone, characterization, dialogue, recurrent images, and symbolism may suggest that this is too simple an interpretation, that such labels as pessimistic or optimistic are misleading, and that the harmony achieved in the novel is one that involves doing full justice to the polar opposites: good and evil; earth and sky; the negative and positive vision.

The particular tripartite structure, as we have seen, was partly determined by the pattern of Forster's introductions to India. Thus, the first part, Mosque, explores the Moslem approach to truth; the second part, Caves, examines the confusion and sterility of the British, or rational Western approach; and the brief third part, Temple, celebrates the comprehensive spirituality of the Hindu approach. The parts also correspond to the three Indian seasons, 'the Cold Weather, the

Hot Weather, and the Rains', as Forster notes in the Everyman edition of the novel. Other interpretations have been offered from time to time, such as the triple division: 'emotion, reason, love'. However, it is less important to define these divisions than to sense the separate tone and atmosphere of each and to see that they are major elements in securing that expansion of meaning that Forster describes in *Aspects of the Novel*.

> Expansion. That is the idea the novelist must cling to. Not completion. Not rounding off but opening out. When the symphony is over we feel that the notes and tunes composing it have been liberated, they have found in the rhythm of the whole their individual freedom.

It is not the immediate effect of the three parts that matters but the impression left when the separate parts have attained their individual freedom in the rhythm of the whole.

Each of the three main parts, Mosque, Caves, and Temple, has a theme, a tone, an atmosphere of its own, while contributing to the total structure of the novel. In each section, the first chapter introduces the main themes and sets its characteristic atmosphere. The most far-reaching in its imaginative effects is the opening chapter of the whole book. Through its description of the contrasting aspects of Chandrapore, the one native, the other official, through its description of the contrasting faces of earth and sky, and its ominous and most carefully placed final allusion to 'the extraordinary caves', it sounds the major themes of the novel and releases its dominant images. Of these it is the images of the undifferentiated earth and over-arching sky that are to become the controlling symbols of the novel. Even at this early stage, the 'dome' of the sky is a richly ambivalent image, suggesting simultaneously the promise of a rounded perfection but also hints of a receding infinite. As the events unfold in the first part, the dome becomes associated with the mosque, with 'the secret understanding of the heart' experienced by Mrs Moore and Dr Aziz, with the quest for the divine through the ideal Friend, in fact, with the way of Islam. An underlying note of intimacy, almost casualness, characterize this opening, which leads on to a series of invitations to harmony, domestic ('bridge parties, tea parties'), and divine ('Come, come, come'). In the first, kindness and spontaneous affection throw a magic bridge across the gulf that separates people; in the second, both absence and presence are seen to be necessary aspects of the divine.

The opening chapter of the second part, Caves, strikes a prophetic and oracular note. The perspective alters. To prepare the way for the ultimate diminishing of human value in the Marabar Caves, the continent of India and all human life is placed in a vast geological perspective. 'Geology, looking further than religion, knows of a time when neither the river nor the Himalayas that nourished it existed, and an ocean flowed over the holy places of Hindustan.' The tone changes to prosaic matter-of-factness in the account of the dimensions of the caves, then gains imperceptibly in intensity as the negative similarity of the caves is stressed and their mystery suggested. 'It is as if the surrounding plain or the passing birds have taken upon themselves to exclaim "extraordinary", and the word has taken root in the air, and been inhaled by mankind.' After this wonderful evocation which picks up the 'extraordinary' of the final sentence in chapter one, comes the description of the interior of the circular chamber.

> There is little to see, and no eye to see it, until the visitor arrives for his five minutes, and strikes a match. Immediately another flame rises in the depths of the rock and moves towards the surface like an imprisoned spirit: the walls of the circular chamber have been most marvellously polished. The two flames approach and strive to unite, but cannot, because one of them breathes air, the other stone (ch. 12).

A perceptive critic of the novel, Malcolm Bradbury, suggests that 'The Platonic romantic gesture of the match in the cave is the dominating ambiguity of the book', and he asks the question 'Does it see *itself* in the polished wall of stone, or is the glimmer of radiance a promise?' (Stallybrass, 1969, p. 142). The novel provides no final answer: the balance between visionary symbolism and ironic comment keeps the question always in doubt. But since the middle section of the novel is to present the extreme challenge of the negative vision for Mrs Moore and Adela, the chapter ends appropriately with a monotonous reiteration of the word 'nothing' and a reference to the hollow boulder, the Kawa Dol, thus preparing the reader for the echoing sound that reduces 'pathos, piety, courage' to hollow nothingness, a nothingness voiced by all the major characters in an earlier manuscript version of the novel, but later given dramatic focus in Mrs Moore's experience in the cave.

The opening of the third part, Temple, is very different from the other openings, since it does not stand alone as a separate atmospheric prelude but merges into the description of the religious ceremonies at Mau. The whole section is exceptionally brief. Asked why he had introduced the ceremonies, Forster replied:

> It was architecturally necessary. I needed a lump, or a Hindu temple if you like – a mountain standing up. It is well placed; and it gathers up some strings. But there ought to be more after it. The lump sticks out a little too much (Cowley, 1958, p. 27).

This last part opens with a sentence that clearly marks off the events to be described from what has gone before, both in time and place. 'Some hundreds of miles westward of the Marabar Hills, and two years later in time, Professor Narayan Godbole stands in the presence of God.' The tone becomes apocalyptic, but after the chant 'Tukaram, Tukaram', celebrating the mystic union of the soul with God, the prose shades off into an ironic account of the tawdry religious ceremonies. For the first time in the novel, religious mysticism and the comic spirit fully interpenetrate. The ironic comedy that is sustained throughout the whole of the last part suggests that a complete vision of life must admit the comic, 'there is fun in Heaven'. Moreover, it permits the novelist to withhold total assent from the Hindu mysticism, against which D. H. Lawrence had warned him in a letter of 2 June 1915, 'above all, don't read the Crown of Hinduism. I can't tell you how I detest things Hindu & things Buddhistic – it is all such ineffable self-conceit as to be overwhelming. Better read Tartuffe' (KCL). It will become apparent that the dialectical structure, which consists of positive affirmation (Mosque), negative retraction (Cavès), muted reaffirmation (Temple), not only determines the meaning of the novel, but is reflected in every detail of the novel's imaginative organization.

Important as the tripartite structure is in creating a synthesis of the negative and positive visions, it is the subtle characterization that supplies much of the vital life of the novel. In view of Forster's frequent references to the importance of characters in his own and other novels, this is not surprising. *A Passage to India* presents a variety of parallel and interlocking relationships: between Ronny Heaslop and Adela Quested; between Dr Aziz and Cyril Fielding; between the rulers and the ruled; and between Moslem and Hindu. The main weight of the book falls on the friendship between Aziz and Fielding, a weight that it fully sustains, from the first spontaneous gesture of friendship through the offer of the collar stud to the last ride together, where the final recapitulatory paragraph recalls all the forces in India that make perfect comradeship between an Englishman and an Indian difficult, but not impossible ('not yet' and 'not there').

> But the horses didn't want it – they swerved apart; the earth didn't want it, sending up rocks through which riders must pass single file; the temples, the tank, the jail, the palace, the birds, the carrion, the Guest House, that came into view as they issued from the gap and saw Mau beneath: they didn't want it, they said in their hundred voices, 'No, not yet,' and the sky said, 'No, not there' (ch. 37).

The mediating voice of the author, transmitting the message of India, confirms the insight of the 'divine fool', Ralph Moore, who also uses the phrase 'Not yet', when Aziz says that '"the two nations cannot be friends." "I know. Not yet."'

Until the action moves from Chandrapore to Mau, in the last part of the novel, the two sets of relationships, those between Ronny and Adela and those between Aziz and Fielding, develop side by side, throwing light on each other. There are revealing contrasts and parallels, especially as far as they reflect the interaction of reason and emotion and the divisive influence of India. Ronny and Adela cannot connect and are unable to grapple with the unknown: Aziz and Fielding at times show themselves able to connect and can accept the irrational and the unseen, Fielding only partially. Adela, who has come out to see Ronny at work as well as at play so that she can decide whether to marry him, believes that nothing is too difficult or mysterious to solve if you worry at it: she is earnest, sincere, full of common sense, fair-minded, but deficient in emotion, imagination, and beauty – a kind of latter-day Hannah More. She has come determined 'to see the real India'. Try seeing Indians, Fielding interjects at the Club, good advice fraught with ironic consequences.

Both Mrs Moore and Adela notice that India has brought out the worst features of Ronny's character, but it is only after his 'gross' insensitivity in breaking up Fielding's successful tea party (a dramatic contrast to Turton's 'bridge party'), that Adela becomes fully conscious of her fiancé's faults: 'His self-complacency, his censoriousness, his lack of subtlety, all grew vivid beneath a tropic sky. . . . It was the qualified bray of the callow official, the "I'm not perfect, but –" that got on her nerves' (ch. 8). The tea party that brings Aziz and Fielding together and suggests the possibilities of human harmony through affection and goodwill, also causes the first serious disharmony in

Adela's and Ronny's relations. As a result, Adela decides that they will not be married after all. However, the 'animal thrill' that passes between them in the Nawab Bahadur's car brings them together again. But it is a 'spurious' unity, an unconscious surrender to instinct, a panic reaction to the mystery of the Indian night; it is not a genuine fusion of mind and body. Adela's failure to connect in this minor moment of panic leads on to the major panic in the caves (Forster's maturest presentation of Pan theme); it leads to her psychic breakdown when she believes she has been assaulted by Dr Aziz in the caves. Just before she enters the cave, she makes the agonizing discovery that she does not love the man she has agreed to marry. Neither she nor Ronny is capable of wholeness of being. Adela, more sensitive than Ronny, has glimpses of the unconscious, but is shocked at such evidence of the irrational, and suppresses it. She cannot understand how she came to blurt out that she would not stay in India, at a tea party, when she had said nothing to Ronny first, and is filled with remorse. She cannot come to terms with the irrational within herself or in the Indian life around her. In her conscious mind Aziz comes to represent India; in her unconscious he becomes associated with the unknown that she represses. All the fears, frustrations and disappointments that she connects with an abstraction, India, become attached to a person: hence her delusion that Aziz has attacked her in the cave. Forster was wise to omit the vivid physical details of an earlier manuscript version, since these made it seem that there must have been an actual assailant ('he got hold of her other hand and forced her against the wall, he got both her hands in his, and then felt her breasts'). And such details also reduced the elements of mystery and suspense so essential to any well-made plot.

The progress of the relationship between Aziz and Fielding, unlike that between Adela and Ronny, makes due allowance for elements not susceptible to reason; it is based on a greater understanding of the interpenetration of reason and emotion, the conscious and the unconscious, although Fielding is never able to transcend the rational bias of his personality completely. Unlike Mrs Moore and Professor Godbole, he cannot develop 'the echo', the negative vision that is the ultimate challenge to his liberal humanism. There is, however, a great difference between the 'bleak definiteness of Fielding's avowal of disbelief' and Forster's own 'reverent agnosticism', as A. H. Smith has remarked (Bradbury, 1966, p. 114). And the difference was intensified during manuscript revisions, as Forster transcended the limitations of his own liberal humanism. Fielding's visit to the sick Aziz, which ends with the Indian showing the Englishman a photograph of his dead wife (a symbolic gesture of brotherhood for a Moslem), marks the triumph of the developed heart, in contrast to the pathetic failure of the undeveloped heart, which is exemplified in the relations between Ronny and Adela. By the end of the visit Aziz has discovered that Fielding 'was truly warm-hearted and unconventional, but not what can be called wise'.

> But they were friends, brothers. That part was settled, their compact had been subscribed by the photograph, they trusted one another, affection had triumphed for once in a way. He dropped off to sleep amid the happier memories of the last two hours – poetry of Ghalib, female grace, good old Hamidullah, good Fielding, his honoured wife and dear boys. He passed into a region where these joys had no enemies but bloomed harmoniously in an eternal garden, or ran down watershoots of ribbed marble, or rose into domes whereunder were inscribed, black against white, the ninety-nine attributes of God (ch. 11).

The domed perfection, in this wonderful harmonizing act of consciousness, comes immediately after a mischievous schoolboy has sown the seeds of suspicion against Fielding. Affection can triumph over corroding suspicion and produce connection and harmony. But the triumph is precarious.

Adela's charge against Aziz, the operatic trial and its consequences, destroy the harmony established in the first part of the novel. Ronny only awaits a suitable moment to break off the engagement after Adela's unexpected retraction of her charge against Aziz; suspicion and misunderstanding threaten the friendship between Fielding and Aziz. At his arrest at the railway station and after the trial, Aziz feels that Fielding has deserted him; subsequently he suspects that self-interest has prompted Fielding to ask him to withdraw his demand for compensation from Adela; yet amid all this confusion something remains of the old relationship. Fielding may complain that Aziz's emotions '"never seem in proportion to their objects"' and Aziz may reply, '"is emotion a sack of potatoes, so much the pound, to be measured out?"', as Masood, in real life, had asked Forster. But both men are frank about their emotions; they preserve an underlying affection for one another, which only needs the good influence of Mrs Moore's memory to reawaken it into vital life. This occurs twice:

163

first when Aziz suddenly gives up the claim for compensation at the thought of Mrs Moore; second when Aziz's words to her son, Ralph Moore, 'then you are an Oriental', bring back the memory of the old Englishwoman's kindness and intuitive sympathy. This memory then leads on to an affectionate reunion with Fielding, after the ritual baptism of reconciliation as the boats collide at the religious festival celebrating the birth of Krishna.

> 'Then you are an Oriental.' He unclasped as he spoke, with a
> little shudder. Those words – he had said them to Mrs Moore in
> the mosque in the middle of the cycle, from which, after so
> much suffering, he had got free. Never be friends with the
> English! Mosque, caves, mosque, caves. And here he was starting
> again (ch. 36).

Aziz's sensibility – touching, impressionable, perhaps a little absurd, but always aesthetic – possesses the potential for achieving harmony and wholeness of being.

In this novel Forster makes a sharp distinction between the attempts to achieve harmony through 'completeness' and through 'reconstruction'. The former is the product of love and affection and imagination, the latter of the intellect. For the reader and for many of the characters in the novel, the people who come closest to expressing the ideal of completeness are Mrs Moore, Professor Godbole, and Dr Aziz, not so much in their ordinary everyday natures, as in the goodness of which they prove capable or which they communicate; and in the visions they enjoy. The two such dissimilar figures, Mrs Moore and Professor Godbole, provide the necessary counterweight to the vast forces of disintegration and division exerted by the chief character in the novel – India. Appropriately it is as felt presences that Forster embodies Mrs Moore and the spirit of India. But to the extent that Mrs Moore's good influence is more obviously a fictional device it may appear the weaker. It is not always noticed, however, that on her departure, Mrs Moore modifies her nihilistic vision of India, her sense of the 'horror of the universe and its littleness'. The sight of a mosque reawakens her interest in the unknown and she longs to stop 'and disentangle the hundred Indias'. Thus, the message of the cave is not the final truth about India and she enjoys benevolent thoughts once again (ch. 23).

In many ways, *A Passage to India* comes closer than the other novels to providing a connection between good states of mind and good actions. Quite rightly critics have drawn attention to the central importance of the passage when Professor Godbole impels the memory of Mrs Moore and a wasp into his consciousness; and, emulating God, loves them equally.

> He had, with increasing vividness, again seen Mrs Moore, and round her faintly clinging forms of trouble. He was a Brahman, she Christian, but it made no difference, it made no difference whether she was a trick of his memory or a telepathic appeal. It was his duty, as it was his desire, to place himself in the position of the God and to love her, and to place himself in her position and to say to the God, 'Come, come, come, come.' This was all he could do. How inadequate! But each according to his own capacities, and he knew that his own were small. 'One old Englishwoman and one little, little wasp,' he thought, as he stepped out of the temple into the grey of a pouring wet morning. 'It does not seem much, still it is more than I am myself' (ch. 33).

This supreme example of the power to connect, dependent for its full effect on the reader's memory of Mrs Moore's loving acceptance of the wasp she finds when she goes to hang up her cloak (at the end of chapter 3) has been much praised. What has not been so frequently noticed is that crucial good actions are preceded by good states of mind in this novel. Adela's good action in withdrawing her charge against Aziz is preceded by a good state of mind, a state in which she achieves a special kind of completeness, because she no longer falsifies what happened on the visit to the caves, as the result of unreal expectations and hidden fears. She connects.

> The fatal day recurred, in every detail, but now she was of it and not of it at the same time, and this double relation gave it indescribable splendour. Why had she thought the expedition 'dull'? Now the sun rose again, the elephant waited, the pale masses of the rock flowed round her and presented the first cave; she entered, and a match was reflected in the polished walls – all beautiful and significant, though she had been blind to it at the time. . . . Her vision was of several caves. She saw herself in one, and she was also outside it, watching its entrance, for Aziz to pass in. She failed to locate him. It was the doubt that had often visited her, but solid and attractive, like the hills, 'I am not —' Speech was more difficult than vision. 'I am not quite sure.' . . . 'I'm afraid I have made a mistake' (ch. 24).

Thereafter, however, she and Fielding follow the path of reconstruction not completion; and they fail. They reach the height of their limited powers in their friendly reconstruction of past events; but it is a friendliness as of dwarfs shaking hands. Their words 'I don't believe in God'

> were followed by a curious backwash as though the universe had displaced itself to fill up a tiny void, or as though they had seen their own gestures from an immense height – dwarfs talking, shaking hands and assuring each other that they stood on the same footing of insight. They did not think they were wrong, because as soon as honest people think they are wrong instability sets up. Not for them was an infinite goal behind the stars, and they never sought it. But wistfulness descended on them now, as on other occasions; the shadow of the shadow of a dream fell over their clear-cut interests, and objects never seen again seemed messages from another world (ch. 29).

The English capacity for easy intercourse and quiet reconstruction, limited as it is in comparison with genuine completeness, awakens Aziz's envy when he reads Adela's letter to Mrs Fielding, 'written in a spirit he could not command'. He discovers that Adela has given Ralph Moore money so that he 'will enjoy his India', thereby paying a debt to India that she will 'never repay in person'. Here one notices once again Forster's insight into the process by which money is substituted for personal relations. At first, Aziz is repelled, and it needs the counterbalancing presence of Mrs Moore's memory for him to achieve completeness and to recognize 'how brave Miss Quested was'. Once he has recognized this, he is filled with generous thoughts and wishes to write to her.

Most of Aziz's good actions are preceded by good states of mind, by visions of potential harmony and completeness. The last of these semi-mystic states, though it does not lead to any single good action but only to renewed intimacy with Fielding, illustrates the free play of mind and emotion, the extreme fluidity of association, necessary for such acts of imaginative synthesis, generated in the first place by affection and memory. When Aziz has finished adding the name of Mrs Moore to his letter to Adela,

> the mirror of the scenery was shattered, the meadow disintegrated into butterflies. A poem about Mecca – the Caaba of Union – the

thornbushes where pilgrims die before they have seen the
Friend – they flitted next; he thought of his wife; and then the
whole semi-mystic, semi-sensuous overturn, so characteristic of his
spiritual life, came to end like a landslip and rested in its due
place, and he found himself riding in the jungle with his dear
Cyril (ch. 37).

As the result of the closer relationship established between states of
mind and action in *A Passage to India*, Forster avoids the suggestions
of internal grace and privileged aestheticism of the earlier novels, and
the tendency, in *Howards End*, to offer states of mind and aesthetic
patterns as valid solutions to problems in society. This marks the final
escape from the lapsed Protestantism of the Cambridge Apostles and
the preciousness of Bloomsbury.

In *A Passage to India*, Forster's understanding of human nature, his
wit, his humour, and his mastery of dialogue preserve the characters
from becoming too representative or symbolic. Dialogue becomes
supremely important. For example, the comment that prompts Aziz
to pour out confidences to Mrs Moore is not one of sweet reasonable-
ness or simple kindness, but an acid reply to polite praise of the atrocious
Mrs Callendar. '"A very charming lady",' says Aziz. '"Possibly, when
one knows her better",' replies Mrs Moore. The dialogue throughout
A Passage to India, apart from creating a sense of living reality, throws
into dramatic relief the contrasting attitudes to life, thus reinforcing
the impression of bewildering diversity. The early scene that presents a
group of Indians discussing the question whether it is possible to be
friends with an Englishman, provides a particularly good example, as
does the episode at Aziz's bedside. In the former, Aziz springs instantly
to life through his playful inconsequential chatter; he is a much more
successful embodiment of vitality and nature than the Italian primitives
and English pagans of Forster's earlier fiction. The ensuing conversation reveals the wide diversity that exists among the Indians on the
subject of friendship with the English and something too of the
unconscious illogicalities of the speakers, especially Mahmoud Ali. The
atmosphere of relaxed intimacy forms a direct contrast to the later
stereotyped exchanges at the English Club, intended to reveal the
unimaginative deadness of the officials and their wives. On his arrival
at Hamidullah's house Aziz cries out: 'Hamidullah, Hamidullah! am I
late?'

'Do not apologize,' said his host. 'You are always late.'

'Kindly answer my question. Am I late? Has Mahmoud Ali
eaten all the food? If so I go elsewhere. Mr Mahmoud Ali, how
are you?'
'Thank you, Dr Aziz, I am dying.'
'Dying before your dinner? Oh, poor Mahmoud Ali!' (ch. 2).

In such conversations as those between the Indians at the beginning of
the novel and at Aziz's bedside, Forster returns – with suitable modifications of rhythm and idiom – to the informal mixture of seriousness and
banter that characterized the talk of his Cambridge youth, as reflected
in *The Longest Journey*, though now there is added a touch of suspicion
and nervous pettiness in the light-hearted exchanges. He makes brilliant
use of dialogue to illustrate the infectious power of idle rumour among
people suspicious of their rulers. But the tone is comic, culminating in
the revelation that what Professor Godbole is suffering from is not
cholera contracted at Fielding's tea party, but that ignoble complaint:
haemorrhoids. It is extraordinary how economically Forster suggests
the flickerings and cross-currents of thought and emotion among a
naturally volatile people. A mischievous schoolboy's remark inflames
the fires of suspicion. The atmosphere of conspiracy seems almost self-
generating, yet the dialogue preserves a delicate balance between
comedy and compassion. An Indian writer, Natwar-Singh has
remarked that the speech of Forster's Indian characters is entirely
convincing, even to Indian ears. Forster's success represents the triumph
of sympathy and artistry. Indeed, it is the lack of sympathy with many
of the minor characters at the English Club that causes their dialogue
to verge on stage caricature.

A Passage to India is a novel with a serious theme, man's relationship
to his fellow man and to the universe, yet the tone of the dialogue is
comic. A series of comic misunderstandings establish that it is the little
things not the large issues that make it difficult for people to communicate; a lesser artist might have felt that only major ideological difference
would sustain his grand theme. Forster's attitude to dialogue changes
from his first novel to his last. In *Where Angels Fear to Tread*, he thinks
of 'the barrier of language' as 'sometimes a blessed barrier, which only
lets pass what is good' (WAFT, ch. 8). In *A Passage to India*, language
comes to stand for everything that divides man: while memory and
silence stand for what reconciles and unites. Most of the differences
that arise between Dr Aziz and Fielding spring from a misunderstanding of idiom, but the idiom itself expresses a whole character or culture.

This may be seen in attitudes towards sex ('she has no breasts'), to art ('post-impressionism indeed'), to truth (the collar-stud). Forster catches the dated slang of his English characters as surely as the excited mishandling of English idioms by the Indians (grown so much worse when he revisited India in 1945). Mrs McBryde, a nurse who has married the chief of police, comes instantly alive through her dated slang: '"Oh, Nancy, how topping! Oh, Nancy, how killing!"' Miss Derek's inanities at the car accident express the essential triviality of her response to life. Mrs Turton's amazed, '"Why, they speak English",' of the Bhattacharyas, epitomizes the haughty insulation of the British wives, their treatment of educated Indians as either clever children or as objects of cruel amusement. The novelist takes care that the mistakes of such sympathetic characters as Aziz and the Nawab Bahadur are either endearing (Aziz to Mrs Moore on the death of her husband, '"Then we are in the same box"' – for 'boat'), or innocently comic (the Nawab's '"half a league onwards"'). He reserves for insignificant servants or mischievous fools phrases like '"I'll take you any dam anywhere"' (the Eurasian chauffeur) or '"I was mislaid"' for 'I was mistaken' (the absurd but mischievous Dr Panna Lal). The crucial dependence of personal relations on communication is finally spelt out in the account of Aziz's suspicions of Adela and Fielding in chapter 31, 'an intonation misunderstood, and a whole conversation went awry.'

A Passage to India is not a political novel but a novel about personal relations. According to Forster, the solution to human misunderstanding lies in human nature, not in political institutions: it lies in man's capacity to transcend human difference by developing the heart and the imagination. Consequently he employs dialogue to show that the misunderstandings involve all areas of life: how we greet each other, our attitudes to art, poetry, religion, love, sex, and marriage. But politics hardly at all. Some critics have said that the almost complete neglect of politics is a characteristic weakness of the English liberal humanist. This may be so. But would it have been a better novel if Forster had filled the Indians' dialogue with the 1920s equivalent of such phrases as 'the trouble is we are all alienated from the decision-making process', or 'it is all a question of destroying an elitist tyranny'? In *A Passage to India*, the reader is made to feel the blindness and stupidity of imperial rule, but it is clear that the removal of that rule would not bring Utopia, only a different set of problems. History has borne this out.

Towards the end of the novel Forster offers the generalization that the characteristic weakness of the East is suspicion, that of the West hypocrisy. True or false as a proposition, it is important that the reader should feel the truth of this remark at the climax of the misunderstanding between Aziz and Fielding. He does so because the dialogue has already expressed every variety of suspicion and hypocrisy. In the English Club, hypocrisy is closely associated with unthinking complacency and stock responses – the habits of judging a man according to whether he is good at games, for example. It is a brilliant invention to make the drunken subaltern praise a polo-playing Indian at the moment he and all the members of the club are condemning Aziz. '"The native's all right if you get him alone, Lesley! Lesley! You remember the one I had a knock with on your Maidan last month. Well, he was all right. Any native who plays polo is all right"' (ch. 20). The reader knows, as neither the subaltern nor any member of the club knows, that the polo-playing 'native' was, in fact, Dr Aziz. This is an example of Forster's long-term strategy in making widely spaced scenes, involving dialogue, mutually self-supporting. This ironic handling of dialogue exposes the soldier's self-contradictory behaviour, the ingrained snobbish racialism that lies behind his stupid protestations of goodwill. It also forces the reader to connect the two scenes, so that he becomes actively engaged in detecting hidden hypocrisies.

Many of the key phrases and images in *A Passage to India* are first expressed or released in the course of dialogue. The effect of this is twofold: first to assimilate the symbolism into the living texture of the novel, and second to form a dramatic context within which the symbols interact. Such key phrases as 'you are an Oriental', 'seeing India as a frieze', 'travel light' (first used between Aziz and Fielding at Aziz's sick-bed and taken up several times later) are all first released through dialogue. The theme of identity offers a particularly good example of this accommodation of the general to the particular through dialogue. It is first announced in conversation between Ronny and Adela in connection with the unidentifiable bird.

'Bee-eater.'
　'Oh, no, Ronny, it has red bars on its wings.'
　'Parrot,' he hazarded.
　'Good gracious no.'
　The bird in question dived into the dome of the tree. It was of no importance, yet they would have liked to identify it (ch. 8).

This theme of objects that escape identification becomes linked with the theme of being labelled. Nothing in India can be labelled, yet the English survive by creating stereotyped roles that can be conveniently labelled; and Adela fears desperately that she will become labelled as the wife of an Anglo-Indian official as soon as she marries Ronny. When Aziz protests that it is impossible that she will become just another Anglo-Indian wife, she replies, '"But I shall; it's inevitable. I can't avoid the label."' But the bird cannot be labelled, neither can the creature that struck the Nawab Bahadur's car; this, we are made to feel, is why 'nothing embraces the whole of India, nothing, nothing.' Because many of the major themes emerge naturally out of conversation, the pattern of recurrent images that constitutes the novel's structure is fully integrated into the minute details of character, motive and action. The symbolism grows out of living speech; it is not imposed arbitrarily from without. And the voice of the novelist supplies the final harmonizing modulation. This is seen most obviously in the great visionary moments of the novel, but also in the poetic evocations of the polar opposites, earth and sky, and the duality within each. Typical of his power to invest earth and sky with a meaning that pierces the heart is his account of the false dawn on the morning of the visit to the caves. Adela, 'exaggerating her enthusiasm', cries out, '"Look, the sun's rising – this'll be magnificent – come quickly – look."' The novelist comments:

> As she spoke, the sky to the left turned angry orange. Colour throbbed and mounted behind a pattern of trees, grew in intensity, was yet brighter, incredibly brighter, strained from without against the globe of the air. They awaited the miracle. But at the supreme moment, when night should have died and day lived, nothing occurred. It was as if virtue had failed in the celestial fount. The hues in the east decayed, the hills seemed dimmer though in fact better lit, and a profound disappointment entered with the morning breeze. Why, when the chamber was prepared, did the bridegroom not enter with trumpets and shawms, as humanity expects? The sun rose without splendour. He was presently observed trailing yellowish behind the trees, or against the insipid sky, and touching the bodies already at work in the fields (ch. 14).

An earlier passage forms a counterbalance to this vision of promise unfulfilled.

171

Mrs Moore, whom the club had stupefied, woke up outside. She watched the moon, whose radiance stained with primrose the purple of the surrounding sky. In England the moon had seemed dead and alien; here she was caught in the shawl of night together with earth and all the other stars. A sudden sense of unity, of kinship with the heavenly bodies, passed into the old woman and out, like water through a tank, leaving a strange freshness behind (ch. 3).

The vision is confirmed in the description of the reflections in the water of the Mau tank, near the end of the novel, where 'earth and sky leant toward one another, about to clash in ecstasy' (ch. 36). The prophetic and mediating voice of the novelist finally reconciles the contraries.

The superiority of Forster's last novel rests as much on the triumph of voice as the triumph of vision. Voice has special importance for Forster. Both in life and in art he identifies and recalls people through voice. Hence of course the supreme importance of dialogue in his novels. And, as omniscient novelist, he mediates between character and reader through his carefully modulated commentary – the assumed voice of the author. As Stephen Wall has noted, Forster was the last English novelist to use the omniscient voice with great success. In *A Passage to India*, compared with the earlier novels, he greatly extends the range of his characters' voices and exercises a surer control over his own, curbing its tendency towards English whimsy and romantic sentiment: it is a wiser voice, less attached to the limited values of the English tradition, as reflected in Cambridge and Bloomsbury, able now to speak for mankind, without strain or insincerity. In this novel, and in his later political essays, he spoke as the conscience of England's better self. It was thus that Forster became – like some of his good characters and the spirit of India – a felt presence, even when he chose to remain silent as a novelist.

9

Criticism and Biography

After the publication of *A Passage to India* in 1924, Forster did not cease to write fiction altogether, but he did not seek publication for the homosexual short stories he wrote from time to time. However, his Commonplace Book shows that he went on considering the possibility of writing another novel. At one time, he was drawn towards writing 'a novel on middle age', choosing as his hero a married man of about fifty 'a robust alert character': perhaps 'the curtain might rise upon him and wifee in their bed.' But three difficulties stood in his way. The first was the recurrent difficulty of making marital relations central when his interest and experience lay elsewhere – 'I must get nearer myself, but how?' The second was how to avoid dullness in treating of middle age; he felt unable, he said, to be a bore, 'from a sense of literary duty', like Thomas Mann. And the third was how to avoid falsity of sentiment, especially how to prevent the experiences of middle age from being transformed into those of a young man: 'all the incidents . . . haloed with a spurious novelty & wonder . . . falsified by "oh this was the first time . . .'', a rejuvenating process which 'insensibly perverts and pervades modern literature', and 'turns the numerous fascinating noises of life into a mechanical morning song.' He, therefore, sternly commended himself to: 'Abjure freshness, underemphasize surprise'; each incident 'should fall on to a thick bed of previous impressions, like the tree on to mould that has been formed by its own dead leaves.' There is in all this a triumph of the critical over the creative spirit; and it is not surprising that nothing came of this particular plan for a novel on middle age. In later years, friends encouraged, chided, and cajoled; but in vain. The Commonplace Book records one such appeal, on 8 March 1943, by Forster's close friend Bob Buckingham. '"Repeat yourself," he said: "it does not matter, so changed are the conditions. Say again that you believe in human relationships and disbelieve in

power."' Forster was not to be tempted by such an appeal to the past.
Yet he adds:

> The plea remains, something that can't be whittled away or
> stated in any other words. And my fear that – in spite of success
> far beyond my hopes and of a gratification far beyond most
> men's – I haven't fully come off, would be laid.

This is a fear that must haunt even the most prolific and successful
novelists. In Forster's case, not even his undoubted success in the
spheres of literary criticism and biography could still it.

Aspects of the Novel

The invitation to give the Clark Lectures at Cambridge in 1927 was a
tribute to Forster's distinction as a novelist and his perception as a
critic; moreover, it re-established his connection with Cambridge that
was to remain close until his death in 1970. After he lost his house on
his mother's death in 1945, King's College elected him an Honorary
Fellow and later provided him with rooms in College. For the Clark
Lectures in 1927, he chose as his topic the Novel; and when the lectures
were published he gave them the title, *Aspects of the Novel*, a modest
title totally in keeping with the personality of the lecturer and his
general tone and approach. In view of Forster's frequent disclaimers to
scholarship (he 'was not a scholar and refused to be a pseudo-scholar',
said Virginia Woolf), it is worth considering what qualifications he
did actually possess. He had knowledge of the novel from the inside,
having written five novels, the last – *A Passage to India* – recognized as a
masterpiece as soon as it appeared in 1924. He had an extensive knowledge of English, American, and European fiction. As a frequent book-
reviewer, he had learnt to seize on essentials in any work, to be sensitive
to nuances of meaning and style, to summarize imaginatively, to select
quotations aptly, and to develop an attractive and flexible prose style
for communicating his acute insights to a wide public. Moreover, he
was already an accomplished lecturer and reader of scholarly papers,
although not a professional academic. He had lectured on a variety of
literary topics to the Weybridge Literary Society, including 'Literature
and the War'; he had addressed the Working Men's College 'On
Pessimism in Modern Literature' and other subjects; he had given talks
on literary topics to students in India. As the result of this very mixed
experience, he had developed his own informal method of speaking

about literature and saw no particular reason to change it for his Cambridge audience. This included A. E. Housman, who, much to Forster's disappointment, came to only two lectures, put off perhaps by the lecturer's informality and self-confessedly 'ramshackly course' of lectures. 'Housman came to two & I called on him on the strength of this, but he took no notice' (CB, KCL).

Forster's approach to the novel was deliberately anti-historical, in marked contrast to his essay on the 'Novelists of the Eighteenth Century and their Influence on Those of the Nineteenth', submitted for an undergraduate prize in October 1899. When he came to give the Clark Lectures he knew that he lacked the range of knowledge and the 'rare gifts' necessary for 'genuine scholarship'. Despising the cataloguing and classifying absurdities of 'pseudo-scholarship', he therefore decided to abandon the historical approach altogether and to imagine all the great novelists of the world writing their masterpieces under the dome of the central reading room of the British Museum. A charming and whimsical fancy that does enable Forster to 'exorcise' the 'demon of chronology' and to concentrate on the novelist's common task of finding in art a mirror for reality – a common task because, unlike History which develops, 'Art stands still' (AN, 'Introductory').

Forster begins by presenting his audience with two passages of introspection, two funeral scenes, and two passages of fantasy about the muddle of life: the first pair are by Richardson and James; the second pair by Wells and Dickens; and the third by Virginia Woolf and Sterne. Forster deliberately withholds the names of the authors to bring out the idea that similarity of vision transcends chronology, yet any well-trained undergraduate today would have little difficulty in showing how deeply the language and sensibility of each passage is rooted in its historic period, and could indeed have been written at no other time. Any connection that the use of unseen passages, the withholding of authorship and the anti-historicism, suggests with the new Cambridge school of 'practical criticism' of the 1920s is utterly misleading. Indeed, Forster's neglect of close linguistic texture ('almost nothing is said about words', complained Virginia Woolf) and his neglect of social context, seriously limit his critical perspective. Of this, Forster was partly aware, regretting that his chosen method ruled out the discussion of literary tradition, especially as this affects a novelist's technique. Reference to tradition, he believed, could show that Virginia Woolf 'belonged to the same tradition' as Sterne, 'but to a later phase of it'. This is indeed a rather special conception of literary tradition. What Forster does not sufficiently appreciate is that the actual material of fiction and the consciousness of the artist are at least in part historically conditioned. It is illuminating to compare his remarks on Richardson with those of Ian Watt in *The Rise of the Novel* or with those of any other modern critic sensitive to the fact that the moral and social values embodied in a novel reflect the unique inter-action of individual sensibility and the temper of an age.

Having – as it were – set his scene in the British Museum and having adopted a French critic's convenient definition of a novel as 'a fiction in prose of a certain extent', Forster focuses on seven formal properties of the novel. These he calls 'Aspects'. They are: 'The Story', 'People', 'The Plot', 'Fantasy', 'Prophecy', 'Pattern', and 'Rhythm'. This chatty, updated Aristotelian approach gives the discussion an air of complete-ness while allowing Forster to speak about what happens to interest him most. The chosen framework might suggest an exclusive concern with form and technique, a concern shared by such novelists as James, Conrad, and Ford Madox Ford, exemplified also in Percy Lubbock's *The Craft of Fiction*. But, in fact, Forster avoids a strictly formalist approach; he maintains a pleasant balance between questions relating to technique and questions relating to truth and reality. At the begin-ning of the lecture on 'Fantasy', he indicates the principle that deter-mines this balance; in the novel itself and in his own approach.

> The idea running through these lectures is by now plain enough:
> that there are in the novel two forces: human beings and a bundle
> of various things not human beings, and that it is the novelist's
> business to adjust these two forces and conciliate their claims.

Ultimately, however, Forster's supreme test is truth to life, an old-fashioned test certainly, but one that is susceptible of considerable refinement in application. But it did not satisfy Virginia Woolf, a close friend and admirer, who asked 'What is this "Life" that keeps on cropping up so mysteriously and so complacently in books about fiction?' (Gardner, 1973, p. 334). Here she was not only continuing the battle against the Edwardian realists, begun in *Mr Bennett and Mrs Brown*, and originally provoked by Bennett's claim that she had failed to create character or reality in *Jacob's Room*, but also remembering Forster's remarks about characters and life in his 1925 essay on her early fiction. 'Why', she asks pertinently of Forster, is reality 'absent in a pattern and present in a tea party?' From this it may be seen that, in spite of the chapter headings drawing attention to the formal properties of the novel, Virginia Woolf regarded *Aspects of the Novel* as typical of the 'unaesthetical' attitude that prevailed in English fiction and which would 'be thought strange in any of the other arts'. To understand her responses here we need to remember her admiration for the contribution made by Henry James and Turgenev to the 'art of the novel' and also her inordinate pride in Bloomsbury aesthetics. Bloomsbury, she believed, was a society 'alive as Cambridge had never been to the importance of the arts'. By contrast, Forster was altogether more sceptical towards Bloomsbury aesthetics and the art of the novel. 'This vague truth about life. Exactly. But what of the talk about art?', he asked Virginia Woolf in a letter. 'Each section leads to an exquisitely fashioned casket of which the key has unfortunately been mislaid and until you can find your bunch I shall cease to hunt very anxiously for my own' (Bell, 1972, II, p. 134). Many years later he summed up his own sceptical pragmatic approach:

> The novel, in my view, has not any rules, and there is no such thing as the art of fiction. There is only the particular art that each novelist employs in the execution of his particular book ('The Art of Fiction', 24 November 1944).

The chief interest of the first chapter of *Aspects* is that it brings out Forster's comparative lack of interest in narrative: 'Yes – oh dear yes – the novel tells a story.' And yet, of course, Forster is himself a brilliant story-teller. But depreciation of this element leads him to reduce Scott's stature to that of a mere entertainer. 'He could tell a story. He had the primitive power of keeping the reader in suspense and playing on his curiosity.' If that summed up the whole of Scott he would certainly not enjoy the acclaim he enjoys today. That Forster allots two chapters to 'People' is an accurate indication of the importance he attributes to character in fiction. In the first chapter on People he breaks new ground by drawing attention to how little of our lives actually gets into fiction. The five main facts of life (birth, food, sleep, love, and death) appear selectively or hardly at all. The brief impressionistic notes on this topic prove that Forster's view of life was not the simple one ascribed to him by Virginia Woolf; they are products of a mind that has brooded long over the contrast between 'Art' and 'Life', that has seen that the novelist's function is 'to reveal the hidden life at its source'. Indeed Forster had recognized as clearly as Virginia Woolf or James Joyce that, by modifications of convention and technique, much more might be achieved to render our experience vivid as we 'move between two darknesses', birth and death. Forster returns to the same 'unavoidable termini', at the end of the essay, 'What I Believe': 'The memory of birth and the expectation of death always lurk within the human being, making him separate from his fellows and consequently capable of intercourse with them' (TCD).

In the second of the chapters on 'People', Forster draws a distinction between 'flat' and 'round' characters. By the first he means Jonsonian, 'humours' characters, 'constructed round a single idea or quality', like Mrs Micawber, for example, with her repeated 'I never will desert Mr Micawber.' These have the advantages that they are easily recognized and easily remembered. By the second, 'round' characters, he means characters that are so fully developed that we can imagine how they would behave in circumstances not actually presented in the novel (this is not quite the Bradley, 'How Many Children had Lady Macbeth?' approach applied to the novel). 'Round' characters also have the 'capacity of surprising us in a convincing way'. This distinction has caught on and become part of the language of twentieth-century criticism. But it lacks precision, is less illuminating than the distinction between 'life on the page' and 'life eternal' made in the Rede lecture on Virginia Woolf, and can at best be regarded as a convenient piece of critical shorthand. In *Aspects*, 'flat' and 'round' are sometimes used as neutral terms to describe differences in technique and sometimes as evaluative terms to award praise or blame. In the first case it is Forster the fellow-novelist speaking, in the second it is Forster the critic. Here is one place where the two do not quite coincide.

It is true that in literary criticism, as opposed to science, definitions can never be more than a rough and ready convenience to facilitate communication. Most readers of *Aspects* probably respond gratefully to the simplicity of Forster's definition of 'Plot' as distinct from 'Story'. 'The king died and then the queen died' is a story; but 'The king died, and then the queen died of grief' is a plot. The time sequence is preserved, Forster remarks, but 'the sense of causality overshadows it.' Beautifully simple. Yet the distinction leads ultimately to curious results. It leads, for example, to a further definition of the plot as 'the novel in its logical intellectual aspect'. But what about the aesthetic patterning function of plot? Forster has little to say about this under the heading of 'Plot'. The reason is that he wants later to make a clear distinction between 'Pattern' (something mechanical and external that determines the shape of Anatole France's *Thaïs* and James's *The*

Ambassadors), and 'Rhythm' (something organic and internal, as in Proust, a process of 'repetition plus variation', and 'internal stitching'). Again, the definition of 'Fantasy' as a form of fiction that 'asks us to pay something extra', is too fanciful itself to take us very far, and the choice of Norman Matson's *Flecker's Magic* as a major exhibit marks a disastrous victory of fashion over sound judgment. It is in the sections on 'Prophecy' and 'Rhythm' that Forster rises to the height of his powers as a critic, combining lucid definitions with beautifully chosen examples. Here his sympathies were fully engaged and he was writing with half an eye on his own work, especially in developing his ideas on 'Rhythm'. The result is criticism of the very highest order. Three examples must suffice. The first comes from his account of Proust's use of rhythm

> . . . what we must admire is his use of rhythm in literature, and his use of something which is akin by nature to the effect it has to produce – namely a musical phrase. Heard by various people – first by Swann, then by the hero – the phrase of Vinteuil is not tethered: it is not a banner such as we find George Meredith using – a double-blossomed cherry tree to accompany Clara Middleton, a yacht in smooth waters for Cecilia Halkett. A banner can only reappear, rhythm can develop, and the little phrase has a life of its own, unconnected with the lives of its auditors, as with the life of the man who composed it. It is almost an actor, but not quite, and that 'not quite' means that its power has gone towards stitching Proust's book together from the inside, and towards the establishment of beauty and the ravishing of the reader's memory. There are times when the little phrase – from its gloomy inception, through the sonata, into the sextet – means everything to the reader. There are times when it means nothing and is forgotten, and this seems to me the function of rhythm in fiction; not to be there all the time like a pattern, but by its lovely waxing and waning to fill us with surprise and freshness and hope.

The second comes from his discussion of the 'prophetic' in Dostoevsky.

> Dostoevsky's characters ask us to share something deeper than their experiences. They convey to us a sensation that is partly physical – the sensation of sinking into a translucent globe and seeing our experience floating far above us on its surface, tiny,

remote, yet ours. We have not ceased to be people, we have given nothing up, but 'the sea is in the fish and the fish is in the sea' (AN, ch. 8 and cf. above, p. 105).

The third example comes from his discussion of Melville. Here he points out the importance of evil in Melville's moral vision and its relative absence in English fiction, a theme brilliantly developed by Angus Wilson many years later in a series of unscripted radio talks.

> It is to his conception of evil that Melville's work owes much of its strength. As a rule evil has been feebly envisaged in fiction, which seldom soars above misconduct or avoids the clouds of mysteriousness. Evil to most novelists is either sexual and social, or something very vague for which a special style with implications of poetry is thought suitable (ch. 7).

Aspects of the Novel has survived remarkably well and continues to be read when more scholarly discourses on the novel gather dust on the shelves. The reasons are not difficult to discover. It is alive on every page; it communicates the author's own enthusiasms; it whets the reader's appetite through apt quotations and skilful commentary, while never doing the reader's work for him, the usual fault of popular literary handbooks. It is genuinely popular without being vulgar. In the simplest possible manner it throws new light on old problems, and it contains original insights into the art of many major novelists, especially Emily Brontë, Melville, Dostoevsky, and D. H. Lawrence. His discriminating praise of two novelists as unlike each other as Jane Austen and Herman Melville illustrates the range of his imaginative sympathies; it also reminds us of his own extraordinary feat in assimilating characteristic features of both into his own art. The pages on Melville repay the closest attention. Here was a writer, Forster realized, who had 'not got that tiresome little receptacle, a conscience', who was therefore able – unlike Hawthorne, or say, Mark Rutherford – to reach 'straight back into the universal, to a blackness and sadness so transcending our own that they are indistinguishable from glory'. Is this not what Forster achieves in *A Passage to India* and in flashes in *The Longest Journey*? His continued admiration for Melville appears in his adaptation with Eric Crozier of Melville's short story *Billy Budd*, 'a remote unearthly episode', as a libretto for an opera by his friend and admirer Benjamin Britten. All three lived in the same house for a month; Forster and Crozier worked from a 'kind of skeleton synopsis', trying all the time to make the words flower into lyricism. 'I felt quite differently to what I have felt while writing other things,' remarked Forster, 'completely different. I was on a kind of voyage' (KCL). The idea of 'song' and a voyage into the unknown are the essential features of Forster's conception of Prophecy.

Aspects of the Novel is not without its faults. Forster brought to his task a mixed bag of likes and dislikes, of discriminating preferences and odd blind spots. His judgment of some major writers is consequently somewhat erratic. He is unfair to Scott, sees only the preacher in George Eliot, finds it difficult to be just to Meredith, his youthful idol, and he uses Henry James almost exclusively as an example of the sacrifice of 'Life' to 'Art', quoting Wells's brilliant but malicious account of the high altar of James's art ('and on the altar, very reverently placed, intensely there, is a dead kitten, an egg shell, a piece of string'), declaring that 'most of human life has to disappear' before James can do us a novel. Yet, notes for the lecture series in his Commonplace Book reveal a sympathetic insight into James's difficulties as a novelist – were they not his own? In these rough notes he considers evil in the English novel and claimants to 'Satanic intimacy', glances briefly at the 'Pan School', petering out in Hichens and E. F. Benson, and remarks perceptively that in *The Turn of the Screw*, Henry James 'is merely declining to think about homosex, and the knowledge that he is declining throws him into the necessary fluster.' It was a pity Forster's personal censor intervened before he actually gave the lectures, since this insight into James's creative psychology was startlingly original at the time.

There are two further weaknesses in *Aspects of the Novel*. Few of the definitions or distinctions, although they have passed into the language of criticism, will stand up to rigorous scrutiny. And ultimately the whole book throws as much light on Forster's own fiction as it does on the Art of the Novel, a point amply demonstrated by James McConkey in his application of the seven different 'Aspects' to Forster's own novels. Yet, with all its obvious limitations and weaknesses, it is a book one finds oneself returning to again and again and always with a sense of new discovery and fresh insight into some major novelist. This capacity to surprise and delight is the combined product of individual taste, personal integrity, and the inveterate habit of looking at life and art from unexpected angles. It is also the product of the crisp sensitive prose style. At a time when extravagant claims were being made in Cambridge for systematic and scientific criticism,

Aspects of the Novel struck a minor blow for the more personal, informal approach.

Forster's earliest writings reveal his gift for recreating the lives of neglected characters from the past. He is obviously attracted to minor figures caught up in major events, to genuine seekers after truth however muddled, to interesting failures rather than to dull successes, to those who have left behind them at least one work that still lives or can be brought to life again. The two essays, 'Gemistus Pletho' and 'Cardan', both published in the *Independent Review* in 1905, illustrate Forster's youthful skill in combining history and biography in a highly entertaining fashion; they also foreshadow his later success in raising the biography of the obscure into a fine art, as in *Marianne Thornton* (1956), and, to a lesser extent, in *Goldsworthy Lowes Dickinson* (1934), although perhaps Dickinson could not be labelled 'obscure' in 1934, since, by then, he had become well known through his work for the League of Nations and through broadcasting.

The essay on Georgius Gemistus recounts the story of this little-known philosopher who was born at Constantinople in 1355 and who spent his life in Greece, but for one important visit to Italy when he helped to found the Neo-Platonic Academy in Florence. What attracts Forster to Gemistus and Cardan, an obscure scientist, is the strange but very human gap between their dreams of truth and the absurd form these dreams often take. Thus, writing of Gemistus' ideal of reviving the religion of Greece by invoking the names of the Greek gods, Forster writes:

> These names had for him a mysterious virtue: he attached them like labels to his uninspiring scheme, while he rejected all that makes the gods immortal – their radiant visible beauty, their wonderful adventures, their capacity for happiness and laughter. That was as much as his dim, troubled surrounding allowed to him. If he is absurd, it is in a very touching way; his dream of antiquity is grotesque and incongruous, but it has a dream's intensity, and something of a dream's imperishable value (AH).

This was written when Forster himself was seeking to recapture the 'radiant visible beauty' of classical mythology, in his short stories and early novels. Throughout these two biographical vignettes, 'Gemistus Pletho' and 'Cardan', there is a delicate balance between sympathy and ironic detachment; a compassionate recognition, too, of the extent to which human beings are limited by their historical environment, by their 'troubled surroundings'. It is the quality of Forster's imaginative sympathy for human weakness and oddity and his refusal to extract easy laughter from the absurdities of the past that chiefly distinguish his biographical essays from those of Strachey. In this he is at one with Virginia Woolf in her biographical essays in *The Common Reader*. The ending of his account of the eccentric sixteenth-century Italian scientist, Cardan, brings out the essential difference between Forster's and Strachey's approach to biography.

> To raise up a skeleton, and make it dance, brings indeed little credit either to the skeleton or to us. But those ghosts who are still clothed with passion or thought are profitable companions. If we are to remember Cardan today let us not remember him as an oddity.

It is as an oddity that Dr Arnold appears, with his too short legs, in Strachey's brief biography, it is as an obsequious oddity that the poet Clough appears in his life of Florence Nightingale. What Forster looked for in biography and the study of the past were 'profitable companions' and not objects of ridicule or ironic contempt. In later years he certainly recognized that Strachey was 'much more than a debunker', that he did 'what no biographer had done before him: he managed to get inside his subject'. By comparison Forster's is a smaller achievement. He was not strongly drawn to biography as a literary form, and he made no startling innovations in technique; but he did write two fine biographies that reveal as much of their author as of their subject.

Goldsworthy Lowes Dickinson

It would have been easy for a less sympathetic biographer than Forster to present Goldsworthy Lowes Dickinson as an oddity, an incurable idealist with little grasp of the actual, an unworldly Cambridge don who thought he knew how to put the whole world to rights where the statesmen of the world had failed, a philosopher who was a prey to every eccentric scheme of thought, including psychical research, 'that dustbin of the spirit', in Forster's phrase. Certainly, in writing of Dickinson, he does not call him a 'modern saint', as he did the unworldly Maharajah of Dewas, in *The Hill of Devi*; but, in both cases, intimate friendship with the subject undoubtedly leads to some overvaluation. Sympathy outweighs detached judgment. Moreover, in the case of Dickinson, affection for the dead and respect for the living, together with a decorous reticence about sex, produce hesitant understatement that detracts from the truth of the biography. In the Preface, Forster states that he has not excluded facts about Dickinson's life with which he was out of sympathy or those 'which might be held to decrease his reputation'. He may not have excluded the hidden life entirely, but the reader needs peculiar skill to read the full story between the lines. In composing the biography, Forster drew heavily from the manuscript autobiography Dickinson had written during the last twelve years of his life, as well as on Dickinson's private correspondence and voluminous published works. The best known of these are *The Greek View of Life* (1896); *The Meaning of Good* (1901), which came out just after G. E. Moore's *Principia Ethica* and sent Forster's friend H. O. Meredith stalking along King's Parade chanting, 'you shall never take away from me my Meaning of the Good'; *Letters from John Chinaman* (1901), the most popular of Dickinson's works, to which Forster later wrote an Introduction; and *A Modern Symposium* (1905), a Socratic dialogue that accurately reflects the range of Edwardian political thought and comes closest to expressing Dickinson's faith through the person of Vivian, the Man of Letters. In addition to drawing on these books and unpublished materials, Forster also drew on a friendship that lasted for over thirty years. The two men were typical products of late-nineteenth-century Cambridge: they shared a common interest in classical culture, they both loved travel, were drawn to the East as a possible source of wisdom, shared a common passion for music and were both good amateur pianists (Forster even sketched out a study of Beethoven's piano sonatas that contains a moving passage on the Fall of France in 1940). After the publication of Dickinson's own autobiography in 1973, it is now, at last, possible to enter the biographer's workshop and witness at first hand Forster's process of selection, reduction, reshaping, and cautious omission.

In writing the early chapters of his biography, it is clear that Forster was working with Dickinson's manuscript autobiography on the desk before him. These chapters deal with Dickinson's family; his cherished memories of his boyhood home called The Spring Cottage; his snobbish first school, the prep school run by E. H. Coleridge, the grandson of the poet; his miserable experiences at his public school, Charterhouse; and his radiant happiness at Cambridge, a happiness similar to Forster's, and noted in the first chapter of this study. It was Dickinson's wish that the manuscript autobiography should not be published in its entirety, but used at his biographer's discretion, for he thought that there could be no question of publishing the frank passages of sexual confession. However, Forster carried out this wish with even greater strictness than was probably intended. Throughout his biography of his friend, Forster keeps close to the original manuscript, lifting whole phrases and sentences when they are especially vivid and reproducing long passages from it. But he either omits altogether or reduces to cryptic understatement Dickinson's frank accounts of his sexual development, his worship of his father, his boot fetishism, and his homosexual relations with Roger Fry, Ferdinand Schiller, and others.

In the manuscript autobiography, Dickinson gives a long and detailed account of the origin of his particular fetish, rejecting psycho-analysis as a possible cure ('I have no curiosity to try that method'), but nevertheless exhibiting frank intellectual curiosity about himself.

It was, and it still is, from this earliest time, boots rather than feet, and polished boots that moved my feelings. And still I have the most curious taste in this matter, and am attracted by some kinds of boots and shoes and repelled by others. Like all forms of fetishism this seems to me odd and unaccountable (Proctor, 1973, p. 43).

Of all this, Forster says nothing directly. And his treatment of Dickinson's love for Roger Fry is the epitome of understatement. In the manuscript autobiography, Dickinson describes

going one night into Roger's bedroom to say good night, and stooping down to kiss his forehead. This was a decisive moment. I went back to my lodgings strangely excited, lay awake reading (I think, Heine's *Reisenbilder*), and said to myself 'I must be in love'. From that time I grew more and more intimate with him (Proctor, 1973, p. 90).

In his biography, Forster simply refers to Dickinson's affection for his Cambridge friends, J. E. M. McTaggart, Wedd, and Fry; and notes that Dickinson's relationship with Fry soon became profound and that they 'lunched and breakfasted together every day', in the academic year 1887–8. This reticence throws some light on his later unwillingness to write the official biography of Roger Fry, a task undertaken by Virginia Woolf in his stead. In dealing with the early episodes in Dickinson's life, it is true that Forster speaks of the gloom that was

increased in Dickinson's boyhood by a prep-school master's 'attempts
to deal with what were still termed "the mysteries of sex"'; moreover
he relates with decorous omissions some of the more amusing episodes
in his sexual development; but he fails almost entirely to convey
Dickinson's capacity for strong passion and pain, the intensity of his
sufferings, his determination to be honest about sex.

In the first chapter of the manuscript autobiography, Dickinson
writes,

> In the midst of these early recollections, there stand out certain
> experiences of sex. And as they were important for my later life,
> I shall speak of them. For it is the object, in these reminiscences,
> to tell what is usually not told. I am, I think, almost entirely free
> from false shame, and the absurd kind of moral judgments
> current on these subjects (Proctor, 1973, p. 43).

His biographer, writing for publication, and not for himself, as in
Maurice and the homosexual short stories, did not feel equally free.
This is understandable, but what is less understandable is Forster's
failure to follow up this important clue to Dickinson's whole development and see its relevance to the man and his works. It seems strange
that someone as sensitive as Forster to the workings of the unconscious
and the influence of sex on the development of the whole personality
should have benefited so little from the evidence provided by the
Dickinson manuscript. Did he wish to spare Dickinson's relations?
Was he afraid of shocking his own mother, who was always a potent
inhibiting force? Or did he mainly fear that the biography might be
censored by his publishers or banned after publication? Was the reason
for the suppression altogether more personal in origin? The latter
probably. Although sexually unorthodox himself, Forster probably
found the accounts of fetishism embarrassingly absurd, while Dickinson's love of men came too close to that part of his own life that he
had decided must remain hidden from the reading public. What, for
example, did he think of Dickinson's distaste at the 'sex-rut' aboard a
cargo ship to America, and the self-knowledge shown in Dickinson's
comment 'To me having the homosexual temperament, it always
requires a slight effort not to be repelled by the spectacle of sex passion
between men and women.' He omitted it. But did he see its relevance
to his own fiction?

Given the state of public opinion in the early 1930s, and that all the
men in Dickinson's life were still alive, Forster could make little direct

use of the four chapters (chs 7–10) that recorded the 'curious, passionate, unhappy, ecstatic story' of Dickinson's love for Roger Fry, Ferdinand Schiller, Oscar Eckhard, Peter Savary, and Dennis Proctor. This was unfortunate, since there was an obvious connection between Dickinson's private agony and his desire to alleviate the sufferings of humanity. 'The pain becomes almost unbearable', he writes of his unrequited love in the manuscript autobiography, 'and I can only stave it off by plunging into some kind of work, which yet must bear upon it.' This statement, which Forster neither quotes nor builds on, throws a quite different light on what lay behind Dickinson's busy life as a writer, public speaker, propagandist for the League of Nations, broadcaster, and tireless world traveller. In his work he sought to escape his private anguish and assuage the agony of the world.

How well does Forster's biography convey the quality of Dickinson's work and thought? The answer is, surprisingly well, considering that he felt out of sympathy with many aspects of it, especially the wishy-washy social idealism and the crankiness over psychical research. His praise of *The Greek View of Life* is sound and judicious: it 'might be called an introduction to translations. It is an attempt to show the non-expert the character and environment of hidden treasures and leave him among them.' He notes perceptively that, when three years later the idea of a series of dialogues came to Dickinson in Greece, the dialogue form 'exactly suited his genius'. But he also notes that none of his speakers is ever female, that 'his people are always sedentary, and the appeal to reason, however much they may ignore it, hangs like a sword over their heads.' Dickinson, unlike Forster, made too little allowance for the non-rational in human conduct. It is this, among other things, that gives almost all Dickinson's writing an air of remoteness and unreality. His ideas would work only in a world of fellow idealists.

At the turn of the century Forster shared Dickinson's faith in a revitalized Liberalism. Consequently, in the biography, he speaks with real warmth of the great days of the *Independent Review*, when Dickinson was a founder member of the editorial board. The review, Forster writes, was

founded to combat the aggressive Imperialism and the Protection campaign of Joe Chamberlain; and to advocate sanity in foreign affairs and a constructive policy at home. It was not so much a Liberal review as an appeal to Liberalism from the Left to be its better self. . . . The first number lies on the table as I write: as fresh and attractive to hold as when I bought it on a bookstall at St Pancras thirty years back, and thought the new age had begun (GLD, pp. 115–16).

Such high hopes could not survive the First World War, and both men turned from the Liberal to the Labour Party, although neither was ever a party man. Dickinson directed his idealism into popularizing the idea of a League of Nations. In spite of setbacks, misunderstandings, hostile criticism, and personal sorrow, he worked tirelessly for world peace. Forster, more sceptical, took no part in this campaign. Consequently, his account of this phase of Dickinson's life is less coloured with the warmth of personal reminiscence than many others. Of special interest is Forster's description of the visit the two men made to India in 1912, since this does not depend on the brief section in the manuscript autobiography, but is largely based on Forster's own memories. It thus fills out the picture of Forster's experience during this crucial first visit. In an anecdote about Dickinson's warm reception in the Mess of the Royal West Kent Regiment, we notice Forster's tendency to find a 'touchstone' of reality in other people on too slender evidence.

They made him swallow prairie oysters. They got rather drunk, in exquisite style, while Bob Trevelyan sported with them, and Dickinson and the C.O. sat apart, a couple of benign but contrasted uncles. Looking back to that jolly evening, I see him then for the first time as a solid figure, who has won his own place in the world, and holds it firmly. This is the time when I begin to use him as a touchstone, and to condemn those who fail to appreciate him (GLD, p. 138).

For both men, but especially for Dickinson, the power of religion in India came as a revelation. They differed fundamentally, however, over the issue of whether it was possible for Englishmen and Indians to be friends. Forster firmly dissented from the kind of view Dickinson expressed in a letter to H. O. Meredith. 'And why can't the races meet? Simply because the Indians *bore* the English. *That* is the simple adamantine fact.'

In later life, Dickinson felt that he had lived in vain, that he had never been loved by anyone, and that all his high hopes for mankind had come to nothing. Yet his own tribute to the brilliant young economist and mathematician, F. P. Ramsey, who died when he was twenty-seven, might appropriately have been applied to himself. There is a certain type, he wrote,

> unworldly without being saintly, unambitious without being inactive, warmhearted without being sentimental. Through good report and ill such men work on, following the light of truth as they see it; able to be sceptical without being paralyzed, content to know what is knowable and to reserve judgment on what is not. The world could never be driven by such men, for the springs of action lie deep in ignorance and madness. But it is they who are the beacon in the tempest, and they are more, not less, needed now than ever before. May their succession never fail.

In his summing up of Dickinson, Forster returns to one of the themes of all his early fiction, the theme of salvation, but here defined in strictly practical terms.

> What he cared for was love and truth. What he hoped for was a change in the human heart. He did not see how the civilization which he had tried to help could be saved unless the human heart changed, and he meant by 'saved' not some vague apotheosis but salvation from aerial bombing and poison gas (GLD, p. 200).

Ultimately, Forster himself came to reject the idea of a change of heart. Instead he placed his faith in the possibility of finding better means to organize the existing good. Here, then, is the essential difference between Forster's tough-minded humanism and Dickinson's gentler old-world liberalism. Thus, in writing the biography of Dickinson, Forster was in part reviewing the traditions from which he himself had sprung. He emerged strengthened and better equipped to understand the full horror of the rise of the totalitarian state in Europe.

Marianne Thornton

Forster's biography of his great-aunt Marianne Thornton is an act of family piety. It was a means of repaying his immense debt of gratitude to the person who alone made his life as a writer possible. Before beginning work on it, he had already paid his tribute to his Thornton ancestors in a number of essays. In 'Battersea Rise', he had sketched briefly the life of his great-grandfather Henry Thornton at the house Battersea Rise, together with his connections with the Clapham Sect

(AH). In two essays in *Two Cheers for Democracy*, 'Bishops Jebb's Book', and 'Henry Thornton', he had filled in further details, and analysed more carefully the characteristic strengths and weaknesses of the family and the Sect: their practical philanthropy and sober devotion offset as it was by their insensitivity to 'poetry, mystery, ecstasy, music'. But Forster had inherited a vast collection of Thornton documents, including journals and letters, now in King's College Library. In these the whole ethos of a past age came vividly alive; moreover, the character of his great-aunt cried out to be given some kind of extended life, if not literary immortality; and so he decided to write her biography, which involved, in part, an imaginative return to the female-dominated world of his boyhood. A number of years before he had declined to write the biography of his great friend Roger Fry, and he had abandoned the plan of editing a volume of T. E. Lawrence's letters, because of possible libel actions. Although he felt no strong attraction towards biography, he threw himself happily into the task of writing the life of his great-aunt. The work has three kinds of related interest. It is worth reading for the extraordinary personality of Marianne Thornton, for the 'pageant' of Victorian domestic life it presents, and for the valuable autobiographical chapters with which it concludes. As a 'domestic biography', it can be read with enjoyment by readers who know nothing of Forster or his works; but for most readers its chief interest will always lie in the extent to which it helps to complete our knowledge of the novelist.

In view of Forster's idea that the dead enjoy a special kind of immortality in the memories of the living, it is illuminating to read that at the centre of the Thornton creed lay an 'unshakeable belief' in immortality. However, where their belief rested on an idea of a future life in which the members of the household would meet each other and recognize each other and 'be happy eternally', Forster's own belief is altogether less materialistic and anthropomorphic, concerned as it is with immaterial presences, voice, and memory.

He sees with absolute clarity the limits of Thornton philanthropy and humanitarianism. Marianne's parents would do anything to remove slavery abroad, yet 'When the slavery was industrial they did nothing and had no thought of doing anything; they regarded it as something "natural", to encounter it was an educational experience, and an opportunity for smug thankfulness' (MT, p. 54). While he does not share the moral indignation of many modern historians in their analysis of the one-sidedness of the Clapham Sect, he agrees with the truth of the analysis, adding, however, the characteristic comment: 'The really bad people, it seems to me, are those who do no good anywhere and help no-one either at home or abroad.'

His great-aunt Marianne did not share her father's complete lack of imagination, although she did regard imagination 'as dangerous because it makes us behave in an unreal way'. The great landmark in her life was her visit to Paris and she insisted that Forster's mother should go there after her marriage to Eddie, her favourite nephew. Marianne travelled to Paris under the wing of her guardian, Sir Robert Inglis, stern defender of the English Church, whose portraits so oppressed Forster's youth that when, later, two came into his possession, he 'took one of them out of its frame, tore it into small pieces, and burnt them in the kitchen range. Duplicates of Sir Robert were too much' (MT, p. 75). But even with so stern a guardian, Marianne enjoyed herself in Paris; it made her gayer and more affectionate. No doubt remembering what travel had meant to himself as a young man, Forster describes Marianne's visit to Paris as a 'heartening vindication of the importance of foreign travel' (p. 95).

Forster does not entirely escape the obvious pitfalls in writing a domestic biography of an insignificant Victorian lady. The first is the inclusion of too much trivial detail; we are reminded that there is more in Jane Austen than the tinkle of the tea-cups. The second is the failure to provide any sense of pattern or development. Of his subject, Forster observes: 'She is so lively and so sociable that one is in danger of becoming desultory about her, and losing the mainstream of her domestic life.' But in fact her life was too uneventful for there to be any sense of a 'main stream'. A third pitfall lies in reproducing material that has become a family legend, but which cannot withstand a more dispassionate gaze. On the whole, Forster avoids this, having suffered enough in boyhood anyway. For example, of one of Marianne's letters that had achieved great prestige in the family he comments ironically: 'It was read aloud to me as a boy and I was told it was the most amusing letter Marianne ever wrote. I would not advance that claim for it.' The fourth pitfall is to exaggerate the importance of certain domestic crises in order to create dramatic highlights. Marianne's disappointment at losing her cherished home is rightly stressed because it gives a mythic stature to her life as a custodian of tradition. But there is certainly a sense of strain in the emphasis placed on the crisis that the younger Henry Thornton's love for his deceased wife's sister caused in the family. Until 1907 the English law forbade such a marriage. Although the incident cannot quite bear the stress it is given, the chapter 'Deceased Wife's Sister' does bring out Marianne's statesmanlike qualities in a family crisis: 'She would push nothing to a conclusion even in her mind.' This section, then, does much to counterbalance the image of her as a wilful domestic tyrant, so that she emerges finally 'as a heroine of the war against panic and emptiness, to stand besides Mrs Wilcox and Mrs Moore' (Ronald Bryden, in Gardner, 1973, p. 423).

When Forster was born, in 1879, his great-aunt was eighty-two. She died when he was eight. In those eight years she imposed her strong will on almost every detail of his family life. Her kindness to his widowed mother turned into domestic bullying. 'Melancholy to relate, in a few years my mother was saying "Monie is a very wicked woman".' After the death of his father, Forster became Marianne Thornton's favourite, 'The Important One', and she overwhelmed him with expensive gifts. It is from the last chapters of *Marianne Thornton* that we get most of the details of the first fourteen years of Forster's life, details that have already been drawn on in the first chapter of this study. Even if the biography is read for no other reason it will continue to be consulted for these reminiscences of the author's early life.

The biography is linked to Forster's other works most obviously by the vision of continuity within a pattern of change. 'We are allowed to see the Tradition from which he escaped, by which he is still held.'

10

Essays, Lectures, and Broadcasts

Forster's essays contain many of the qualities that establish his novels as modern classics. There is a similar combination of imaginative insight and ironic detachment, a similar fidelity to the complexity of human experience, a similar integrity of language. During his lifetime the novelist made two collections: *Abinger Harvest* (1936), which brings together essays written between 1903 and 1936; and *Two Cheers for Democracy* (1951), which contains prose written between 1936 and 1951, together with three earlier pieces not included in the earlier collection. The title of the first volume was prompted by the name of the village where many of the essays in the first collections were written; and it ends fittingly with 'The Abinger Pageant', for which Vaughan Williams wrote the music. The title of the second, suggested jokingly by a young friend, epitomizes Forster's qualified enthusiasm for popular liberal ideals. The two volumes do not include all Forster's occasional prose however. They omit all his undergraduate journalism; they include only one *Egyptian Mail* essay, 'The Scallies', and give an inadequate impression of his range and skill as a broadcaster. Not much is lost by the first two omissions, as may be seen from published selections made in 1971 by G. W. Thomson. But the omission of much of the broadcast material is another matter. Two typescript volumes, containing talks given over the radio between 1930 and 1960, now in King's College, Cambridge, throw new light on Forster's collected prose and exhibit his mastery of the spoken word.

The comparatively late date of *Abinger Harvest* and *Two Cheers for Democracy* might suggest that Forster's career as an essayist began when he ceased to publish fiction in 1924, but this is not the case. Several of the essays in *Abinger Harvest* were first published in the *Independent Review* as early as 1903–5; they were therefore contemporary with his early short stories and novels. The truth is that, from his undergraduate days almost until his death, Forster turned naturally to the essay as a congenial form in which to express his views on life and art. Since the essays span the whole of his life, they provide a critical perspective on what he called 'the sinister corridor of our age'.

Abinger Harvest

The fact that certain favourite themes recur in *Abinger Harvest* gives it a coherence that similar collections of essays usually lack. Moreover, through what has been called the 'Art of Rearrangement', Forster has ordered the pieces within the main section to achieve 'a genuine continuity, a unity of attitude, a permanence of tone' (Joseph, 1964, p. 131). It thus contains something of the diversity and the internal stitching of Forster's fiction.

> With as much variety as the novels, *Abinger Harvest* is also concerned with the Englishman's sense of separation and apartness. It, too, examines the English character from different points of view, and, after sections devoted to the present, to books, to the past, and to the East, Forster returns in the fifth section to Abinger, for it, like each of the novels, has roots in the soil of England (Joseph, 1964, p. 7).

A brief glance at the contents of *Abinger Harvest* immediately reveals this connection with the fiction, while closer study discloses a satisfying internal coherence. In reading the collection for the first time, however, one is more aware of the diversity than the underlying unity. But it is undoubtedly there, and imparts additional significance to the individual items and to the collection as a whole.

Appropriately enough, the first part of the collection, 'The Present', begins with Forster's 'Notes on the English Character' and ends with 'Liberty in England', an address that he gave to the International Congress of Writers, in Paris, in 1935. The general argument of the 'Notes' – fully illustrated in the novels – is that 'the Englishman is an incomplete person.' His failure to connect, resulting in hypocrisy and prudery, is then illustrated in the ensuing essays from a number of odd and unexpected angles, culminating in the accusation, in 'Liberty in England', that the Englishman's traditional love of freedom is only partial, because it is both 'race-bound' and 'class-bound'. Yet, for Forster, the most insidious enemy of liberty in England is neither class nor race, but 'the dictator spirit working quietly away behind the façade of constitutional forms', imposing political and psychological censorship. He was to develop the full political implications of this in *Two Cheers for Democracy*. In the essays and talks in *Abinger Harvest*, he was more concerned with the conscience and psychology of the writer and with the state of post-war culture in the 1920s and 1930s. Certainly, his protest at the Paris Congress that 'creative work is hampered' in England, because writers 'can't write freely about sex', illustrates this fact. Today the emphasis assumes a new significance in the light of what we know about the damaging effect of censorship on Forster himself. In pursuance of a saner attitude towards sexuality in literature, he seized every opportunity to protest against the principle of censorship and must have been especially disappointed when Bernard Shaw of all people declined his invitation to appear as a witness for the defence in the trial of Radclyffe Hall's *The Well of Loneliness* in 1928. Many years later, Forster was one of the prominent witnesses for the defence in the famous *Lady Chatterley's Lover* trial.

The cool savage irony of the essays in the first part of *Abinger Harvest* suggests that the First World War and its aftermath opened Forster's eyes to the gross fatuities of England's class system and the ineffable complacency of its ruling caste. In a talk to the Weybridge Literary Society on 'Literature and the War [1914–18]', he praised literature's power to rise above the wartime spirit of fear and hatred, its power to demonstrate 'that beauty and truth and goodness exist apart from the Tribe.' In many of his published writings after the war, it was the failings of his own tribe that he chiefly attacked. The third piece in *Abinger Harvest* is an attack on a bishop who, in 1926, had written to *The Times* to censure the profanity of members of the Labour Party. It takes the form of a piece of lively doggerel verse, first published in the *New Leader*.

It is different for me. I have earned the right,
Through position and birth to be impolite . . .
I can bully or patronize, just which I please;
I am different to them. . . . But those Labour M.P.'s
How *dare* they be rude?

A visit to the Royal Academy in 1926 to see the paintings of the fashionable portrait painter Sargent provides the occasion for extending the attack on the self-righteousness and hypocrisy of the ruling classes in England. The modest, self-deprecating opening, 'I have a suit of clothes. It does not fit', forms a bland introduction to the caustic attack on the rich, the successful, the well-born, whose portraits in splendid clothes hang on the walls. They are the 'Them' of the title of the essay, 'Me, Them and You'.

> The portraits dominated. Gazing at each other over our heads, they said, 'What would the country do without us? We have got the decorations and the pearls, we make fashions and wars, we have the largest houses and eat the best food, and control the most important industries, and breed the most valuable children, and ours is the Kingdom and the Power and the Glory.'

Here is the 'voice' of the unredeemed Wilcoxes who have survived the war and now 'inherit' England. The 'You' of the title refers to the figures in the largest painting of all, entitled 'Gassed', which unconsciously epitomizes the ruling caste's polite and hypocritical escape from reality, its habit of casting a spurious romance over everything.

> You were of godlike beauty – for the upper classes only allow the lower classes to appear in art on condition that they wash themselves and have classical features. These conditions you fulfilled. A line of golden-haired Apollos moved along a duck-board from left to right with bandages over their eyes. They had been blinded by mustard gas. . . . No one complained, no one looked lousy or over-tired, and the aeroplanes overhead struck the necessary note of the majesty of England.

This bitter essay and the dialogue written in 1922 between the dead British soldier and the dead Turkish soldier, in 'Our Graves in Gallipoli', with its ironic references to 'Lloyd George, prudent in counsels' and 'lion-hearted Churchill', and its attack on false heroics ('Nothing for schools, nothing for houses, nothing for the life of the body, nothing for the spirit. England cannot spare anything except for heroes' graves'), makes it a matter of regret that Forster never published a post-war political novel.

'Me, Them and You', like the seven pieces under the heading, 'Our Diversions', reveals Forster's capacity to judge a whole culture as it gives itself away in its art and popular pastimes. He does more lightly what Orwell did so portentously in his essays on boys' comics and the vulgar seaside picture-postcards of Donald McGill. One of the best illustrations is his account of a visit to the Queen's Dolls' House at the

Empire Exhibition. The essay, 'The Doll Souse', exposes the unreality of imperialism, the sheeplike mentality of the public as it files through the turnstiles, and the absolute nullity of the royal exhibit: 'the apotheosis of non-being'. The recurrent undertone to all the essays in the first part of *Abinger Harvest* is the belief that the gulf between 'Them' and 'You' must be bridged. Yet how? Forster can offer no positive solution. But he takes comfort in the liberal idea that there is in everyone the dream of some 'magical island', and that this may help to 'bring humanity's dream closer to fruition'. One must behave 'as if one is immortal, and as if civilization is eternal', and thus keep 'open a few breathing holes for the human spirit.'

One way of keeping open such breathing holes is through reading the great writers of the past and the best works of one's contemporaries. In a Prefatory Note to the second part of *Abinger Harvest*, 'Books', Forster restates, in a form acceptable to modern sensibilities, Matthew Arnold's faith in literature's power to 'prop' the mind. The help comes neither directly nor automatically, as Mr Pembroke in *The Longest Journey* believed. 'The arts are not drugs. They are not guaranteed to act when taken. Something as mysterious and as capricious as the creative impulse has to be released before they can prop our minds.' At Lahore, Forster warned Indian students not to read literature to increase their own importance or to feed their vanity, but to read it because 'a book is really talk, glorified talk' – 'you must read it with the knowledge that the writer is talking to you' ('The Enjoyment of Literature', a paper read to B A and M A classes, 3 March 1913, KCL). In selecting items for inclusion in this section of *Abinger Harvest*, Forster concentrates on writers who speak with an individual voice (Forrest Reid, Ibsen, Proust, Conrad), writers who lift the spirit through their belief in personal integrity, who have faith in their craft. The possession of these qualities links such dissimilar writers as Jane Austen and Ronald Firbank.

The essays on Ibsen, T. S. Eliot, Proust, and Virginia Woolf are all in some way concerned with the modern artist's task of creating a new medium to render contemporary consciousness. Ibsen and Virginia Woolf have a special interest, for in both the poet and the realist struggled for mastery, as they did in Forster himself. He draws attention to the 'subterranean' quality in Ibsen, to his 'impassioned vision' of 'dead and damaged things', the way people and objects in Ibsen's realistic settings are 'watched by an unseen power which slips between their words' – all qualities found in Forster's own fiction. He praises

Virginia Woolf's courage in trying 'to advance the novelist's art' through poetry and vision and believes that if only she could retain her own wonderful new method and form and yet 'allow her readers to inhabit each character with a Victorian thoroughness', she would inaugurate a new literature. His final verdict in the Rede Lecture of 1941, that she was 'a poet' who wanted 'to write something as near a novel as possible' and who could not create in any character 'life eternal', suggests no radical change of mind since the 1925 judgment on the early novels. In T. S. Eliot he sees a major interpreter of the age. But he makes two qualifications in the 1928 essay that once seemed erratic, yet these the subsequent publication of the manuscripts of *The Waste Land* have confirmed. He sees that, for all Eliot's prescriptive talk of tradition and order, *The Waste Land* is as much 'a personal comment on the universe as Shelley's *Prometheus*'; he also sees that the stress placed on tradition was partly 'a case of an American romanticising the land of his adoption'. In general, Forster is not easily taken in by fashionable opinion; he excels in entering a quietly worded minority report. How refreshing it is to read that Conrad 'is misty in the middle as well as at the edge' and how welcome to have the question of his obscurity raised so pertinently: 'Is there not also a central obscurity, something noble, heroic, beautiful, inspiring half a dozen books; but obscure, obscure?'

The third part of *Abinger Harvest*, 'The Past', begins with a warning against the false consolations of history, especially against the illusory comforts that pity and condescension bring. Forster himself is rarely guilty of patronizing the past. The evocations of historic people and places in 'Macolnia Shops', 'Cnidus', 'Gemistus Pletho', and 'Cardan' – all written about 1903–5 – have the same consciously achieved balance between imaginative sympathy and ironic detachment that appears in his fiction. 'Macolnia Shops', a charming essay that describes a beautiful bronze toilet-case bought by a wealthy Roman matron, Dindia Macolnia, for her daughter, contrasts the poetic figures on the case with the down-to-earth motives of the purchaser. The figures tell the story of the punishment of Amycus by Pollux. When the Argonauts asked for water on landing they were refused by Amycus, who was then bound to a tree by Pollux, the boxer. For the essayist the minor figures in the design celebrate the praise of water and the praise of friendship. In expanding this interpretation, he responds to the 'perfect physical bliss' of the male figures who have filled their jars and, 'having reached the goal of their desire', find 'its happiness not illusory'. The scene becomes for Forster a celebration of the wisdom of the body: 'cherish the body and you will cherish the soul. That was the belief of the Greeks.' The second theme, the praise of friendship, has an even greater imaginative appeal to the writer. Two figures represent the ideal of 'comradeship', 'standing together, leaning on their spears, with the knowledge that they have passed through one more labour in company'; clearly they are classical analogues of the later Maurice and Alec. Finally, as a sceptical corrective to this exercise in Keatsian empathy with the figures on the case, comes Macolnia's imagined retort. 'Praise of Water! Praise of Friendship! . . . I bought the thing because it was pretty, and stood nicely on the chest of drawers.'

Empathy and ironic detachment also interact in the essay 'Cnidus', an atmospheric account of a visit to the site of the Cnidian Demeter. The party arrives at the wrong place in heavy dropping rain. All that could be heard was the 'rapture of competent observers, who had discovered that the iron clamps were those used in classical times, and that we were straining our ankles over masonry of the best period.' But of Cnidus Forster could see nothing

> for the land was only an outline, and the sea ran into the sky.
> And who would expect visions from a dripping silhouette, when,
> time after time, the imagination has dwelt in vain desire amidst
> sun and blue sky and perfect colonnades, and found in them
> nothing but colonnades and sky and sun? But, that evening, under
> these weeping clouds, the imagination became creative, taking
> wings because there was nothing to bid it rise, flying impertinently
> against all archaeology and sense, uttering bird-like cries of
> 'Greek! Greek!' as it flew, declaring that it heard voices because
> all was so silent, and saw faces because it was too dark to see.
> I am ashamed of its outbreak, and will confine myself to facts,
> such as they are.

From the hasty visit, spoilt by bad weather and rendered absurd by the incongruity between the trivial present and the hallowed past, two episodes stand out: the sight of the ruined site of the Cnidian Demeter, and the mystery of the extra person who entered the boat on the return. The first prompts an ironic reflection on the contrast between the Cnidian Demeter's original home and her present site in the British Museum, where she is 'dusted twice a week, and there is a railing in front, with "No Admittance".' It also produces a profound meditation on Demeter's universal appeal, a theme more personally explored through the imagery of *The Longest Journey*. The second episode concerning the mysterious stranger gives us an insight into the kind of experience that inspired Forster's early short stories.

> It is well known (is it not?) who that extra person always is. This time he came hurrying down to the beach at the last moment, and tried to peer into our faces. I could hardly see his; but it was young, and it did not look unkind. He made no answer to our tremulous greetings, but raised his hand to his head and then laid it across his breast, meaning I understand, that his brain and his heart were ours. Everyone made clumsy imitations of his gesture to keep him in a good temper. His manners were perfect. I am not sure that he did not offer to lift people into the boats. But there was a general tendency to avoid his attentions, and we put off in an incredibly short space of time. He melted away in the darkness after a couple of strokes, and we before long were back on the steamer, amid light, and the smell of hot meat, and the pity and self-congratulations of those who had been wise enough to stop on board.

In the essays that follow Forster turns from the world of his early travels and classical studies to a more recent past inhabited by such figures as Voltaire, Gibbon, Coleridge, Keats, and Mrs Hannah More. The two essays on Voltaire become a vehicle for warning the reader against patronizing the past, but also for saying important things about the literary man's interest in science. After recreating the atmosphere of Cirey, the great house where Voltaire and Madame du Chatelet, both indefatigable inquirers after truth, pursued their curious researches, Forster warns: 'We find them funny because we know more, but if we patronize them for not knowing more it is we who become funny.' Limited by the scientific knowledge of his day and by personal temperament, Voltaire nevertheless 'did science one good turn: he impressed the general public with her importance. This is all that a literary man can do for science, and perhaps only a literary man can do it.' He thus takes his place in a long tradition stretching from Lucretius to Samuel Butler, Aldous Huxley, and Gerald Heard, and 'must be honoured as an early popularizer.' The judgment made in the 1931 essay that Voltaire loved freedom above all things explains why ten years later Forster hailed him as 'the complete anti-Nazi', 'two hundred years before the Nazis came', one of the two people he would name to speak for Europe at the Last Judgment.

The essay on the English Voltaire, Gibbon, characteristically focuses on a neglected aspect of Gibbon's life. It reveals what the eminent historian gained from 'three apparently wasted years in the militia'. This essay and the two essays that follow on Coleridge and Keats exhibit Forster's natural inclination to look at the great from an oblique angle and also his favourite and somewhat overworked device of hiding the identity of his subject until the end. Both devices work better in the Keats than in the Coleridge essay, which is flawed by a kind of knowing whimsy. In 'Mr and Mrs Abbey's Difficulties', Forster continues his critique of the characteristic weaknesses of the English middle class by presenting a view of Keats through the eyes of his obtuse materialistic guardian, Mr Abbey, who failed to recognize the young poet's genius, as in another context Mr Pembroke saw only misapplied talents in Rickie's short stories. Finally the whole section of 'The Past' ends with two very personal pieces, a brilliant evocation of the busy philanthropy of Hannah More, a godmother of the author's great-aunt, and a nostalgic but shrewd account of the life led by the Thornton family and the Clapham Sect at Battersea Rise. Both essays glance affectionately but perceptively at the blind spots of Forster's Thornton ancestors and their circle: their inveterate distrust of pleasure and their failure to recognize the importance of emotion and imagination. The existence of the undeveloped heart and the failure to connect within his own family tradition undoubtedly gave a special urgency to his attempt to analyse these limitations in the English middle classes and to transcend them.

In India, we are reminded in the final section of *Abinger Harvest*, people do not believe in 'weighing' their emotions. For Forster, the Orient clearly provided a corrective to the limitations of the Western tradition, and the miscellaneous essays grouped under the heading 'The East' all in some way pay tribute to this alternative way of life. The conclusion to 'Salute to the Orient' (1923) has an obvious bearing on *A Passage to India* and on one of the master themes of Forster's fiction.

So if we say of the Oriental, firstly, that personal relationship is most important to him, secondly, that it has no transcendental sanction, we shall come as near to a generalization as is safe, and then it will only be safe in the nearer East. Farther afield, in Persia and India, another idea, that of Union with God, becomes prominent, and the human outlook is altered accordingly.

Again, the essay on the Mosque at Woking links up with the theme of memory in the Indian novel. The suggestion that a Mosque 'attaches no sanctity to it beyond what is conferred by the presence of the devout' offers a useful key to the natural reverence that unites Aziz and Mrs Moore when they encounter each other at the mosque at Chandrapore. Even the characteristic Western vices achieve a kind of nobility in the East. Heroic action leads not to shoddy imperialism but to the three reasons given in the Bhagavad-Gita why Arjuna must fight: because death is negligible, because it is the soldier's duty, because he will renounce the fruits of victory and by renouncing them 'attain to eternal peace'. Yet, there is obviously much that bewilders and repels Forster in India, as these essays in *Abinger Harvest* make clear: 'there is scarcely anything in that tormented land which fills up the gulf between the illimitable and the inane, and society suffers in consequence. What isn't piety is apt to be indecency, what isn't metaphysics is intrigue.' Whereas in Europe the continuity of past and present seems to give some hope for the future, in India 'the hand of the past divides the rulers when they attempt to discuss the present.' In spite of such differences, it is nevertheless the sense of the past, awareness of the continuity of tradition, and a special feeling for a way of life in harmony with the natural rhythms of the earth that links Forster's understanding of India and England. The reason why the Prince of an Independent Indian State still commands the loyalty of his people, according to Forster, is that 'like them he is rooted in the soil'. The 'Pageant', with which *Abinger Harvest* closes, offers a view of the English people rooted in the soil from earliest time as a valid alternative to the England of 'hotels, restaurants and flats, arterial roads, by-passes, petrol pumps and pylons'. The Woodman, who speaks the Epilogue, asks the audience if these are to be man's final triumphs.

> Look into your hearts and look into the past, and remember that all this beauty is a gift which you can never replace, which no money can buy, which no cleverness can refashion. You can make a town, you can make a desert, you can even make a garden; but you can never, never make a country, because it was made by Time.

The appeal has lost none of its urgency with the passage of the years. Ultimately the qualities that guarantee the survival of *Abinger Harvest* as a collection of essays are the author's profound understanding of the contradictions and paradoxes in the English and Indian traditions, his obvious integrity, and the complete absence of any falsity or over-emphasis.

Two Cheers for Democracy

Two Cheers for Democracy, like *Abinger Harvest*, is a carefully composed volume not a random collection of essays. In the Prefatory Note, Forster explains that a chronological arrangement would have been simpler but that he was 'anxious to produce a book rather than a time-string, and to impose some sort of order upon the occupations and preoccupations, the appointments and disappointments, of the past fifteen years.' There are two main sections, 'Part 1 The Second Darkness' and 'Part 2 What I Believe'. The first, as its title suggests, contains essays written in response to the growing Nazi threat to freedom during the 1930s and essays and talks written under the cloud of war. The second begins with Forster's now famous credo 'What I Believe', first published in 1938 and since available on a long-playing record (Argo, PLP 1152); it continues with sections on 'Art in General', 'The Arts in Action'; and with 'Places' – no Forster collection would be complete without some tribute to travel and the spirit of place.

It is a more substantial volume than *Abinger Harvest* and contains some of Forster's best writing. Just as the novelist's two visits to India challenged him to re-examine all his assumptions about man and nature, so later the growing menace to European freedom provided the occasion for him to re-examine and vindicate the principles of his liberal humanism: to assert, in spite of all the signs to the contrary, the importance of individualism, tolerance, sensitiveness, the capacity to enjoy and endure, personal relations, resistance to authority, and scepticism towards political panaceas (noting how soon 'the New Jerusalem becomes a more ordinary city, where the party leaders book the best rooms'). He still speaks with a private voice, but it carries further, because he addresses mankind in the midst of a life-or-death struggle instead of quietly chiding his countrymen for their typical middle-class faults. A second reason for the more substantial nature of *Two Cheers for Democracy* lies in the fact that it contains public lectures and broadcasts as well as brief essays and book reviews. As his fame increased, Forster was invited to give public lectures in Britain and America. He was also asked to broadcast on crucial national issues. The three anti-Nazi broadcasts contain the main elements of his political faith, while the lectures and other pieces in the section, 'The Arts in General', contain the essence of his aesthetic theory, although he would have strenuously disavowed possessing such an unnecessary encumbrance.

The theoretical pieces on the arts reveal Forster's interest in music and painting as well as literature. They also reveal his radical scepticism towards criticism. Behind his own critical practice lies a general acceptance of the main tenets of Romanticism: the theory of inspiration, the function of the unconscious in creative activity, the unique order created by art, the existence of an internal coherence as the main formal principle in all aesthetic works. The emphasis on inspiration comes as no surprise in view of the part played in his works by visionary experiences, the spirit of place, and the sudden irruptions of panic, fear and violence. Moreover, in relegating criticism to the minor role of helping the artist to correct small faults (the excessive use of 'but', in his own case), he suggests that the only real remedy for a defect is inspiration ('The *Raison d'Être* of Criticism in the Arts', TCD), a typically Romantic rather than classic solution to the problem. To illustrate the play of the unconscious in creativity, he consistently uses the image of the bucket lowered into the deep well of the unconscious, influenced by the *Road to Xanadu* rather than by Freud, and takes as his model Coleridge's dream composition of 'Kubla Khan' – 'the creative state of mind is akin to a dream'. Yet the intervention of the unconscious, he believes, does not lead to eccentric subjectivity, but rather to the anonymity and universality of great art. Indeed, the early essay, 'Anonymity: An Enquiry', first published in the *Atlantic Monthly* in 1925 and reprinted in *Two Cheers for Democracy*, draws a valuable distinction between the truthful anonymity of art and the deceitful anonymity of the press. Rephrasing Pater's famous dictum, Forster suggests that 'all literature tends towards a condition of anonymity.' The whole essay throws light on the novelist's own constant striving for impersonality and detachment, but it does not quite explain how the personal voice often survives in the most anonymous art, a problem of special interest in relation to Forster's own writing in which voice plays so important a part.

Forster's belief that art alone creates a valid order for man finds definitive expression in the 1949 address given in New York, called provocatively 'Art for Art's Sake'. After dismissing the claims of politics, science, and religion to create order, he claims that art is the 'one orderly product which our muddling race has produced', that works of art 'are the only objects in the material universe to possess internal order.' In all this, he seems perhaps insufficiently aware of the artistic dangers of reconciling the disharmonies of life into the harmonies of art, of expecting the literary imagination to do what is mainly appropriate for the political imagination, although his own novel *Howards End* exemplifies the danger. It is one thing to reveal the need for imagination in all spheres of life, including business and politics, but it is quite another to substitute aesthetic patterns ('internal stitching') for the social harmony that must largely be created by the political imagination.

Forster accepts that the artist's role in society must be that of the 'outsider, the parasite, the rat'. When so many ships are sinking he would prefer to be 'a swimming rat than a sinking ship'. As an individualist by nature and conviction, and an anarchist by artistic profession, he is sceptical towards two claims often made: that the artist has a duty to serve the state and that the state has a duty to support the artist. Such claims cannot be sustained, he believes, since they are based on a false view of the nature both of the artist and the state. Advocates of state support are ignorant of the conditions under which creation actually takes place. He is rightly suspicious of all authoritarian patronage and interference in the arts. Abroad, in Nazi Germany, Hitler and the state condemned free artistic expression as degenerate and insane and sponsored the production of worthless art. At home, he feared that the BBC and other official bodies, especially in time of war, might stifle genuine creativity through the assumption of omniscience, through the enjoyment of monopoly rights and through various forms of censorship. In contrast, the London Library, which was a body that was 'typically civilized', avoided the characteristic faults of most public institutions, because it insisted on including all points of view and was prepared to take risks. When the Library was in financial difficulties in 1960 and hit on the idea of raising money by auctioning objects given by well-wishers, Forster presented it with the manuscripts of *A Passage to India*. These sold for £6,500, a new record price for the manuscripts of a living author (Stallybrass, 1969, p. 144).

Like his friend Dickinson and many of his contemporaries, Shaw for example, Forster recognized the potential of broadcasting and achieved great success with listeners at home and overseas, because he always gave the impression of speaking to the individual and not to a generalized public, and because he took immense pains to achieve lucidity and absolute naturalness. George Orwell and John Arlott, who were responsible for the main series in which Forster appeared, have spoken with authority of his skill and integrity as a broadcaster. But he was highly critical of the BBC and felt that it must be kept aware of its high responsibilities. Two aspects of its religious policy incensed him. The first was its all-pervasive religious influence on the whole nation – 'dripping away like a tap'. This was repugnant to his agnostic temper of mind, his strong belief that the individual should be left to make up his own mind about religion. The other and related aspect was the BBC's inveterate habit of arranging discussions on religious or philo-sophical issues so that provision was made for a magisterial summing up by a clergyman or some other establishment figure, who was thus given 'the insidious advantage of the Last Word'. The talk he gave on the fifth anniversary of the BBC Third Programme, on 29 September 1951, comes closest to defining what he thought should be the BBC's role as a reconciler of majority and minority interests.

> Quality is everywhere imperilled in contemporary life. Those
> who value it, as I do, are in a vulnerable position. We form as it
> were an aristocracy in the midst of a democracy, yet we belong
> and desire to belong to the democracy. Such conflicting loyalties
> cannot always be reconciled. They can be in British Broadcasting
> more easily than elsewhere, for the reasons that there are three
> programmes: Home, Light, and Third.

In the argument that follows he makes out a strong case for minority culture in a democratic society and for the unique role that the Third Programme might play in maintaining and fostering it. The state, he observes,

> Anxious, when it is not killing people, to feed and house them
> properly, . . . has assumed that values will look after themselves,
> or that what 'the people' want will be *ipso facto* culture. It ignores
> the pioneer, the exceptional, the disinterested scientist, the
> meditative thinker, the difficult artist, or it contemptuously
> dismisses them as 'superior'. One trusts that they are superior.
> They are certainly the types who have helped the human race
> out of the darkness in the past. And if they vanish now, if they
> dissolve into the modern world's universal grey, what is to happen
> to the human race in the future? Into what final darkness will it
> disappear? (*Listener*, 4 October 1951).

This is an eloquent plea that has lost none of its original urgency, but Forster saw that it was possible to be too solemn about culture and to claim too much on its behalf. His essay 'Does Culture Matter?' is one of the least stuffy contributions ever made to the great twentieth century debate on culture and society; yet it is clear that Forster gave a great deal of thought to the issue throughout his life. In Leonard Bast he shows how the vague yearnings for culture among the newly educated become mixed up with both romantic escapism and the desire for social status, and all his novels contain warnings against making culture only a means towards a material end. 'Culture, thank goodness, is no longer a social asset', he remarks in 'Does Culture Matter?', 'it can no longer be employed either as a barrier against the mob or as a ladder into the aristocracy', not seeing that it would become a ladder into the meritocracy. The 'growth of the idea of enjoyment' has put paid to uncritical acceptance and to smartness and fashion, but has also created the problem of the democratic piper calling the tune. With absolute candour he admits that at any time 'cultivated people are a drop of ink in the ocean', and that for someone to try to foist culture on those who don't want it is to act like a fidgety aunt trying to dispose of unwanted parcels. But culture is infectious. The desire to communicate is an impulse not a duty. 'The appreciator of an aesthetic achievement becomes in his minor way an artist; he cannot rest without communicating what has been communicated to him.' Since works of art have this 'peculiar pushful quality', we really have no choice but to take our share in the co-operative venture of transmitting culture.

It was this infectious quality of culture, 'the zest to communicate what had been communicated', that made Forster give up so much of his time to writing book-reviews (for the *Listener*, under the literary editorship of J. R. Ackerley, and for the *New Statesman*, under Raymond Mortimer). Ackerley described him as 'the greatest journalistic catch' during his twenty-five years as literary editor of the *Listener*. 'If you could land him for an article, or a book review, you landed the whale and were the envy of every other literary editor in London.' The zest to communicate also explains why he gave up so much of his time to lectures and radio talks. Two pieces in *Two Cheers for Democracy*, 'John Skelton' and 'George Crabbe and *Peter Grimes*', both given as lectures at the Aldeburgh Festival, exhibit Forster's capacity for communicating his literary enthusiasms and insights in the simplest, most compelling manner. In fact, it was an essay on Crabbe, published in the *Listener*, that first attracted Benjamin Britten to Crabbe's poem as a suitable story for an opera and possibly gave him the necessary 'shove' to return to England from America in 1942; and Forster's infectious enthusiasm for *Billy Budd*, in *Aspects of the Novel*, may have led Britten to Melville for another. 'I've often asked myself whether it was the passage in *Aspects of the Novel* . . . that reminded me of this extraordinary short story of Melville's', the composer confessed when discussing the origin of the opera with Forster, one of the two librettists. It was undoubtedly the infectious quality of culture that led Forster to give frequent book-talks to listeners in India and the Far East. For a number of years he gave a monthly talk, choosing whatever books or plays took his fancy and talking informally but brilliantly about just what it was that had given him pleasure. These talks contain some of his most perceptive criticism and only a small part of it has so far found its way into print.

Although the range of subject matter is very wide in these overseas broadcasts, certain underlying themes persist. Of these the most striking are the concern with the abuses of power and respect for personal relations, tolerance, and justice. In a review of Rex Warner's collection of essays, *The Cult of Power*, he makes an interesting comparison between Warner's analysis of power and Lord Acton's famous dictum, 'All power corrupts. Absolute power corrupts absolutely', and recalls that as a young man he went to Acton's lectures at Cambridge and heard him, 'humped up, bald, bearded', say 'every villain is followed by a sophist with a sponge.' Forster adds that 'some of the things he said remained with me through life.' He condemns James Burnham's *The Managerial Revolution* (a book that partly prompted Orwell's *Nineteen Eighty-Four*) for ignoring personal relations. On another occasion he retells the whole story of *Animal Farm*, just then published, and compares Orwell with Swift. After seeing a production of *Heartbreak House* in June 1943, he observes that Shaw 'is no poet' and has 'filled in the outline with wisecracks and scraps of farce', an illuminating judgment on another artist's attempt to represent the future of England through the fate of a house, as Forster himself had done in *Howards End* a few years before Shaw and Ford Madox Ford was to do in *Parades End*. Of Whitman, he says that there is 'no-one who can so suddenly ravish us into communion with all humanity or with death' and notes his own debt to Whitman's poem 'Passage to India'. He makes an incisive comparison between Voltaire and Strachey in terms of Voltaire's superior 'passion for justice'. The birthdays and deaths of famous literary men drew from him generous and discriminating praise. On Shaw's ninetieth birthday, he pays tribute to his 'gaiety, seriousness, courage, and humanity'. On the death of H. G. Wells, he regrets that his prophetic warnings against science have not been heeded, and tells the anecdote of Wells 'calling after me – not so long ago – calling after me in his squeaky voice "Still in your ivory tower?" "Still on your private roundabout", I might have retorted.' The death of the German refugee writer, Stefan Zweig, evokes a moving tribute to the virtue of tolerance 'as the major instrument in the upward movement of our race'.

A wonderful combination of ripe reminiscence and shrewd criticism characterizes these broadcast talks. In July 1943, looking back on two years of broadcasting to India, Forster defined his double aim: 'to show you in India that there is such a thing as culture over here, even in wartime', and to 'assure you that we are interested in your culture'. 'Culture', he remarked 'is a greatly-abused word, and I used to fight shy of it but I just howl it into the microphone to-day. I believe in culture, and in art, and in the many coloured flags of the spirit.' At first he found the microphone – that 'petrified pineapple' – inhibiting; but he soon discovered that it provided him with another passage to India, a means of breaking down the barriers of communication and establishing a genuine cultural exchange.

Concern with the survival of freedom and Western culture gives unity to the political essays in *Two Cheers for Democracy*. As a Prelude comes 'The Last Parade', an impressionistic account of the Paris Exhibition of 1937. Forster presents the array of national stands as the apotheosis of money and materialism, a machine culture on the point of collapse. In the whole tasteless display there are but two sources of hope: the paintings of Van Gogh and some aspects of the Soviet Pavilion. Van Gogh becomes an exemplary symbolic figure representing an alternative to the Europe of the Paris Exhibition. 'He has got round money because he has sought suffering and renounced happiness.' The Soviet Pavilion 'is trying, like Van Gogh, to dodge money and to wipe away the film of coins and notes which keeps forming on the human retina.' The reference to the Soviet system is a useful reminder that in the 1930s Forster was drawn to Communism as a radical solution to Europe's gross materialism and social injustice, especially through his association with Auden and Isherwood, although usually 'adding, *sotto voce*, that the communist future would be lacking in almost everything for which he cared', says Stephen Spender. In any case, he felt too old and settled in his principles to join the Communist Party; in the inter-war years, growing old became an obsession, and he admitted in his Commonplace Book that far too much creative effort had gone into trying to remain young. An alternative to

Communism was Fascism. Over the whole Paris Exhibition, Forster observes, looms the figure of Satan (Mussolini). 'He has only one remark to make: "I, I, I". He uses the symbols of the sacred and solemn past, but they only mean "I".' The inability to say 'I' in the Wilcoxes represents the absence of the personal in their response to life, the repeated 'I' of the totalitarian leader signifies his monstrous egotism and lust for dominance. Whereas Van Gogh symbolizes the vitality and integrity of European culture, Mussolini symbolizes the stupidity and megalomania of the totalitarian idea that threatens to pervert or destroy that culture for ever. The succeeding essays in *Two Cheers for Democracy* amplify the conflict between individual integrity and totalitarian power.

Some material not included in *Two Cheers for Democracy* or in any other collection places Forster's views of his age in a wider perspective. A survey, written in the early 1920s and called 'English Literature since the War [1914–1918]', sums up the crucial difference between the lofty aspirations of the Victorians and the almost total absence of aspiration in the Moderns. It ascribes the change to the years before the war, yet admits that 'those four years accelerated it'; and asks the question: 'To what end should the twentieth century aspire when the high-minded efforts of the nineteenth have ended in a cataclysm?' Three lectures, probably written in 1938 and beginning with the words 'in the early years of this century', strike an even more despondent note. They label the Edwardian period an age of Hope without Faith, the 1920s an age of Curiosity, and the 1930s an age of Faith without Hope. These tags are of less interest than the analysis of the collapse of the old-fashioned liberalism of Forster's youth. On his first visit to India, Forster still accepted the naïve liberal view that 'if the English would only behave more politely to the Indians, the difficulties between the two races would be solved. Good manners were to do the trick.' By the end of his second visit he knew better. Out of the wreck of old-fashioned liberalism there remained only faith in a spiritual aristocracy and belief in personal relations. 'My own relations with people have brought the only happiness I have found worth having or recommending – not a flash-in-the-pan happiness either', but 'solid achievement'. In retrospect, he sums up the period he has lived through as a tragedy in three acts.

In the first act the individualist hopes to improve society, in the second he tries to improve himself, in the third act he finds he's not wanted, and has either to merge himself in a movement or to retire. One has to face facts, and it seems to me that my particular job is to retire (KCL).

But, in fact, far from retiring, Forster emerged in the late 1930s as the chief spokesman of a revived liberal humanist tradition. He had seen that the old tradition that he had been brought up in meant nothing to the post-war generation of the 1920s: Liberalism 'was full of hope, blown out with hopes like an old gentleman with fat.' Consequently, he felt ill-equipped to grapple with the main issues of the age in the early 1930s. Then, on the eve of the Second World War, the very magnitude of the threat to everything he valued seems to have given him new heart to pit the whole strength of the humanist tradition, based on 'curiosity, a free mind, belief in good taste, and a belief in the human race', against 'The Second Darkness', represented by the rise of Nazism.

The radical distrust of group activity that kept Forster from merging with popular left-wing movements in the 1930s gave him a deep insight into the compulsive attraction of Nazism for many. This distrust comes out in unexpected ways, in his scepticism towards Gerald Heard's faith in group therapy, for instance, and in his scepticism towards the value of group deputations. In 'Our Deputation', an account of group visit to a Government Ministry, he uses modest deflationary tactics to suggest how easily the exercise of democratic rights may turn into polite but meaningless ritual.

> Civilities were re-exchanged, time was up, we thanked and were counter-thanked, our opinions were to be given their full weight, and . . . the Minister slipped from the room. He had performed his duty, and we ours. We went to the tree which had all the time supported our greatcoats, we unwound our mufflers from its branches and placed our hats upon our heads, and we passed down the stairway back into the snow and dirt outside, and resolved into our component parts.

Such passages as this often make their point more effectively than the formal arguments, perhaps because they draw on the art of the novelist and render in simple concrete terms the contrast between seductive political abstractions and the dull, recalcitrant facts of individual life. From the novels, too, the politically conscious writers of the 1930s took strength and inspiration. In 1938, for instance, W. H. Auden dedicated the China travel documentary, *Journey to a War*, to E. M. Forster. His sonnet forms a striking testimony to the quiet carrying power of Forster's voice, to the moral reverberations of his fictional universe.

> Here, though the bombs are real and dangerous
> And Italy and King's are far away,
> And we're afraid that you will speak to us,
> You promise still the inner life will pay.

The closing lines of the sonnet, which recall the climactic incident in *Howards End*, sum up the novelist's potential for saving the English middle classes from complicity in the 'international evil' destroying the world.

> But, as we swear our lie, Miss Avery
> Comes into the garden with the sword.

Although Auden tampered with the text over the years, weakening the whole point of the conclusion by substituting 'a sword' for 'the sword', the 1938 version stands as a representative tribute to Forster's moral vision from the left-wing poets of the 1930s.

It says much for Forster's perception and courage that he frequently declared that the same psychology lay behind group activity in England as totalitarian conformity abroad and warned his readers against the growth of 'Fabio-Fascism' in England, as George Orwell was to do in his essays and political fables, notably *Nineteen Eighty-Four*. Everywhere man 'has disguised the fear of the herd as loyalty to the group.' Individualism is too lonely and too difficult a course for most people who crave for strong leadership. But the wish to love is as strong as the wish to be free. And, Forster confesses, 'because Auden once wrote "We must love one another or die", he can command me to follow.' The hope expressed in 'The Menace to Freedom' that in the future the desire for individual freedom and the desire for love will combine to overcome the external threats to freedom may seem to lack any strong foundation, but what gives special strength to all the political essays in *Two Cheers for Democracy* is Forster's refusal to externalize the problems of freedom and order. He does not treat these problems as if they were exclusively political and had nothing to do with the struggle between the forces of light and darkness within the individual psyche; hence his appeal to a Freudian generation that believed that the solutions to crime and world anarchy lay in psychology and psycho-analysis, although he himself makes no direct use of Freud. Sceptical of all political panaceas and recognizing the imperfect nature of man, he reminds his readers at the outset of the essay 'The Menace to Freedom' that the threat cannot be defined 'in terms of political or social interference – Communism, Fascism, Grundyism, bureaucratic encroachment, censorship, conscription, and so on', or in terms of a mad tyrant escaped from the 'bottomless pit'. The truth is 'our freedom is really menaced today because a million years ago Man was born in chains.'

Here, however, we come across a startling paradox. In his political essays, Forster consistently regards force and violence as the darkest threat to freedom: the ultimate problem as he sees it in the essay, 'What I Believe', is how 'will Man shut up Force in its box'? Yet, in his novels, Forster places a high value on instinctive energy and physical strength, not to say actual violence and cruelty. One explanation for this discrepancy is that the disproportionate emphasis on force and brutality in the fiction is a dramatic device for shocking both his characters and his readers into seeing what polite society chooses to ignore. Thus the fight between Gino and Philip, in *Where Angels Fear to Tread*, was necessary, he explained to R. C. Trevelyan, because

> P. is a person who has scarcely ever felt the physical forces that are banging about in the world, and he couldn't get good and understand by spiritual suffering alone. Bodily punishment, however unjust superficially, was necessary too: in fact the scene – to use a heavy word, and one that I have only just thought of – was sacramental (letter, 28 October 1905, in Gowda, 1969, p. 129).

The emphasis on brutality in the novels is also related to a particular pattern of sexuality that Forster found attractive in fiction and in life. In the contradictory attitudes towards force in the novels and essays we see focused in a single gentle sensibility the tragic disparity between culture and cruelty that has haunted the European mind since Auschwitz and Buchenwald. However, Forster is totally free from anti-Semitic prejudice, unlike many Edwardian and Georgian writers; this may be seen from the two essays 'Jew Consciousness' and 'Racial Exercise' both of which make anti-Semitism ridiculous as well as contemptible, as ridiculous as being ashamed of sisters or mothers at boarding school. And the high regard for the instinctive and unconscious in man never led Forster to flirt with extreme right-wing, Fascist ideas as Lawrence, Eliot, Pound, and Wyndham Lewis were tempted to do at various stages in their careers. In all his political writing, he is totally opposed to force, brutality and authoritarian order, yet he thought that the Nazis were right to say 'that instinct is superior to reason, and character better than book-learning', a surprising, perhaps a shocking statement in its historical context, but completely in line with the moral vision of his fiction, which approves Ansell's instinctive laughter at the loss of the learned thesis and endorses Stephen Wonham's instinctive pagan virtues.

When Forster speaks on public issues he makes it clear that he speaks as an individual and as a writer, with no pretentions to expert knowledge on politics or economics. This is the keynote of the three 'Anti-Nazi Broadcasts', published in a variant form as a wartime pamphlet, *Nordic Twilight*. In the first talk, called 'Culture and Freedom', he argues that the writer needs an atmosphere of freedom in order to be creative, that he needs the freedom to tell the public what he is feeling and thinking, and that the public needs to be free to read what it likes or it will become inhibited and immature. Great works have certainly been produced under conditions far from free, but the works produced under Germany's authoritarian rule have been contemptible. Forster goes on to draw a distinction between a culture that is genuinely national and therefore capable of becoming super-national, and one that has become governmental and consequently falsified, as in Germany. Throughout the broadcasts Forster never makes the mistake of minimizing Germany's past contribution to European culture, a contribution amply recognized in *Howards End* and based partly on his stay in Germany in 1905, when he acted as a tutor for the children of the author of *Elizabeth and her German Garden*, at Nassenheide. In the second radio talk, he reminds his listeners that 'Germany had to make war on her own people before she could attack Europe', and speaks of the infamous Burning of the Books in May 1933, the steady increase in control and indoctrination. Turning to the question, 'What Would Germany Do to Us?', in the third talk, Forster refrains from talk of atrocities and speaks quietly of the likely effects of Germany's control of education and the press on the free spirit of England, concluding, 'This being so, I think we have got to go on with this hideous fight.' To many, to young men anxious not to be hoodwinked like their fathers into fighting a 'war to end all wars', the argument that what we were fighting against was not a nation but an evil principle seemed conclusive. The argument still stands up to critical scrutiny; the voice is still as quietly persuasive as ever.

A pre-war essay 'What I Believe' (1938) and a post-war essay 'The

Challenge of Our Time' (1946) come close to defining the essence of
Forster's liberal humanist creed as it had been tested by the terrible
events of the twentieth century. Any summary of the arguments of
'What I Believe' must totally misrepresent its meaning. It achieves its
validity through a special tone of voice: it convinces as much through
its characteristic withdrawals and reservations as through its positive
affirmations. Its hesitant scepticism and saving irony, its shocks and
surprises ('if I had to choose between betraying my country and
betraying my friend I hope I should have the guts to betray my
country'), its slanginess, irreverence, and colloquial vigour are all
exhilarating. From the first affirmation of agnosticism to the last
contemptuous dismissal of the dictator-hero, the essay engages our
whole moral being: intellect, passion, and will. The first paragraph
expresses great vigour of mind, depth of feeling, and complexity of
attitude, with the direct opening, 'I do not believe in Belief', the stern
admonishment of Science, 'who ought to have ruled', but who 'plays
the subservient pimp', the ambivalent image of the liberal virtues of
tolerance, good temper and sympathy as 'no stronger than a flower,
battered beneath a military jackboot', and the wry, regretful recognition of the need for Faith, as 'a sort of mental starch'. By comparison,
the writing of most of Forster's contemporaries seems to involve only
part of the whole personality, of both writer and reader.

In spite of the proclaimed disbelief in belief and the dislike of Faith,
the essay 'What I Believe' does state Forster's creed. He begins, as we
might expect, with a statement of his faith in personal relations.

> Starting from them, I get a little order into the contemporary
> chaos. One must be fond of people and trust them if one is not
> to make a mess of life, and it is therefore essential that they should
> not let one down. They often do. The moral of which is that I
> must, myself, be as reliable as possible, and this I try to be. But
> reliability is not a matter of contract – that is the main difference
> between the world of personal relations and the world of business
> relations. It is a matter for the heart, which signs no documents.

The second article in his creed is a belief in Democracy, not for the
usual empty pompous reasons, and expressed with a conspicuous lack
of enthusiasm.

> So two cheers for Democracy: one because it admits variety and
> two because it permits criticism. Two cheers are quite enough:

there is no occasion to give three. Only Love the Beloved
Republic deserves that. [The phrase, a favourite of Forster's,
comes from Swinburne's 'Hertha'.]

Before defining the third main article, a belief in a spiritual aristocracy,
Forster turns aside to ask the question: 'What about Force, though?',
always the chief challenge to the liberal humanist. A second-generation
Bloomsbury friend, Julian Bell, who was killed in the Spanish Civil
War, once wrote to Forster saying that the first weakness of liberal
politics was the neglect of force and power and the second the disregard
of the real sources of power. In the essay 'What I Believe', Forster
regretfully admits that force is the ultimate reality and hopes that
mankind will make the most of the brief periods when it is absent:
'I call them "civilization".' From Great Men nothing can be expected
but a desert of uniformity and 'often a pool of blood too, and I always
feel a little man's pleasure when they come a cropper.' Forster's aristocracy is not 'an aristocracy of power, based upon rank and influence,
but an aristocracy of the sensitive, the considerate and the plucky. Its
members are to be found in all nations and classes, and all through the
ages, and there is a secret understanding between them when they
meet.' Readers of *A Passage to India* have already experienced such an
instant recognition in the secret understanding of the heart reached by
Dr Aziz and Mrs Moore in the Mosque. But the passage may be
susceptible to other interpretations, more limiting and damaging to
Forster's universality. Such instant recognitions are especially applicable
to the sexual freemasonry of male comrades, as the relations between
Maurice Hall and Alec Scudder or those between Sir Richard Conway
and Arthur Snatchfold, the obliging and quixotic milkman, reveal.
Moreover, there is also perhaps something over-precious, self-regarding
and exclusive about Forster's picture of the 'invincible army' – 'the
aristocrats, the elect, the chosen, the Best People'. But he adds 'all the
words that describe them are false, and all attempts to organize them
fail.' The qualifications save the passage. As the 'reflections of an
individualist', the essay 'What I Believe' speaks to the individualist in
us all, not to a privileged elite. It possesses a timeless strength and
integrity.

In the period of reconstruction after the Second World War there
was no shortage of plans for creating a new Europe out of the ruins of
the old. In 1946, Forster contributed a talk to a series of eleven broadcasts by distinguished scientists, politicians and others called 'The

Challenge of Our Time': 'no one could tackle better than he in the course of a short essay or broadcast the big words or overworked themes like the Artist and Society or the Challenge of Our Times – ghastly titles that remind one of school exercises' (Annan, 1970). In this broadcast, Forster confronts more directly than ever before the conflict between individualism and state planning. His solution is for men 'to combine the new economy and the old morality', arguing that old-fashioned *laissez-faire* no longer works in the material world but is the only doctrine that seems to work in the world of the spirit. It is unusual for Forster to brandish slogans, yet on this occasion, as if to beat the post-war slogan makers at their own game, he offers his own: 'We want the New Economy with the Old Morality.' However, in accepting the need for social planning and government control, he recognizes that it must impinge on the private life of individuals and returns once more as a writer to the one free order that cannot be destroyed by external controls or pressures, the self-contained harmony of art.

> Art is valuable not because it is educational (though it may be), not because it is recreative (though it may be), not because everyone enjoys it (for everyone does not), not even because it has to do with beauty. It is valuable because it has to do with order, and creates little worlds of its own, possessing internal harmony, in the bosom of this disordered planet.

A writer's duty, Forster believes, exceeds his duty to society; artistic integrity is deeper than moral integrity; the order of art will outlast all other manmade orders. Proust's great novel provides the example, for it is 'based on an integrity in man's nature which lies deeper than moral integrity, it rises to the heights of triumph which give us cause to hope' ('Our Second Greatest Novel', TCD).

Two Cheers for Democracy demonstrates Forster's power to transform confessions of weakness into an armoury of strength. He evolved, as Stephen Spender has pointed out, a subtle strategy in which 'he wore his own ineffectiveness like a cap of invisibility'. 'Under the guise of a defeated liberal', he remained 'alive and kicking', when more positive thinkers proved a spent force (Spender, 1970, p. 3). Orwell in defeat turned sour, Eliot orotund and evasive, Bertrand Russell abstract and arid. It is true that in comparison with the left-wing poets of the 1930s or the early Orwell, Forster appears to give away too much to the opposition, to have no positive alternative to offer, and to accept too readily a quietist position. But appearances are deceptive. In his social essays, as in his novels, there is a peculiar blend of toughness and tenderness. The very absence of specific programme or forceful rhetoric becomes a strength; 'the whisper is tremendous', but never rises to a shout. He pioneered a new style for talking simply but memorably about ultimate issues. In *Enemies of Promise* (1938), Cyril Connolly hailed his prose as a 'major revolution' against the Mandarin style that the Moderns had inherited from the nineteenth century and from which they struggled to break free. The source of his strength as a novelist and publicist is the same: it lies in his capacity to create rhythms of thought and emotion that go on sounding and expanding in our minds long after we have ceased to read the actual words. It was thus that he became an influence for good, quietly working underground, making both his presence and his absence felt, his utterances and his silences, and always with a preference for the 'slighter gestures of dissent', like the early Eliot, 'interposing' rather than 'imposing' his views, as V. S. Pritchett has shrewdly observed. What Forster said of the Greek poet C. P. Cavafy might with equal justice be said of Forster himself: his is 'an achievement which is a pattern, not a sum'.

I I

Conclusion

E. M. Forster is the voice of our shy unofficial selves: the self that seeks fulfilment through beauty, love, and friendship, and is suspicious of the state's attempts to organize people into good citizens through conformity to its official laws and codes. The novels up to *A Passage to India* assume the existence of several codes. There is the code of conventional middle-class society and the tribal laws by which it lives and judges conduct. There are the codes of those who retreat from middle-class conventions into even more restrictive social or aesthetic groups; and there is Forster's own code, critical of society, but free from sectarian exclusiveness. His novels are comedies that involve the reader in an act of quiet complicity against the idols of the tribe. For as long as he reads, he is made an honorary member of Forster's spiritual aristocracy: to refuse such an honour would be to resist the whole joyful strategy and gentle rhetoric of the novels and to enrol in the legions of the benighted who follow neither the head nor the heart. The quiet controlling voice of the author ensures that we commit no such folly.

The recognizable characteristics of Forster's spiritual aristocracy are imagination, warmth of heart, and tenderness for others. But in addition to possessing these human qualities, his spiritual aristocracy is responsive to the elemental, the instinctive, and the unseen: to the visionary moments that transfigure the ordinary world and invest it with value and meaning. There are occasions, however, even under the quiet spell of the author's voice, when the reader may wonder whether sufficient distinction has been made between the beauty of instinctive passion and the dark forces of violence and brutality (which Forster opposes in the political essays but either condones or approves in the fiction). The dramatic emphasis on symbolic moments of choice causes every minute of life to be fraught with potential spiritual significance; but there will always be readers who find that such a moral vision is difficult to sustain and at variance with their own experience, where less seems to depend on response to unique moments of choice and where there is the continuous possibility of a change of direction. Yet the 'salvationism' is always modified by what Spender calls a 'stoic awareness that one cannot expect too much of the truth' (Spender, 1953, p. 86).

One great difference between *A Passage to India* and all the other novels is that the theme of personal salvation plays no part in it. Personal relations, yes; personal salvation not at all. The invitations to enjoy beauty, love, and friendship are as appealing as before, although the approach is more difficult and the invocations to the infinite more mysterious and compelling; but the religious terminology that Forster inherited in a secularized form from the nineteenth century has largely disappeared, driven out by the immensity of India's challenge, a challenge that arose not only from its size and diversity, but also from the living strength of its own religious traditions, Moslem and Hindu. In such a world it was possible for Forster to forget that he was a lapsed Protestant or a lapsed anything and to commit his whole imaginative being to mirroring the polarities of existence. *A Passage to India* is the testimony of a mind that has learnt to live without props, the final triumph of Forster's humanist imagination.

In most of his novels Forster transposes the temperate ideals of classical humanism into a more dynamic and romantic context. The belief that man is the measure of all things, the importance of keeping proportion, the pursuit of truth and the avoidance of error receive only a qualified assent. His is the double vision not the single vision of rationalism and 'Newton's sleep': 'The whole human race is illogical. We are all in one boat here; now we look inward at our fellow passengers, now outward at the infinite sea . . . it is a proof of our double vision' ('Feminine Note in Literature', KCL). A life that fails to admit the unseen is necessarily incomplete. 'To have felt it, if only for a moment, that this visible world is only an illusion, to have conceived, however faintly, that the real is the unseen, to have had even a passing desire for the One, is at once to be marked off from all who have not thus felt' ('The Poems of Kipling', KCL). Forster's own idea of the unseen has at least three dimensions: the hidden mysteries of the unconscious, which assume a growing importance in his work; the world of internal states of being arising from the pursuit of beauty and personal relations; and the various intimations of a supernatural world, expressed in the early fiction through Greek mythology, but later through voices, presences, memories, goblin-footfalls, echoes from the Marabar Caves. The third of these, the supernatural, represents not so much a belief in external powers as the creation of personal mythology on the model of the Greek to externalize the mystery within. Moreover, Forster's notion of proportion is romantic rather than classical. To begin with proportion, as Margaret Schlegel knows, is sterile; dynamic harmony comes through heroic not temperate endeavour. Harmony is to be attained, if ever, through uniting the conscious and the unconscious elements in the human psyche, and through an imaginative accommodation of the seen to the unseen. All Forster's main characters are actively engaged in the process of fusing their natural and social selves and with finding their part in a universe that simultaneously diminishes and confirms their human stature. 'It is the private life that holds out the mirror to infinity; personal intercourse, and that alone, that ever hints at a personality beyond our daily vision' (HE, ch. 10). In every novel one is conscious of a contrast between two responses to life in the novelist, between two moods, two tones of writing. The one is a glad acceptance of life expressed in buoyantly confident prose, edged with irony. The other is a sadder response that springs from deep disappointment when the promised moment of happiness or transfiguration fails. The desolating emptiness that follows expectation denied, experienced by Rickie, and Maurice, and Margaret Schlegel, culminates in the hollow echo of the Marabar Caves. These two sides of Forster's writing are reflections of the double vision; they also represent the delighted ironist and the disappointed visionary. But the visionary element has a positive as well as a negative side.

Forster's much praised moral realism arises from his presentation of 'the contradictions, paradoxes and dangers of living the moral life' (Trilling, 1944, p. 12), rather than from the assertion of a positive moral creed. In the short stories and early novels genuine complexity is occasionally sacrificed to spiritual melodrama or the simplifying solutions of Greek myth, with a consequent upsetting of the moral balance. Later, however, the Paterian emphasis on the intensity of response to life's offered moments, the preoccupation with personal salvation, becomes subsumed into a more complex world in which the virtues of tolerance, sympathy, and saving others – not only oneself – assume a greater importance. It is a moral world in which there is less talk of judgment and more of love; a world, too, in which there is a closer interaction between private and public life. In the early 1930s, Forster appeared to Stephen Spender – and he here speaks for his generation –

'the best English novelist of this century and one of the most acute of its moralists' (Spender, 1951, p. 167).

But the moral realism has a second origin. It arises as much from Forster's honesty in presenting failure as from his skill in rendering complexity. Failure is perhaps too strong a word to use. But even the most successful attempts to connect must be judged only qualified successes: this is as true of Margaret and Helen in *Howards End*, as it is of Aziz and Fielding in *A Passage to India*. With Alec and Maurice we have to take so much on trust that at best their attempts to connect must be called a notional success. Although none of the characters achieves full harmony with others, with nature, or within the self, the final effect of Forster's fiction is not pessimistic, because the struggle to achieve harmony releases heroic energies and because the radiant promise is never entirely withdrawn, as the characters look beyond 'the flaming ramparts of the world', towards their cherished ideal of harmony. In addition, the continuous play of irony on the deceptive surfaces of life gives a fresh and exhilarating insight into the hidden significance of the dramatic conflict of characters. A combination of high-spirited comedy with mischievous malice lights up the familiar domestic world so that it becomes irradiated with Forster's joy in creating a universe that obeys its own laws and possesses a strict internal harmony.

The ideal of a dynamic harmony, as we have seen, is part of Forster's Romantic inheritance; so, too, is his belief in the power of art to create internal order. His novels imply but never categorically assert a connection between the transfiguring acts of consciousness enjoyed by some of the characters, as they struggle to harmonize the disparate elements of their experience, and the unifying process of the literary imagination. The descriptions of such harmonizing acts of consciousness as those experienced by Margaret Schlegel in *Howards End* and Aziz in *A Passage to India*, form a close parallel with Forster's accounts of how the artist's mind works. Such moments of imaginative harmony are enjoyed by a wide variety of characters, from the youthful, unformed Lucy Honeychurch to the mature Helen Schlegel, from the unsophisticated naturals of the short stories to such complicated and deeply intuitive characters as Professor Godbole, and, pre-eminently, by Forster's elderly sybils, Mrs Wilcox and Mrs Moore.

But where Art can give permanence to such visions of harmony, Life cannot. Yet the promise of harmony beckons and helps to shape and order men's lives. Philip Herriton illustrates the misguided attempt to turn Life into Art. Through him Forster divests himself of his *fin de siècle* aestheticism; and neither *Howards End* nor *A Passage to India* is much concerned with contrasting life as aesthetic spectacle and life as personal commitment. But something of the aesthetic taint remains, with the result that in *Howards End* the final answer to social fragmentation is offered by aesthetic patterning, not by a commitment of the characters or the author to any policy of radical reform, either of themselves or society.

Inherited traditions, the influence of Cambridge, personal temperament, and the actual conditions of the Modern Age all led Forster to emphasize the need 'to connect'. Additional light on this preoccupation comes from the posthumously published fiction. It is now clear that, because of the strong sexual taboos in society, Forster himself found it peculiarly difficult to unite the social self with what Stuart Hampshire has called the 'subterranean' and 'proletarian self' of the unconscious. His literary salvation lay in exploiting familiar conventions of domestic comedy and transposing the pattern of relations that interested him most into the more familiar patterns of love and romance. Social and literary taboos however stood in the way of achieving personal salvation by discovering his true nature. The early fiction brings the buried self to the light and reconciles the rival claims of nature and culture within the bounds of orthodox literary conventions. The obscure sense of belonging to a misunderstood minority obviously sharpened and deepened Forster's insight into the stultifying effects of conventional morality on personal development that make it difficult to achieve wholeness of being. A comparison of the male friendships in *The Longest Journey* with those in *Maurice* reveals that they conform to a similar structure. But the structure in the first is disguised while in the second it is overt. Yet, in *Maurice*, the novel not intended for publication, the critique of social conventions, because more open and narrowly focused, becomes propaganda for a minority cause rather than a general, ironic exposure of the rigidity of social norms. Whatever the union of Alec and Maurice may have represented for the life of the author, it did not provide a sound basis for the further development of Forster's art. *A Passage to India* marks a return to the art of obliquity and subtle suggestion, a working through literary and social conventions, not an open rebellion against them.

The failure of Forster's characters to connect is not only the product of his extreme moral realism, a frank recognition that in the moral life a man's reach exceeds his grasp, but also in part a reflection of his own failure to connect 'the monk and the beast in man'. In spite of his love, his compassion, and his humanity, Forster was to some extent an example of the undeveloped heart. For many years he felt unable to develop the full range of his emotions or to express them in his works because they were homosexual. He had the misfortune to live at a time when it was peculiarly difficult for a man of his temperament to achieve wholeness of being; consequently he was never able to give an entirely convincing account of a perfect harmony between the wisdom of the mind and the wisdom of the body, although the pursuit of this elusive ideal provided him with the major theme of all his fiction and a particular angle from which to view it. Like Cavafy, he 'stands at a slight angle to the universe' and to society.

The wisdom and pleasure that the novels communicate do not, in fact, depend on whether the author or the characters succeed in attaining harmony. Forster's achievement as a novelist depends mainly on his powers of characterization, his mastery of dialogue, his delicately poised irony, his flexible prose, and his ingenuity in unfolding major themes so that each novel has a meaning that transcends the sum of its parts. The distinguishing feature of his characterization is the combination of sympathetic inwardness with ironic detachment, found in his major and minor characters alike. His clergymen and schoolmasters are seen mainly from the outside, it is true; but with even so unpleasant a character as Miss Bartlett, who uses her self-appointed martyrdom as a means of manipulating Lucy, there is an unexpected degree of inwardness in the creation. From the first novel to the last, dialogue brings the characters to life and releases the major themes. Forster's dialogue has the virtue of good stage dialogue (put to the proof in stage adaptations); it possesses economy, naturalness, pattern, and point. Benjamin Britten has noticed how skilfully Forster 'our most musical novelist', varies the pattern of his dialogue and has drawn an illuminating analogy with the alternation of recitatives, arias, and large ensemble groupings in classical opera (Stallybrass, 1969, pp. 82-3). Forster's revisions in his later novels show what care went into deciding whether dialogue, narrative, or commentary was most suitable at any one point for achieving maximum economy and expressive power. The extreme lightness and flexibility of touch in most of the passages of commentary in the early novels ensures that the author's voice blends with those of the characters to produce a unity of tone. Similarly in *Howards End* and *A Passage to India* a fine critical sense directs the modulations of tone in relation to the development of the more serious themes in these two later novels. A comparison of the welter and confusion of recurrent motifs in *The Longest Journey* with the beautifully controlled and sparingly used motifs in *A Passage to India* demonstrates the final mastery he achieved in assimilating 'Rhythm' ('music is the deepest of the arts') into the structure of his novels. And the gain in artistry involves no loss of spontaneity; there is a perfect harmony between conscious order and free-flowing energy.

Throughout Forster's career as a writer there was a fruitful interaction of the critical and the creative, the full extent of which is only beginning to emerge with access to the original manuscripts. From a comparison of the early versions of *A Room with a View* with the published novel, it is clear that the novelist was striving to achieve a firm antithetical structure instead of a series of episodes, that he consistently sought greater detachment and subtlety of suggestion, especially in presenting the underground workings of Lucy's mind. The manuscript of *Where Angels Fear to Tread* reveals numerous felicities in revision and a true craftsman's decision to shorten Philip's explicit analysis of who was responsible for the baby's death. In the first three novels there is strong evidence of Forster's battle against derivativeness, against what he called the tug of 'anti-literature'. The Abinger Edition of *The Manuscripts of Howards End* provides fascinating evidence of the interaction of the critical and the creative in the composition of this fine novel; and J. P. Levine's study of *A Passage to India* carefully documents Forster's inspired craftsmanship, most of which affected character and plot, although careful revisions also secured the novelist's distance from his *alter ego*, Fielding, the humanist educator, and therefore affected the maturity and complexity of the final vision.

A similar interaction of the critical and creative sides of Forster's nature gives special distinction to his critical essays. He does not, like T. S. Eliot, make extravagant claims for the superiority of practitioner's criticism, but he does bring to his critical writing a sympathetic professional understanding of the technical problems of a wide range of writers. Yeats, he remarks, was 'a man whose make-up was so strange that a certain amount of mystification and faking seemed to help his genius'; of Proust's technique of using the 'little phrase' from the music of Vinteuil, he observes that 'it gives the memory a shock' and that 'these shocks and their consequences are Proust's main concern'; of Virginia Woolf's problem of dealing with madness, he writes 'she pared the edges of this particular malady, she tied it down to being a malady, and robbed it of the evil magic it has acquired through timid or careless thinking'; of D. H. Lawrence as a prophet he writes that he 'is irradiating nature from within, so that every colour has a glow and every form a distinctness which could not otherwise be obtained'; and finally an observation on Kipling's failure to assimilate the subject of empire into poetry: 'An Empire is a very difficult subject for poetry. Unless the poet possesses an exquisite taste and deep inspiration, he will fall into Kipling's error, and praise it because it is big and can smash up its enemies' ('The Poems of Kipling', KCL). The adverse judgment on Kipling here is a reminder that the quality of Forster's criticism does not depend entirely on the interaction of the creative and critical sides of his mind but on a humanist concern with freedom, truth, and justice. After reading Forster, Natwar-Singh came to realize

> that it was he who had taught thinking and sensitive people in England to disengage themselves from their imperial burdens, emotionally, intellectually, and practically. To a generation fed on the offensive and offending jingoisms of Kipling, Forster's civilized and hopeful alternatives, debunking the Flag, the Stiff Upper Lip, the Clergy, came as a blessed relief (1964, p. 66).

The interaction between the critical and the creative appears in yet one more aspect of Forster's work: in his attitude towards the various traditions that formed part of his cultural heritage as a creative writer. Indeed, he was far more deeply aware of the limitations of these traditions than has been supposed by hostile critics like F. C. Crews and C. B. Cox, who have attributed to him some of the very weaknesses that he analysed and avoided. He was aided in the task of revaluing and revitalizing the humanist tradition, as A. H. Smith has shown, by a distinguished line of earlier writers who had confronted an alien machine culture with the two voices of a revived humanism: the voice that offered an alternative through imagination and instinctive wisdom and the voice that offered goodwill plus culture and intelligence. In some of these writers, for instance Mill, Matthew Arnold, and Mark Rutherford, the two voices blended as they do in Forster (Bradbury, 1966, pp. 109–16). Of all Forster's recent critics perhaps Malcolm Bradbury comes closest to summing up his relationship with the nineteenth century and the Modern Age.

> If Forster is indeed a Victorian liberal, as some of his critics charge, he is also deeply marked by the encounters that the moralized romantic inheritance must make with those

environments which challenge it in matters of belief, technique, and aesthetics. . . . Forster's confession that he belongs to the fag-end of Victorian liberalism does express a real inheritance; but that end is also the beginning of new forms of belief and of new literary postures and procedures . . . he emerges not as a conventionally modernist writer, but rather as a writer who has experienced the full impact of what modernism means – hope for transcendence, a sense of apocalypse, an *avant-garde* posture, a sense of detachment, a feeling that a new phase of history has emerged – while retaining (with tentative balance that turns often to the ironic mode) much that modernism would affront (Stallybrass, 1969, pp. 125–6).

What the judgment of posterity will be we cannot know. Yet it seems as certain as anything can be that Forster's novels will survive changes of fashion and that his critical and social writings will continue to be read both for their originality of thought and expression and for their historical interest. It was the worst misfortune, Forster thought, for a writer to be considered typical of his age. That fate he certainly should escape, since his personal voice constantly affirms that he speaks not for an age or a social class, but for himself. The preservation of that voice from the bland assurance of privilege and the insidious falsities of mass culture is his greatest single triumph and the final vindication of his faith in individualism. 'E. M. Forster does not want a statue', observes the Indian novelist Raja Rao, 'but infectious laughter and a corner of silence in a friend's heart.'

Bibliography

Editions

Forster's works are published by Edward Arnold, London, with the following exceptions:

Alexandria: A History and a Guide, Whitehead Morris, Alexandria, 1922 and 1938; Anchor Books, Doubleday & Co., New York, 1961, reprinted Peter Smith, Gloucester, Mass., 1968.

Pharos and Pharillon, Hogarth Press, London, 1923 and 1961.

Collected Short Stories, Sidgwick & Jackson, London, 1948.

The Uniform Edition by Edward Arnold appeared in 1924, and the Pocket Edition by the same publisher in 1947; it is still in print.

The Abinger Edition, edited by Oliver Stallybrass, Edward Arnold, will contain virtually all Forster's writings, including hitherto unpublished writing, for example the unfinished novel *Arctic Summer*, and also material that has only been available in back issues of newspapers and periodicals. Several volumes have already appeared and should be consulted for superior text, valuable introductions, and full indexes, where appropriate.

Paperback editions: Penguin Books reprint all Forster's novels, *Collected Short Stories, Aspects of the Novel, Two Cheers for Democracy*, and *The Hill of Devi.*

Bibliography

Gerber, H. E. (1959), 'E. M. Forster: an annotated checklist of writings about him', *English Fiction in Transition*, Spring; regular bibliographical lists by F. P. W. McDowell in subsequent numbers of *English Literature in Transition.*

Kirkpatrick, B. J. (1965), *A Bibliography of E. M. Forster*, Hart-Davis, London, second revised impression, 1968.

Background Studies

The reader will find the following books and articles provide an up-to-date picture of the social and literary background. It is important to consult recently published works, since the whole period during which Forster wrote has been the subject of continuous and radical reassessment.

Annan, N. G. (1951), *Leslie Stephen: His Thought and Character in relation to his Time*, MacGibbon & Kee, London; for relation of Clapham Sect to Bloomsbury and therefore the connection between Forster's Thornton ancestors and his own circle.

Annan, N. G. (1970), 'Morgan Forster remembered by Lord Annan', *Listener*, 18 June.

Bell, Q. (1968), *Bloomsbury*, Weidenfeld & Nicolson, London; lively, impressionistic account.

Bell, Q. (1972), *Virginia Woolf: A Biography*, 2 vols, Hogarth Press, London; provides background to Virginia Woolf's and Forster's critical writings about each other.

Daiches, D. (1969), *Some Late Victorian Attitudes* (The Ewing Lectures, 1967), André Deutsch, London.

Ellmann, R. (1960), 'The Two Faces of Edward' in *Edwardians and Late Victorians*, ed. R. Ellmann (English Institute Essays, 1959), Columbia University Press, New York; traces assimilation of nineteenth-century religious terms into a secular context as well as portraying complexity of the period.

Holroyd, M. (1967, 1968), *Lytton Strachey: A Critical Biography*, 2 vols, Heinemann, London; documents Bloomsbury and Strachey's relations with Forster.

Hynes, S. L. (1968), *The Edwardian Turn of Mind*, Princeton University Press and Oxford University Press; a major reassessment, it corrects popular misconceptions about the age, and provides information about political societies, political movements, the Edwardian 'seers and prophets', and major and minor writers.

Johnstone, J. K. (1954), *The Bloomsbury Group: A Study of E. M. Forster, Lytton Strachey, Virginia Woolf, and Their Circle*, Secker & Warburg, London; for the ideas of G. E. Moore and Roger Fry, but it exaggerates the uniformity of Bloomsbury aesthetics and the actual influence of Moore and Fry on Forster and others (Forster never read Moore).

Lester, J. A. (1968), *Journey Through Despair 1880–1914: Transformations in British Literary Culture*, Princeton University Press; a challenging critical survey.

Masterman, C. F. G. (ed.) (1901), *The Heart of the Empire: Discussions of Problems of Modern City Life in England. With an Essay on Imperialism*, T. Fisher Unwin, London; reprinted Harvester Press, Sussex, 1973.

Masterman, C. F. G. (1902), *From the Abyss. Of its Inhabitants. By one of them*, R. Brimley & Johnson, London.

Masterman, C. F. G. (1904), 'The English City' in *England: a Nation*, ed. L. R. F. Oldershaw, R. Brimley & Johnson, London.

Masterman, C. F. G. (1909), *The Condition of England*, Methuen, London;

reprinted with an Introduction by J. T. Boulton, Methuen, London, 1960.

Priestley, J. B. (1970), *The Edwardians*, Heinemann, London; a good pictorial introduction to the age.

Proctor, D. (ed.) (1973), *The Autobiography of G. Lowes Dickinson*, Duckworth, London.

Read, D. (1972), *Edwardian England, 1901–1915: Society and Politics*, Harrap, London; excellent brief introduction to the period.

Woolf, L. (1960), *Sowing: An Autobiography of the Years 1880–1904*, Hogarth Press, London.

Woolf, L. (1961), *Growing: An Autobiography of the Years 1904–1911*, Hogarth Press, London.

Woolf, L. (1964), *Beginning Again, 1911–1918*, Hogarth Press, London.

Woolf, L. (1967), *Down Hill all the Way, 1919–1939*, Hogarth Press, London.

Critical Studies

Beer, J. B. (1962), *The Achievement of E. M. Forster*, Chatto & Windus, London; stresses the visionary element but gives a balanced account of romantic, comic, and moral aspects of Forster's art.

Bradbury, M. (ed.) (1966), *Forster: A Collection of Critical Essays*, Prentice-Hall, Englewood Cliffs, N.J.; includes representative essays, discriminating Introduction, and Selected Bibliography.

Bradbury, M. (ed.) (1970), *E. M. Forster: 'A Passage to India': A Casebook* (Casebook Series), Macmillan, London; contains essays on composition, essays showing contemporary reception, and examples of recent studies.

Brander, L. (1968), *E. M. Forster: A Critical Study*, Hart-Davis, London.

Cecil, Lord David (1949), *Poets and Storytellers: A Book of Critical Studies*, Constable, London; contains a brief but comprehensive essay on Forster's fiction.

Colmer, J. (1967), *E. M. Forster's 'A Passage to India'* (Studies in English Literature, 30), Edward Arnold, London.

Connolly, C. (1938), *Enemies of Promise*, Routledge & Kegan Paul, London.

Connolly, C. (1945), *The Condemned Playground Essays: 1927–1944*, Routledge & Kegan Paul, London.

Cox, C. B. (1963), *The Free Spirit: A Study of Liberal Humanism in the Novels of George Eliot, Henry James, E. M. Forster, Virginia Woolf, Angus Wilson*, Oxford University Press; argues that Forster failed to apply his liberal ideas to social reality.

Crews, F. C. (1962), *E. M. Forster: The Perils of Humanism*, Princeton University Press and Oxford University Press; an adverse judgment on Forster's humanism.

Ellem, E. (1971), 'E. M. Forster: The Lucy and New Lucy novels: fragments of early versions of *A Room with a View*', *Times Literary Supplement*, 28 May.

Ellem, E. (1973), 'E. M. Forster's *Arctic Summer*', *Times Literary Supplement*, 21 September.

Enright, D. J. (1957), 'To the Lighthouse or to India' in *The Apothecary's Shop: Essays on Literature*, Secker & Warburg, London; an illuminating comparative estimate of Forster and Virginia Woolf.

Gardner, P. (ed.) (1973), *E. M. Forster: The Critical Heritage*, Routledge & Kegan Paul, London; valuable for early reviews and for tracing development of Forster's reputation.

Gowda, H. H. (ed.) (1969), *A Garland for E. M. Forster*, Mysore; contains perceptive critical essays and a selection of unpublished letters from Forster to R. C. Trevelyan.

Gransden, K. W. (1962), *E. M. Forster* (Writers and Critics Series), Oliver & Boyd, Edinburgh (revised edition 1970); a valuable introduction.

Hampshire, S. (1969), *Modern Writers and Other Essays*, Chatto & Windus, London; the essay on Forster is one of the most incisive to be written.

Joseph, D. I. (1964), *The Art of Rearrangement: E. M. Forster's 'Abinger Harvest'*, Yale University Press, New Haven and London.

Kermode, J. F. (1962), *Puzzles and Epiphanies: Essays and Reviews, 1958–1961*, Routledge & Kegan Paul, London; sees Forster as a symbolist writer.

Kermode, J. F. (1970), 'Forster', *Listener*, 18 June.

Klingopulos, G. D. (1961), 'Mr Forster's Good Influence' in *The Modern Age* (The Pelican Guide to English Literature, vol. 7), ed. Boris Ford, Penguin, Harmondsworth; balanced and perceptive essay on Forster as a novelist and publicist.

Leavis, F. R. (1952), 'E. M. Forster' in *The Common Pursuit*, Chatto & Windus, London; an evaluation in terms of the balance of poetry and realism.

Levine, J. P. (1971), *Creation and Criticism: 'A Passage to India'*, Chatto & Windus, London; valuable study of the background and genesis of the novel.

Macaulay, R. (1938), *The Writings of E. M. Forster*, Hogarth Press, London; interesting as the first book-length study.

McConkey, J. (1957), *The Novels of E. M. Forster*, Cornell University Press, Ithaca; an application of Forster's 'Aspects' to his own novels, together with suggestive remarks on 'Voice'.

McDowell, F. P. W. (1969), *E. M. Forster* (Twayne's English Authors Series), Twayne, New York; reliable guide, with excellent bibliography.

Martin, R. (1974), *The Love that Failed: Idea and Reality in the Writings of E. M. Forster*, Mouton, The Hague and Paris; carefully documented, but does not encompass posthumously published works.

Natwar-Singh, K. (ed.) (1964), *E. M. Forster: A Tribute. With Selections from his Writings on India*, Harcourt Brace, New York.

Pritchett, V. S. (1965), *The Working Novelist*, Chatto & Windus, London; the essay on Forster combines literary and political acumen.

Pritchett, V. S. (1971), 'The upholstered prison', *New Statesman*, 8 October; places *Maurice* in relation to Forster's other works and vision of life.

Rutherford, A. (ed.) (1970), *Twentieth-Century Interpretations of 'A Passage to India'*, Prentice-Hall, Englewood Cliffs, N.J.

Shahane, V. A. (1962), *E. M. Forster: A Reassessment*, Kitab Mahal, Delhi.

Shahane, V. A. (1968), *Perspectives on E. M. Forster's 'A Passage to India': A Collection of Critical Essays*, Barnes & Noble, New York.

Spender, S. (1951), *World Within World*, Hamish Hamilton, London; the autobiography records the impact of Forster's writings and personality on Spender and his generation in the 1930s.

Spender, S. (1953), 'Personal Relations and Public Powers' in *The Creative Element*, Hamish Hamilton, London.

Spender, S. (1970), 'E. M. Forster (1879-1970)', *New York Review of Books*, 23 July; one of the most discriminating obituary essays.

Stallybrass. O. (ed.) (1969), *Aspects of E. M. Forster*, Edward Arnold, London; the essays cover all aspects, including Bloomsbury, music, broadcasting, and humanism.

Stone, W. (1966), *The Cave and the Mountain: A Study of E. M. Forster*, Stanford University Press; draws on unpublished material, is lavishly illustrated and offers a coherent psychological interpretation of Forster's development and works.

Thomson, G. H. (1967), *The Fiction of E. M. Forster*, Wayne State University Press, Detroit; interprets the novels as 'romances' and draws on manuscript evidence for *A Passage to India*.

Thomson, G. H. (ed.) (1971), *'Albergo Empedocle' and Other Writings*, Liveright, New York; prints Forster's undergraduate journalism and should be consulted in relation to Thomson's 'A Forster Miscellany: thoughts on the Uncollected Writings' in Stallybrass (1969).

Trilling, L. (1944), *E. M. Forster: A Study*, Hogarth Press, London; launched the revival of interest in Forster, especially in America; it is incisive on works and intellectual and political background, especially valuable for the introductory chapter 'Forster and the Liberal Imagination', also reproduced in Bradbury (1966).

Warner, R. (1950), *E. M. Forster* (Writers and Their Work, No. 7), Longmans, London (revised 1954).

Wilde, A. (1964), *Art and Order: A Study of E. M. Forster*, New York University Press; Peter Owen, London, 1965; excellent on Forster's aesthetics.

Woolf, V. (1942), *The Death of the Moth and Other Essays*, Hogarth Press, London; Quentin Bell provides the necessary background in his biography of Virginia Woolf.

Bibliography

Interviews

Cowley, M. (ed.) (1958), *Writers at Work: the 'Paris Review Interviews'*, Secker & Warburg, London.

Gransden, K. W. (1959), 'E. M. Forster at eighty', *Encounter*, January.

Jones, D. (1959), 'E. M. Forster on his life and his books', *Listener*, January.

Orr, P. (1961), Discussions between E. M. Forster and Peter Orr, recorded in Mr Forster's Rooms in King's College, Cambridge, on 19 December, for the British Council. Available on tape in the series 'The Art of the Novelist', Nos 497, 498, 499 and 929. Also extracts, with commentary, on tape from Radio University VL5UV, University of Adelaide.

Wilson, A. (1957), 'A conversation with E. M. Forster', *Encounter*, November.

Index

I E. M. Forster

Life:

birth, 1; female-dominated, 1; schools, 4–5 (reflected in LJ, 5, 75–6, and in M, 4); departure 'Rooksnest', 3–4; Cambridge, 6–9; visited Italy and Greece, 19–20, 25–7, 42, 137, Germany, 214, India, 20, 137–42, 188, 210, Alexandria, 4, 20, 137, 142–4, India again, 20, 151–4, 210; gave up publishing fiction after 1924, 24, 173–4; elected supernumerary Fellow of King's College, Cambridge, and gave Clark Lectures, 21, 174; President, National Council for Civil Liberties, 21; addressed Writers' Conference, Paris, 21, 129, 195; broadcast monthly on BBC Eastern Service, 22; gave Rede Lecture on Virginia Woolf, 21, 198, Ker Lecture on 'English Prose between 1918 and 1939', 21, 146; Honorary Fellow of King's and took up residence in Cambridge, 174; third visit to India, 22; visits to America, 22–3; support for Aldeburgh Festival, 23, 112, 180–1; made Companion of Honour, 24; President, Humanist Society, 21; awarded Order of Merit, 24; death, 19

Tastes, activities, friendships:

agnosticism, 7, 21, 215; anti-imperialism, 3, 10–11; attitude to poor, 17; as biographer, 182–92; Bloomsbury, 13–14; book reviews, 208–9; as broadcaster, 22, 23, 193, 205–7, 216–17; as critic, 174–83, 203–5, 225–6; dislike of Christ, 7; distaste for women, 25, 108; as Edwardian novelist, 16–18; friendships with, Ansell, 3, Dickinson, 183–5, D. H. Lawrence, 10, H. O. Meredith, 7; homosexuality, 113, *and see* ch. 6; humanism, 40, 220; struggle against

muddle, 43; 'not really a novelist', 63; operatic quality of writing, 76, 224; pacifism, 4; Pan worship and Lawrence, 18; private income, 19; belongs to no school, 17–18; sense of continuity, 92, 148, 202; symbol of liberal conscience, 24, 211–12

Works:

Short Stories

The Celestial Omnibus, 27, 29, 30–5; title story, 34; 'Other Kingdom', 28, 34–5, 46; 'The Other Side of the Hedge', 16, 28; 'The Road from Colonus', 26, 28, 30, 32–4, 55; 'The Story of a Panic', 26, 27, 28, 30–2, 47, 55
The Eternal Moment, 27; title story, 28, 36; 'The Machine Stops', 39–40, 46; 'Mr Andrews', 38; 'The Point of It', 38; 'The Story of the Siren', 35–6
The Life to Come and Other Stories, vii, 3, 27, 36, *128–36*; 'Albergo Empedocle', 27, 34–5, 128; 'Ansell', 3, 35, 150; 'Arthur Snatchfold', 120, 128, 131–4; 'The Classical Annex', 128; 'Dr Woolacott', 128, 129; 'The Obelisk', 128, 129–30; 'The Other Boat', 128, 131, 134–5; 'The Purple Envelope', 29, 128; 'The Rock', 30, 32–4, 128; 'The Second Course', 128; 'The Torque', 128; 'What does it Matter?', 3, 128, 130

Novels

A Room with a View, 1, 9, 15, 16, 19, 24, 27, 36, 42–53, 57, 65, 72, 149, 225; 'Lucy', 42; 'New Lucy', 43, 49, 52
Where Angels Fear to Tread, 9, 15, 16, 19,

II General Index

Index

Index

Index

Love, 2, 12, 57, 59, 69, 79, 101, 125–6, 165, 212, 219; and conditioning, 123–4; and death, 104; Forster mythologizes, 47, 53, 55–6. *See also* Money
Lowes, J. L., 204
Lubbock, P., 176
Ludolf, G. H., 149

Macaulay, Zachary, 9
McConkey, J., 181
Machen, Arthur, 29
Machine age, 12, 18, 75, 209, 226; 'The Machine Stops', 39–40
Madingley Dell, 69, 72
Maharajah of Chhatarpur, 140
Maharajah of Dewas Senior, 20, 140, 151, 152–3, 154, 183
Mann, Thomas, 173
Mansfield, Katherine, 89
Masood, Syed Ross, 138, 141–2, 152, 155, 163
Masterman, C. F. G., 10, 11, 17, 87–8, 103–4; *The Condition of England*, 10, 87; *From the Abyss*, 17, 88, 103, 104
Materialism, 13, 59, 209; and culture, 85–8, 91, 207
Matson, Norman, 179
Maupassant, 28, 132
Melville, 180. *See also Billy Budd*
Memory, 2, 165, 166, 168, 190, 202, 221
Menon, Narayana, 151
Meredith, George, 12, 18, 29, 46, 68, 75, 181; *The Ordeal of Richard Feverel*, 12, 75
Meredith, H. O., 7, 70, 184, 188; *Maurice* based on, 113
Merrill, George, 109
Michelangelo, 104
Middle classes, weaknesses, 4, 5, 6, 15, 21, 25, 42, 201
Mill, J. S., 9, 49, 226
Milner, Lord, 145
Money, 18, 27, 69, 70–1, 98–104, 209; agent of corruption, 32; and death, 104; substituted for love, 2, 100–11, 116, 166
Money, L. C. C., *Riches and Poverty*, 87
'Monk and the beast', 80, 93, 224; idealism and brutality, 118
Monteriano, 36, 53, 56, 58
Moore, G. E., 7, 184
Moore, George, 7; *Evelyn Innes*, 19
Moore, Mrs, 2, 6, 14, 41, 156, 158, 159, 161, 164, 165, 166, 167, 168–9, 172, 192, 216; and negative vision, 41, 159

More, Hannah, 161, 200, 201
Morris, William, 102; *News from Nowhere*, 39
Mortimer, Raymond, 207
Muddle, 43, 47, 51, 67, 74, 93, 117, 152; and baptism, 1; and fantasy, 28; Forster guilty of, 54–5; defeated by love and truth, 43, 48; and mystery, 151, 152, 154
Muir, Edwin, 39
Munch, Eduard, 76
Munro, H. H. (Saki), 88
Music, 22, 50, 158, 179, 181; 'our most musical novelist', 224
Mussolini, 210
Myth, 26, 35, 61–2, 182, 220, 221; and love, 47, 52, 55; and Maurice and Alec, 115, 122, 127

Nation, 21
Nature, 9, 18, 27, 32, 48, 51, 58, 66, 69, 79, 167; and convention: in Lucy, 44–5, 51; in Gino, 55, 63, 66; in Stephen Wonham, 74–5; and culture, 66, 223
Natwar-Singh, K., 168, 226
Nazism, 203, 210, 211, 212, 213, 214
New Statesman, 207
Nietzsche, 99
Nordic Twilight (Three Anti-Nazi Broadcasts, TCD), 214

'Only connect', 6, 66, 89, 92–4, 96, 98, 109, 147, 150, 151, 161, 165, 222–3; failure to connect, 6, 48, 94, 187, 201, 223–4
Orwell, George, 39, 196, 205, 217; *Animal Farm*, 208; *Nineteen Eighty-Four*, 208, 212
Overarching sky, 19, 93, 119, 123, 158; and infinite, 40, 119, 123

Paganism, 6, 18, 34–5, 73, 74–5, 79
Pan, 6, 18, 29, 30, 75, 127, 181; fashionable guise for Unseen, 41; 'the little God Pan', 47; panic fear, 31, 162, 204; pantheism, 30; in 'The Story of a Panic', 30, 32
'Panic and emptiness', 41, 85, 101, 192
Paris Exhibition, 209–10
Past, 20, 26, 37, 67, 79, 92, 198, 200–1; in Forster's art, 37–8; and present, 92, 120, 148, 150, 202
Pastoral, 53, 84, 93, 127
Pater, W., 204; the 'present moment', 12, 221; *Marius the Epicurean*, 6, 37
Pembroke, Agnes, 5, 40, 46, 49, 67–84, 91

Index